TWO CENTURIES OF
MANCHU WOMEN POETS

TWO CENTURIES OF MANCHU WOMEN POETS

An Anthology

Translated by Wilt L. Idema

UNIVERSITY OF WASHINGTON PRESS

Seattle & London

Publication of this book was made possible in part by a grant from the Chiang Ching-kuo Foundation for International Scholarly Exchange.

Printed and bound in the United States of America

21 20 19 18 17 5 4 3 2

University of Washington Press
www.washington.edu/uwpress

Library of Congress Cataloging-in-Publication Data

Names: Idema, W. L. (Wilt L.) translator.
Title: Two centuries of Manchu women poets : an anthology / translated by Wilt L. Idema.
Description: Seattle : University of Washington Press, [2017] | Includes bibliographical references and index.
Identifiers: LCCN 2016035714 | ISBN 9780295999869 (hardcover : alk. paper)
Subjects: LCSH: Chinese poetry—Qing dynasty, 1644–1912—Translations into English. | Chinese poetry—Women authors—Translations into English.
Classification: LCC PL2537 T96 2017 | DDC 895.11/480809287—dc23
LC record available at https://lccn.loc.gov/2016035714

The paper used in this publication is acid-free and meets the minimum requirements of American National Standard for Information Sciences—Permanence of Paper for Printed Library Materials, ANSI Z39.48–1984. ∞

CONTENTS

ACKNOWLEDGMENTS

As the following pages will make only all too clear, I am not a specialist in Qing history or Manchu studies. I came to the topic of Manchu women poets of the Qing dynasty in an indirect way. When I participated in the conference on Chinese women's biography at Laguna Beach, California, in March 2006, I presented a paper on the "One Hundred Poems Lamenting My Husband" (Kufu shi) by the late-Ming woman poet Bo Shaojun. When I pursued the development of this genre I discovered that Lady Tongjia, an eighteenth-century Manchu woman poet, had published not only an even larger set of poems lamenting her husband, but also several other collections during her lifetime. I became more fascinated by the topic of Manchu women poets during the conference "Traditional Chinese Women through a Modern Lens" at Harvard in June 2006 because of Ding Yizhuang's presentation on the life and poetry of the Mongol-Manchu poet Naxun Lanbao. The availability of several important collections of Manchu women poets at the Harvard-Yenching Library facilitated my initial research, and the library staff was extremely helpful in procuring copies of other collections from China. When I was invited by Grace Fong to McGill University to deliver the annual Hsiang Lecture on Chinese Poetry in 2007, I used that opportunity to organize my thoughts on the topic for the first time.

In the years since then, many colleagues, students, and friends have helped me pursue my research on this topic. Without their help this project would never have reached its present shape, but of the many names I can mention only a few. I have greatly benefitted from the many publications on Manchu society of Mark Elliott, as well as from my conversations with him. Ellen Widmer has continuously prodded me to find Manchu women poets outside Beijing and to complete the project. Ma Xiaohe has gone far beyond the call of duty in procuring materials from Chinese libraries. Hu Qiulei and Zhang Yinzhi have helped me in reading prefaces that were printed in cursive script. Xia Xiaohong and Fu Xianglong, Chen Yuehong and Fang Jingjing, and especially Yan Zinan, along with other scholars kindly helped provide access to some pre-1800 texts by transcribing them for me. Yan Zinan was also very helpful in drawing my attention to some relevant recent publications that had escaped my attention. Xu Yongming alerted me to the master's thesis of Zhu Jiji. Hu Siaochen provided me with materials from Taiwan, and my graduate student Sun Xiaosu has been very helpful in hunting down articles and other materials. An invitation to visit China by the China International Culture Association allowed me to consult some rare materials in the National Library of in Beijing in September 2014. The indexing of this volume was supported by a generous subsidy from the Fairbank Center for Chinese Studies, Harvard University. The two anonymous readers for the Press not only spotted numerous typos but also made a number of very useful suggestions. Needless to say, all remaining shortcomings of this book are very much my own.

As always, it has been a great pleasure to work with the extremely professional staff of the University of Washington Press.

CHRONOLOGY OF DYNASTIES AND QING REIGN PERIODS

Shang ca.	1460–1045 BCE
Zhou	1045–256 BCE
Qin	221–207 BCE
Han	202 BCE–220 CE
Western Han	202 BCE–9 CE
Eastern Han	25 CE–220
The Three Kingdoms	
Wei	220–265
Wu	220–280
Shu-Han	221–263
Jin	266–420
Western Jin	266–316
Eastern Jin	317–420
Northern and Southern dynasties	317–589
Sui	581–618
Tang	618–907
The Five Dynasties	907–960
Song	960–1279
Northern Song	960–1127
Southern Song	1127–1279
Liao	916–1125
Jin	1115–1234
Yuan	1260–1368
Ming	1368–1644
Qing	1644–1911
Republic of China	1912–
People's Republic of China	1949–

REIGN PERIODS OF THE QING DYNASTY

Shunzhi	1644–1661
Kangxi	1662–1722
Yongzheng	1723–1735
Qianlong	1736–1796
Jiaqing	1797–1820
Daoguang	1821–1850
Xianfeng	1851–1861
Tongzhi	1862–1874
Guangxu	1875–1907
Xuantong	1908–1911

DATES AND NAMES

THE CALENDAR AND COUNTING YEARS

The traditional Chinese year is a lunar year made up of twelve months of twenty-nine or thirty days. In order to correct the difference between the lunar year and the solar year, the Chinese calendar added intercalary months (named after the preceding months) when necessary. The date of Chinese New Year shifts considerably from year to year and can correspond to any day in the period from January 20 to February 20. The first three months of the year are spring, the next three summer, the following three fall, and the final three winter. This means that the seasons in the traditional Chinese calendar tend to start more than a month earlier than the seasons in the Western calendar.

Years are counted as years of reign periods. Each reign period has its own name, usually a felicitous phrase. Under earlier dynasties rulers changed their reign periods at irregular intervals, but starting from the Ming each emperor on his accession chose a reign period title that was maintained throughout his reign. Since that time emperors usually have been referred to by the name of their reign period.

Years may also be counted using a cycle of sixty two-character combinations consisting of one of the ten characters of the "Heavenly Stems" and one of the twelve characters of the "Earthly Branches." The twelve characters of the Earthly Branches are also used to number the twelve hours of the day.

A baby is said to be one year of age (to be in the first year of its life) from the moment of birth, and adds one more year on the first New Year's Day. This means that in the Chinese counting, men and women will be at least one year older than they are in Western counting. In extreme cases the difference may mount to almost two years.

SURNAMES AND OTHER NAMES

Most Chinese surnames (*xing*) consist of only a single syllable (e.g., Wang, Zhang), but two-syllable surnames are also found (e.g., Sima, Ouyang). The surname precedes the personal name (*ming*), which will consist of one or two syllables. On reaching adulthood, a man also may take a style name (*zi*). Many literati also use one or more *hao* (artist's name, pseudonym), which in many cases has a connection to the name of their study or garden; they may also assume religious names. Chinese women may also adopt a *hao* alongside their personal name. In many contexts, both before and after marriage, women are designated only by their surname (e.g., Li Shi, the woman surnamed Li: Miss Li, Madam Li, Lady Li).

Manchus have a clan name (e.g., Gioro); lineages within clans are distinguished by prefixing a second term to the first (e.g., Aisin Gioro). Manchu men may have names taken from a wide range of words (e.g., Dorgon, which means *badger*) and are in general designated by their personal name without the use of their clan or lineage name. After 1644, once the Manchus had entered China proper and moved their capital to Beijing, they increasingly came to use names made up of one or more auspicious Chinese characters, and also style names and *hao*. To distinguish the names of Manchu men from Chinese names in this volume, the syllables of the names of Manchu men are in transcription linked by a hyphen (for ease of reference in the bibliography, however, the hyphen is omitted). As this book is primarily based on works originally composed in Chinese by Manchu women who most likely did not know any Manchu, and as I am no Manchu scholar, I have not tried to identify the Manchu form of these names.

Manchu women are, like Chinese women, often designated by using their lineage name only (e.g., Miss Nalan, Madam Zhaojia, Lady Zhoujia, Lady Tongjia, Lady Husihali).[1] Only in rare cases are women referred to by clan name and personal name (e.g., Wanyan Jinchi). In some cases women are customarily referred to by a combination of personal name and *hao* (e.g., Baibao Youlan, Duomin Huiru, Lingwen Zhuyou). In a few other cases women are only known by their personal name (e.g., Xiguang) or their *hao* (e.g., Sibo, Mengyue, Bingyue). Yangyizhai Zhuren/Nüshi (Mistress/Female Scribe of the Study of Nurturing Simplicity) and Lanxuan Zhuren/Nüshi (Mistress/Female Scribe of Orchid Pavilion) are only known by their study names, while Guizhen Daoren (The Person of the Way Who Seeks Refuge in the Truth) is best known by her religious name.

TWO CENTURIES OF MANCHU WOMEN POETS

Introduction

IN THE THIRD MONTH OF 1873, THE MONGOL WOMAN POET Naxun Lanbao composed a preface to the poetry collection of her Manchu grandmother Wanyan Jinchi.[1] In it she confessed that she had long desired to compile an anthology to be titled *Anthology of Poetry by Manchu Women* (Manzhou guige shichao)—literally, *Anthology of Poetry from Manchu Inner Chambers*—and that she was now printing this collection of her grandmother as the first installment. In the same month she also wrote a preface to the poetry collection of her good friend Baibao Youlan, presumably the second installment of her planned anthology. It may come as something of a surprise that it was a Mongol woman, a proud descendant of Chinggis Khan, who conceived the idea of an anthology of Manchu women poets, but Eastern Mongols and Manchus had been close allies since the earliest days of the Qing dynasty, an alliance that was cemented by systematic intermarriage between the Manchu and Mongol elites. When she was still a toddler, Naxun Lanbao's father had been summoned in 1828 from Kulun (present-day Ulan Bator) to serve in the imperial guard in Beijing, and she had grown up in her grandmother's house, never to visit Mongolia again. Married to a Manchu official in the capital, and the mother of Manchu sons, Naxun Lanbao closely identified herself with the Qing dynasty and its Manchu rulers. Alas, her anthology project never progressed beyond the first two installments, because she died later that year.

Naxun Lanbao's anthology of poetry by Manchu women, if realized, would have consisted of poetry written in Chinese. The Manchu language had had its own script since the early seventeenth century, and written Manchu continued to be widely used in the administration of the Qing empire. There also existed a considerable body of Manchu translations from Chinese literature. Manchu as a written language, however, remained very much tied to the administration of the empire, and by the early eighteenth century, when Manchu men not only had become accustomed to speaking Chinese but also had started to study Chinese literature in increasing numbers, Manchu had become a second language for them at best.[2] While Manchu men were repeatedly urged by their rulers not to forget their ancestral tongue, Manchu women were allowed to speak Chinese, read Chinese, and write Chinese. In the course of my research I encountered only two women who had mastered written Manchu.[3]

AN ANTHOLOGY OF POETRY BY MANCHU WOMEN

The title of Naxun Lanbao's envisioned anthology, *Anthology of Poetry by Manchu Women*, clearly derives from the *Anthology of Poetry by Women of the Present Dynasty* (Guochao guige shi chao) of 1844, compiled by Cai Dianqi. This large anthology brought together shortened versions of the collections of a hundred leading women poets of the Qing dynasty.[4] Although it did not include the complete collections of the authors, it clearly tried to allow its readers to gauge the qualities of these women poets in all their variety by offering substantial selections from their works. In this respect it was different from the *Correct Beginnings by Ladies of the Present Dynasty* (Guochao guixiu zhengshi ji; hereafter *Correct Beginnings*), printed in 1831, an earlier large-scale anthology of women's literature of the Qing dynasty. This anthology, which contained more than 1,700 poems by 933 authors, was compiled by Yun Zhu (1771–1833), a (Han) Chinese woman who had married into a Manchu family. *Correct Beginnings* tried to demonstrate the transformative impact of the ruling dynasty throughout the empire; it included as many individual poets as possible from every nook and cranny of the empire, but it selected only a very small number of poems (six at the most) for each included poet, showing a preference for poems with a virtuous content.[5] Yun Zhu's anthology included some Manchu women poets (and also a few Mongol female poets), but they were scattered amid the much more numerous Chinese women poets. It is unlikely that Naxun Lanbao was unaware of *Correct Beginnings*, but she does not mention it anywhere in her writings.

In the preface to her grandmother's collection, Naxun Lanbao mentions Yuan Mei (1716–1798) and Tie-bao (1752–1824) as supporters of women's poetry. Yuan Mei, the most famous poet of the eighteenth century, had upon his retirement from the imperial bureaucracy settled in Nanjing, where later in life he started to accept female disciples. Even though Nanjing had a Manchu garrison, none of his female disciples was a Manchu, so no Manchu woman poet was included when he compiled an anthology of poems by these women.[6] Yuan Mei was associated with the flourishing scene of women's literature in the

Jiangnan area by the end of the eighteenth century; Tie-bao's appreciation of women's literature was used to stress the quantity and quality of women writers in Beijing. Tie-bao was a Manchu official who spent most of his career in northern China. Because of his literary talents he was charged with many editorial projects, among them the compilation of *Elegant Chants of Prosperous Times* (Xichao yasong ji; 1804; hereafter *Elegant Chants*). To this anthology of poetry by Manchus and the descendants of their Chinese and Mongol allies from before 1644, he added a two-chapter supplement of poetry by their womenfolk, "Elegant Chants of Prosperous Times, an Additional Collection" (Xichao yasong ji yuji), but he included only female authors who already had passed away.[7] This anthology presented poems by a fair number of Manchu women poets, but the authors with the largest selections, Cai Wan (1695–1755) and Gao Jingfang (first half of the eighteenth century), belonged to the so-called Chinese banners.[8]

The Chinese banners were a component of the multiethnic coalition that had established the Qing dynasty. When Nurhaci, the founding ancestor of Manchu power, had early in the seventeenth century imposed a uniform organization on the disparate tribes and ethnic groups under his command, his Jürchen-speaking warriors and their dependents had been organized as the Manchu banners, his Mongol allies and their dependents as the Mongol banners, and his Chinese subjects as the Chinese banners. By the time the Qing invaded the territory of the toppled Ming dynasty in 1644, there were eight Manchu banners, eight Mongol banners, and eight Chinese banners (collectively designated as the Eight Banners), and it was this multiethnic coalition under Manchu leadership that succeeded in conquering China. Following the conquest, the Manchu and Chinese banners settled in China as garrisons, with the majority concentrated in Beijing.[9] While many Manchus already were bilingual in Manchuria, settlement in China spurred on their use of Chinese, but that process would have been quicker for men than for women (who had fewer social interactions requiring use of Chinese), so it should be no surprise that the earliest women poets among the Eight Banners belonged to Chinese families that had joined the Manchu state before 1644. Cai Wan and Gao Jingfang, who occupy such a prominent place in Tie-bao's anthology, are also the only banner women to be included in the *Anthology of Women Poets of the Present Dynasty*.

Strangely enough, Naxun Lanbao makes no reference to Tie-bao's anthology of poetry by banner women. Her conviction that Manchu women poets are ignored by the available anthologies would appear to be primarily based on their absence in the *Anthology of Women Poets of the Present Dynasty*. And so she starts the preface to her grandmother's collection with the following words:

> There is no lack of gentlemen and dignitaries amongst those who are registered in our banners who are renowned for their poetry. But when I start counting, there reigns an absolute silence in the inner chambers, except for Lady Cai and Lady Gao.

Yet, when planning her own anthology, she chose a narrower focus than the Eight Banners by limiting herself specifically to Manchu women poets. In this she may well be a typical representative of intellectual currents of the second half of the eighteenth century and later. Whereas the Yongzheng emperor (r. 1723–1735) had downplayed the distinction between Chinese and outsiders, his son and successor the Qianlong emperor (r. 1736–1795) had consistently stressed the racial uniqueness of the Manchus, downplaying the role of the Chinese banners in the conquest, to the extent that he took various measures to decrease the size of the Chinese banners and to encourage the members of the Chinese banners to abandon their status as bannermen and join the common Chinese population.[10] The violent outbursts of anti-Manchu sentiment during the massive rebellion of the Heavenly Kingdom of Great Peace (Taiping Tianguo; 1849–64) in the middle of the nineteenth century only further strengthened Manchu feelings of ethnic self-awareness, that were maintained throughout the many years of the Qing dynasty by a separate legal status and segregated dwelling spaces.[11]

As is clear from Yun Zhu's *Correct Beginnings* and other large-scale anthologies, women poets were found throughout the length and breadth of the Qing Empire, but the overwhelming majority were concentrated in the Jiangnan region, and the works of the Jiangnan women poets dominated and still dominate the general opinion on women's poetry of traditional China. Naxun Lanbao was therefore quite justified in claiming a larger space for Manchu women poets by inaugurating a large-scale anthology. In her preface to the poems of Baibao Youlan, she stressed the moral qualities of her author, but in initiating her anthology she also might have stressed some distinctive characteristics of Manchu women's poetry. Practically all of the Manchu women poets whose works have survived spent all or at least most of their lives in Beijing, and in their poems describe the landscape and seasons of this northern city and its surrounding sights, such as the Western Hills. While a few of them traveled widely through China, they did so as the wives, daughters, or daughters-in-law of Manchu officials. In the eighteenth century especially, the lives of some of these Manchu women poets were greatly impacted by the vagaries of court politics, such as the factional struggles preceding and following the Yongzheng accession and the reformulation of Manchu identity during the Qianlong reign, and these sudden reversals of fortune were of course reflected in their poetry. While a few of the Manchu women poets died at an early age, before or after marriage, and a few of them appear to have led a long and happy married life, many of them were widowed at an early age and had to raise their sons and daughters in relative poverty. Their collections tend to be small, and consist almost exclusively of *shi* poems, the most common genre of traditional Chinese poetry. The most notable exception in this respect is of course Gu Taiqing (1799–1877), the concubine of Prince Yi-hui (1799–1833). The background of Gu Taiqing has puzzled scholars for generations.[12] She most likely grew up at least partly in the Jiangnan region, and even after she moved to Beijing she primarily associated with women poets from that region.[13] Like many women poets from that region she wrote not only hundreds of *shi*, but also excelled in the writing of *ci* lyrics.[14] As has become clear in recent years, her writings also include plays and a novel.[15] Because she is so much a representative of the Jiangnan tradition of women's literature (and also because she has been studied and translated extensively), she will not be treated in this volume. But while I have excluded Gu Taiqing, I have included two women writers who were very much part of the community of Manchu women writers even though they were not Manchu in the strict sense of the word. The first of these is of course Naxun Lanbao; the second is Guizhen Daoren, whose father belonged to one of the Chinese banners. Guizhen Daoren was a contemporary of Yun Zhu and Gu Taiqing, but unlike them, she interacted intensively with the other Manchu women writers of her day in Beijing.

To a certain degree this work is the realization, albeit in English, of Naxun Lanbao's *Anthology of Poetry by Manchu Women*. It presents substantial selections from the poetry collections of most of the Manchu women poets whose collections were accessible to me. But it is also more. My selection of poems was guided not only by their literary quality and their translatability, but also by their value as documentary evidence of the experiences and thought of these women. Many of these Manchu women poets not only reflected on their experiences of the moment, but also wrote long poems or sets of poems looking back on their own life, strengthening the autobiographical nature of their collection. I have also included selections from their prose writings if these were available. A number of the collections contain prefaces by their authors, female friends, or male relatives, which at times are very informative about the circumstances of their lives and their own conceptions of their literary activities; I have included such materials in complete translation. Where a more detailed discussion of the political circumstances of their lives was called for, I have provided that information. Historians of Manchu society and culture have often deplored the absence of information on the lives of Manchu women during the Qing dynasty, so I hope that this volume will help to fill that gap.

CATALOGS AND COLLECTIONS

When disclosing her plans for an anthology of Manchu women poets, Naxun Lanbo states that she has already collected quite a number of collections. Unfortunately, she does not list the names of the poets or the titles of their works. One of the earliest surveys of women poets of the Eight Banners was provided by the Mongol scholar Fashishan (1753–1813).[16] Fashishan belonged to a family of Mongols who had settled in Beijing after 1644, and whose members served as officials. Fashishan was adopted at birth by his uncle Heshun, whose wife Lady Han was born in one of the Chinese banners. This widely read woman was an accomplished poet and played an important role in Fashishan's early education.[17] Starting from 1780 Fashishan had a splendid career, inside and outside the Hanlin Academy. He often was involved in large-scale compilation projects, which accorded well with his voracious reading appetite. His *Poetry Talks of Wumen* (Wumen shihua) contains at its end a section devoted to women poets of the Eight Banners.[18] This survey opens with Cai Wan and covers twelve names; the most extensive item, as might be expected, is devoted to Lady Han's poetry. Of these twelve names only five are explicitly identified as Manchu. Fashishan also collaborated with Tie-bao in the compilation of *Elegant Chants*. This compilation contained the works of fourteen banner women. Of the three poets included in the first scroll, only one was Manchu; of the ten poets in the second scroll, five were Manchu. The selection of each included poet is preceded by a short biographical note. However, the notes tend to be somewhat more informative in the descriptions of the collections included in the *Comprehensive Treatise on the Eight Banners* (Baqi tongzhi), an exhaustive compilation on the history and organization of the Eight Banners that was commissioned in 1786 and printed in 1799, a project for which Tie-bao served as one of the directors.

Yun Zhu's *Elegant Beginnings* adds many more names of Manchu (and Mongol) women poets, because she also includes women who only left a handful of poems or as little as a single verse. But Yun Zhu does not place the women poets of the Eight Banners together in a special category, so one has to go through the complete collection in order to retrieve the relevant information. All together she includes over twenty Manchu women poets, and a few more names are found in the sequel put out by her granddaughter. Shen Shanbao's (1808–1862) voluminous *Poetry Talks on Famous Women* (Mingyuan shihua) also does not set aside a separate section for a discussion of the works of women of the Eight Banners. While she was personally acquainted with Gu Taiqing and spent some years in Beijing, she does not seem to have had close personal contacts with many other Manchu women poets of her day, and her few comments on other Manchu women poets tend to be very short.[19]

Up to the middle of the nineteenth century, the overwhelming majority of the known Manchu women were Beijing based. This makes sense because ever since the early years of the Qing dynasty, the largest number of Manchus were settled in the capital. From the second half of the nineteenth century we also know the names of a few Manchu women poets from Hangzhou. The Manchu woman poet with the largest collection, Lady Husihali (1848–1896), hailed from the northeast; both she and her husband belonged to Manchu families living near Shenyang and she spent part of her youth and adult life on the Liaodong Peninsula. Lady Husihali is also the last Manchu woman poet in this selection. In some poems of the final years of her life she laments the incursions of the Japanese army into Manchuria during the Sino-Japanese War (1894–95), bitterly complaining about the ineffectiveness of the troops of the Qing. Unfortunately, we have no Manchu woman poet who lived through the final years of the Qing: the Boxer Rebellion and the flight of the court to Xi'an, the frantic modernization of the last decade, and the establishment of the Republic of China that turned the Manchus from masters into second-class citizens for many years to come.

The earliest work exclusively devoted to women poets of the Eight Banners was not published until after the fall of the Qing dynasty. This is Zhen-jun's (1850–1920) *Short Biographies of Women Poets of the Eight Banners* (Baqi shiyuan xiaozhuan), which was included in *Tales of People of the Qing, Second Compilation* (Qingren shuohui erbian) of 1917.[20] Closer inspection reveals, however, that *Short Biographies* is extracted from a 1907 nostalgic compilation on banner lore by that same antiquarian scholar, titled *Anecdotes from Close to Heaven* (Tianzhi ouwen).[21] It collects anecdotes concerning twenty female authors, of whom half are Manchu. Manchu women poets are also included in Shi Shuyi's (b. 1878) *Brief Accounts of Poets of the Inner Apartments of the Qing Dynasty* (Qingdai guige shiren zhenglüe; 1922). Notices on four of them are included in the main body of the work, but the largest number is found in the appendix, which opens with biographical notices on eleven Manchu women poets. A much more comprehensive survey is found in the *Classified Catalog of Literary Works by Members of the Eight Banners* (Baqi yiwen bianmu), published in 1941 by En-hua.[22] A special section this work lists fifty-six titles of collections by banner women (it should be noted that some authors left more than one title). A more recent survey of collections by banner women writers is found in section 21 of Hu Wenkai's *An Inquiry into the Writings by Women of the Successive Dynasties* (Lidai funü zhuzuo kao), which was first published in 1957, reissued in an expanded edition in 1985, and recently revised by Zhang Hongsheng (2008).[23] The most comprehensive list of Manchu and Mongol women poets yet has recently been provided by Du Xun in his *Songs from the Ocean of Inner Apartments* (Guihai yin; 2012). His list reaches fifty-four names, of which six are Mongol women.[24]

But not all women listed by Du Xun left a collection, and not all collections that are known by title have been preserved. This anthology deals primarily with the Manchu and Mongol women poets whose collections have been preserved and are accessible in major libraries. The National Library in Beijing and the Harvard-Yenching Library have been my primary sources.[25] In the cases of the Madam Zhaojia and Xiguang, my discussions are based on their poems in *Elegant Chants.*

Most of the extant collections have been preserved in print, but a few survive in manuscript. One instance is Mengyue's *Selected Poems of the Bamboo Lodge* (Zhuwu shichao), preserved only as a manuscript that had been prepared with publication in mind; it carries not only Mengyue's own preface of 1808 but also an elaborate set of "editorial principles" (*fanli*). Lady Husihali's two collections, *Small Drafts from Leisure after Needlework* (Xiuyu xiaocao) and *A Record of Accompanying My Husband to His Official Posting in Jiangxi* (Jiangyou suihuan jishi), which together contain almost one thousand poems and are easily the largest collections in our corpus, were printed upon her death in 1896 by woodblock technology, but quickly reprinted in 1903 by the then quite modern method of lithography.[26] The other printed editions that have been preserved were printed by the traditional woodblock technology. All printed collections appear to have been printed privately.

In many cases a woman's poetry collection was printed only upon her death, by her husband, her son, or another male relative. The first example of such a publication is the printing by Yong-shou (1702–1731) of his maiden aunt Miss Nalan's collection *Poetry Drafts from Leisure after Needlework* (Xiuyu shigao). This collection contained 120 poems composed by his aunt, who passed away at an early age. Miss Nalan was a daughter of the wealthy high Manchu official Ming-zhu (Mingju, 1635–1708), and a younger sister of the famous lyricist

Nalan Xing-de (Naran Singde, 1655–1685) and the well-known poet and official Kui-xu (1674–1717). Her collection is the earliest surviving poetry collection by a Manchu woman poet. Naxun Lanbao's collection of poetry, *Preserved Poems of the Hall of Fragrant Rue* (Yunxiangguan yishi), was printed upon her death by her son Sheng-yu (1850–1900) in 1874. In some cases a considerable period of time elapsed between a poet's death and the posthumous publications of her works. For instance, Wenhuang Xianghua's (1783–1837) collection *Drafts from Leisure after Needlework of the Wearing Orchids Studio* (Peilanxuan xiuyu cao) was put in order by her son Qing-yue but appears to have been printed only in 1883 (in this case the title page informs us that "the printing blocks are stored at home" [*benzhai cangban*]).

In some cases such a posthumous publication of a woman's collection was part of a larger filial project to publish the writings of one's ancestors. At the end of the eighteenth century Neng-tai included the collections of his grandmother, the Mistress of the Study for Nurturing Simplicity (Yangyizhai Zhuren), and mother, the Mistress of Orchid Pavilion (Lanxuan Zhuren), when he had the poetry collections of his grandfather, father, and uncle edited and printed. Tie-bao's son Rui-yuan appended *Ruting's Poetry Drafts* (Ruting shigao), the collected poems of Tie-bao's wife Yingchuan, to the collected writings of his father when he had those published upon his death. The publication of the first collection of Bingyue's poems as *First Draft of Cold Study Chantings* (Lengzhaiyin chugao) probably was closely connected with her younger brother-in-law Yi-xing's (Gui-pu; 1747–1809) project to have the writings of his late father printed. By including the collections of female members of the family in larger publication projects, these Manchu gentlemen followed a trend that can also be observed in the publication of women poets in the Jiangnan region.[27]

More rarely, a family published a woman's collection during her lifetime. The first edition of Baibao Youlan's collection *Collected Poems of Cold Reds Studio* (Lenghongxuan shiji) was printed in 1857 after decades of delay (her own preface was dated 1837), but when it appeared it carried prefaces by some of the most-honored names in the realm, including her brother-in-law Prince Gong. Likewise, when Lingwen Zhuyou's collection was printed in 1884, most likely on the occasion of her fiftieth birthday, it came with a preface by the famous statesman Peng Yulin (1816–1890). Not all women poets were delighted with such a present, as we know from Yun Zhu's reaction when her sons had her poems printed ("These are not worthy to be transmitted, and even if transmitted it should be only a few. Hereafter don't print any of my personal works!"), but then it was good breeding for a woman to be modest about her poetic achievements (Yun Zhu also may have thought the effusions of her youth too frivolous).[28]

As in the case of Naxun Lanbao, women on occasion were active in the publication of poetry collections by other women.[29] Some went so far as to publish their own collections during their lifetimes. For instance, Yong-shou's widow Sibo published first a collection of her own poems together with those by her close friend Gong Danting, titled *Preserved Together: A Selection of Poems* (Hecun shichao). She later also published a small collection of prose essays by herself, Gong Danting, and one of her own daughters, a pupil of Gong Danting. Even more self-promoting was Lady Tongjia. She too published a small anthology of her own poems together with those of the female tutors who had taught her or had been hired by her as *A Combined Selection from the Poetry-Instruction Loft* (Wenshilou hexuan); she earlier had published a collection of poems lamenting her parents (*Preserved Drafts of Crow-like Attachment* [Wusi cuncao]) and another lamenting the loss of her husband (*Tearful Drafts from beside the Coffin* [Suiwei leicao]). Her *Family Instructions from the Hall for Cherishing Goodness* (Baoshantang jiaxun) date from 1800 (by that time her son had been raised to the rank of Prince Rui); after the death of her son she published the poems she had written during the year following his passing as *A Heart Ripped Apart* (Liexin ji). Her collected poems from her widowed years were published as *Elegant Pastimes by the Empty Window* (Xuchuang yake) and appeared with a preface and postface by high-ranking Manchu officials.[30] Bingyue too may have played an active role in the publication of her two collections of poetry.

In a few rare cases, collections by Manchu women writers were even reprinted during the Qing. The poems of Lady Tongjia in *A Combined Selection from the Poetry-Instruction Loft* (Wenshilou hexuan) were also included in her *Elegant Pastimes by the Empty Window* (Xuchuang yake). Yun Zhu's collection was first printed by her son Lin-qing (1791–1846) in 1814, then reprinted in 1866. Baibao Youlan's collection was first published by her son in Jinhua in 1857, then later (in 1875) published in Beijing in a pared-down edition prepared by Naxun Lanbao. That edition was then reprinted in 1882 by Baibao Youlan's only surviving younger brother.

Many of these collections come with extensive paratextual materials in the form of prefaces and postfaces.[31] When such texts are written by close relatives or friends these may be very rich in biographical details. Texts that were printed by the authors or during their lifetimes may also include prefaces by the authors themselves, which can be quite enlightening with regard not only to their lives but also to their opinions on poetry. The prefaces by high-ranking officials, whether Chinese or Manchu, or well-known literati of the time are usually less helpful in this regard because they tend to expound on the value of women's poetry (often by mentioning that Confucius had included works by women in *The Book of Odes*), stressing the moral stature of the author's works that set her collection apart from the common run of women's poetry.[32] The only exception is Peng Yulin's preface to the collection of Zhuyou, because in his first job he had been her tutor and so he could write about her character as a teenager. These prefaces by high officials and well-known literati would have helped to raise the status of women's poetry in the Manchu community. By the early twentieth century, women poets were even sufficiently esteemed to be received at court. Two women from the Hangzhou Manchu garrison were among the women artists received in audience by Empress Dowager Cixi in 1903: Wang Shao, the author of a poetry collection, *Poems from the Green-in-Winter Hall* (Dongqingguan shi), and Hualiang, who is best known as a painter and who compiled a handbook titled *Painting Models from the Studio for Surpassing Models* (Chaofanshi huafan).[33]

Most collections are quite small and are not subdivided into *juan* (scrolls), but a few larger ones are. Many collections arrange their contents in order of composition, which turns the collection into something like a cross between a diary and an autobiography (and, in view of the many descriptive poems inspired by the change of seasons and personal travels, a collection of snapshots). While the collections, of course, are very selective in the subjects covered, they often provide a fairly detailed image of the author's life and her experiences, especially when the collection also includes long autobiographical works in which the author looks back on her life.[34] In some cases collections arrange their contents by genre. Old-style poems in lines of five syllables tend to precede those of seven syllables; as for modern-style poetry, the same applies both for eight-line regulated poems and four-line quatrains (the two styles of poetry are discussed in the following section). If lyrics are included at all, they will be interspersed with the *shi* poems in chronologically arranged collections. In the case of the first editions of Baibao Youlan's *Collected Poems of Cold Reds Studio* (Lenghongxian shiji) they are grouped together in a special section at the end.

WRITING POETRY

The poets collected in this volume almost exclusively composed *shi* poetry, both old style and modern style. All *shi* is distinguished by a fixed line-length. While *shi* with a fixed line length of three, four, and six syllables exist, the most common line length is either five syllables or seven syllables. In lines of five syllables there is a caesura following the second syllable; in lines of seven syllables there is a caesura following the fourth syllable. Each line forms one or more sentences (or exceptionally, a clause of a complex sentence) and in the original Chinese, enjambment does not occur. A poem consists of at least four lines, and the even lines are expected to rhyme. A rhyme may be repeated any number of times, but in longer poems a change in rhyme is often used to mark a change of subject; in the translations in this book such a shift of rhyme is indicated by a line space. During the fifth and sixth centuries Chinese poets became increasingly aware of the tonal nature of their language and rules for tonal alternation and contrast were formulated for euphonic effects. The *shi* poems that adhered to these rules were eventually called modern-style poetry, while the poems that did not adhere to these rules were classified as old-style poetry (both kinds continue to be written into the 21st century). In modern-style poetry the commonly practiced genres are the four-line quatrain (*jueju*) and the eight-line regulated poem (*lüshi*). The regulated poem had as an added requirement that both the second and third couplet each should consist of parallel lines. Such parallel lines, which share a similar grammatical construction but display contrasting content, are often used for description, aiming to represent totality by naming contrastive elements. Parallel couplets were used for a variety of purposes inside and outside poetry, and pupils were trained from an early age to construct such couplets. A modern-style poem of ten lines or more (with more than two parallel couplets between the opening couplet and the final two lines) was called a *pailü*, but I have encountered only a few examples of the genre in the collections canvassed for this volume.[35] *Pailü* invited the use of contrasting allusions in their parallel couplets, and such a self-conscious display of erudition was probably considered unseemly for a woman. Longer poetic compositions in modern-style verse could, however, easily be created by arranging quatrains or regulated poems into sets.

With the exception of course of Gu Taiqing, Manchu women poets rarely ventured into the composition of lyrics (*ci*). Lyrics originated as popular songs in the ninth and tenth centuries, and each melody came with its own pattern prescribing the number of lines for each stanza, the places of rhyme, and the use of tones. To write lyrics apart from the most common patterns must have been much easier for speakers of southern dialects—which had in many ways stayed closer to the vernacular of the Tang and Song dynasties—than for the speakers of northern Mandarin with its many multisyllable words and simplified tonal system. The Jiangnan region had seen a revival of lyrics in the seventeenth century, and many women poets in the Jiangnan area also took to the genre, especially because the genre had clear feminine associations. As popular song, *ci* had from the thirteenth century on been replaced by *qu*, a genre that also was practiced by some Jiangnan women, but by none of our Manchu women poets, despite the genre's links to northern China. One Manchu woman poet, Lady Husihali, as late as 1895 warned the Chinese women of Yuanzhou, Jiangxi, where her husband served as prefect, against reading "lascivious lyrics" and listening to "seductive songs," suggesting that some Manchu women poets at least may have shied away from these genres as too frivolous.

Manchu women writers learned to read and write at home. The eighteenth-century poet Mengyue wrote that she was allowed to attend school with her brothers while dressed as a boy, until she became a teenager and had to switch to female attire—and that may well have been common. But many women poets came from noble families that were able to hire first-rate tutors. Both Miss Nalan and Sibo belonged to the household of the immensely wealthy Ming-zhu, who is known for having hired for his sons the best Chinese tutors money could buy. When Sibo became a widow, she hired a female tutor for her daughters and nieces. This woman, Gong Danting, was the widow of a district magistrate and would stay with Sibo for ten years until Gong's son had passed the metropolitan examinations. We know the names of three Chinese women Lady Tongjia hired as tutors for her children. After Chinese had become the native language of Manchus, we find fewer references to such Chinese tutors and more girls appear to have studied with male and female relatives—in highly educated families there must always have been an ample supply of suitable candidates. Some of our poets started to write at an early age: Lady Tongjia's earliest preserved poems date from her thirteenth year, while Lady Husihali's collection includes poems written at the age of eleven (by Chinese count, so probably at age ten or even nine). In what would appear to be an exceptional case, Tie-bao informs us that his wife Yingchuan was illiterate when they were married and that he taught her to read and write.

But while many Manchu women learned to compose parallel couplets and poems because that was part of the standard educational curriculum, this does not mean that all families encouraged their daughters to write poetry. Many families may well have warned their daughters away from poetry once they reached marriageable age, as we learn from a comment by Naxun Lanbao in the preface to her grandmother's collection of poetry:

> I have observed that when daughters of family and relatives enter school and recite books they often are equal to boys—but they distinguish themselves by the virtuous beauty of their customs. However, when these daughters reach

> marriageable age their parents as a rule do not allow them to practice poetry, and if these daughters occasionally do write poems, their parents warn them not to show them to outsiders, and for that reason few of their poems are transmitted.

Many parents may well have felt that reading and writing could have a negative impact on a woman's work of running the household. If women continued to write poetry nevertheless, they often emphasized that they dashed off their scribblings only after they had finished their needlework. Many titles of women's collections contain the phrase *xiuyu* (leisure after needlework). Preface writers do not tire of emphasizing that the authors of the collections were dutiful daughters and wives, filial in their duties toward their parents-in-law, effective as household managers, and devoted to the education of their children.

Scholars working on women's culture of the Jiangnan region have emphasized the importance of female networks and poetry clubs for women writing poetry.[36] In his famous novel *Dream of the Red Chamber* (Honglou meng; also known as *Story of the Stone*), the eighteenth-century author Cao Xueqin (1715–1764) provides detailed descriptions of the poetry clubs organized by the young women in the Grand Prospect Garden. In view of the persistent widespread distrust of women practicing poetry even in nineteenth-century Beijing, the importance of a supportive environment for aspiring young female poets is evident. Many Manchu and Mongol women poets lived in families in which poetry was intensively practiced by other male and female relatives. Women often partook in more informal social gatherings at which poetry was composed, as we learn from prefaces such as the following from the collection of Mengyue:

> On the third day before Double Ninth my full elder brothers Tong-yuan and Jing-ting visited me at my home after dinner for a chat. When we noticed that it would be still some time before the chrysanthemums by the eastern hedge would bloom, we came up with the theme of "Questioning Chrysanthemums." Each of us would write one regulated poem, to be completed before the candle had burned out—the fine was to provide fat crabs and good wine to be consumed together on the Ninth. Thereupon I recorded this event as our pleasure of the moment.[37]

Even though we do not have the names of formal poetry clubs organized exclusively by Manchu women, many women poets had more or less intensive contacts with other women poets.[38] Sibo exchanged poems with her close friend Gong Danting, a daughter of whom was one of the teachers hired by Lady Tongjia. Nurturing Simplicity and Orchid Pavilion were mother-in-law and daughter-in-law. Lady Tongjia's mother-in-law, Lady Zhoujia, also was a prolific poet. Late in life Lady Tongjia became good friends with Bingyue, after she had read her first collection. Bingyue was also a close friend of Guizhen Daoren, who late in life also was acquainted with Naxun Lanbao. Naxun Lanbao's grandmother Wanyan Jinchi may have also been acquainted with these three ladies. Baibao Youlan and Naxun Lanbao became close friends after Baibao Youlan had settled in Beijing, and they continued to correspond after Baibao Youlan had followed her son to his posting in the Jiangnan area. Intensive interactions between these poets are also suggested by a number of shared titles, which indicate common activities, such as shared excursions to the Western Hills outside Beijing. One way in which intense friendship might be expressed between friends was by writing mourning poems for each other while still alive. Sibo has left us an essay in which she defends this practice with the argument that mourning poems are precisely the venue to speak one's true feelings without any impediment, and that they therefore are a perfect vehicle for friends to disclose their deepest feelings to each other. In the collection of Bingyue almost a century later, we find examples of such mourning poems for her good friend Guizhen Daoren.

The literary contacts of Manchu women poets were primarily with other banner women. Surprisingly, none of the works of the women in this collection suggests any direct contacts with either Yun Zhu or Gu Taiqing.[39] Recorded connections with well-known Chinese women poets are rare, but Lady Tongjia's *A Combined Selection from the Poetry-Instruction Loft* (Wenshilou hexuan) contains a postface by the Suzhou woman poet, painter, and calligrapher Cao Zhenxiu (1762–1822), who spent a number of years in Beijing during the final years of the eighteenth century.[40] Bingyue (and perhaps also Lady Tongjia) wrote poems inspired by works of the much more widely known Jiangnan woman poet Luo Qilan (1756–after 1813),[41] but Luo was an inveterate networker who had her poems and paintings widely circulated, inviting endorsements.[42] Wenhuang Xianghua was acquainted with the Shanghai woman poet Xie Lijuan; Naxun Lanbao's collection contains a poem thanking Zhang Qieying (1792–after 1863) for an inscription on a portrait.[43] There is also very little evidence on the readings in women's poetry of these Manchu women poets. They exchanged their publications among each other, and wrote flattering poems on reading each other's collections.

Many of the women poets in this volume must have spent considerable time and energy writing, and some even confess to an addiction to poetry. Wanyan Jinchi, who was chided by her granddaughter for ridiculing the women who submitted their poems to the judgments of Yuan Mei and Tie-bao, left a defiant poem:

Written in Jest

> For women the chanting of poems may only be an avocation,
> But I always admire them for each having a particular strength,
> And I'd rather be robbed by my intelligence of all my luck
> Than have to accept that my natural inspiration is suffocated.

At the same time, many of these poets displayed a cultivated modesty in public. Wuyunzhu, the wife of the grand secretary Yi-sang-a (1638–1703) and perhaps the earliest known Manchu woman poet, reportedly once said:

> If a person of the inner chambers can compose poetry, that is of course a beautiful thing. But she can [use her poetry] only to receive the instructions of her father and elder brothers and match songs with her elder and younger sisters. How could it be a thing for women to follow teachers and form societies?[44]

Wuyunzhu authored a collection of poems "but did not show it to others." Fashishan describes his adoptive mother Lady Han's behavior as follows:

> She understood the Classics and Histories and was skilled in rhymed compositions. But whatever she wrote she did not show to others. She threw [her compositions] in an ancient jug and on the first and the fifteenth of each month she would draw fire and burn them, saying, "Where are the traces and images of flowing water and blooming flowers preserved? But the radiant splendor of the white moon and clear breeze stays on." Those who heard her say this considered it words of insight.[45]

Several of the poets in this volume explicitly ordered their descendants not to publish their scribblings, which in the prefaces by relatives and filial offspring often leads to considerable soul-searching: should they heed their mother's or wife's instructions while alive or should they broadcast her virtue and talent now that she had passed away? Women who published their own collections felt challenged to defend their actions, but this rarely results in a more probing discussion of the nature of poetry.

GENDER ISSUES

The women discussed in this volume were almost all born to families of serving officials and there is no indication that their birth was not welcomed. In contrast, Mengyue recounts that her parents were elated at her birth, which followed that of several elder brothers. Manchu girls were not subjected to the gruesome process of footbinding. This made it easier for them to join their brothers and cousins in their youth in games and sports, and some women, such as Mengyue and Yingchuan, prided themselves in their equestrian abilities. Mengyue also mentions her skill at the martial sport of archery. A sizable number of these women poets traveled extensively, accompanying their fathers, fathers-in-law, husbands or sons to their official postings.[46] Most appear to have learned to read and write as children at home, occasionally under female tutors, at other times under male tutors, and in some cases together with their brothers. Lady Tongjia stresses that she received the same education as her brother, and that no difference was made because she was a girl. We know, however, that Yingchuan was illiterate when she was married, even though she was raised in a prestigious family.

Two eighteenth-century Manchu women, Sibo and Lady Tongjia, have left us essays on the education of girls.[47] Sibo, addressing her daughters on the eve of their marriage, warns that although they have been pampered at home, they will have to strictly abide by the norms for female behavior as set down in the Classics upon joining their husbands' families. She stresses the need to practice frugality, urges them not to shirk physical labor, and warns them not to pride themselves on their pedigree and look down on their husbands' families. The final warning might have special relevance for Manchu brides, because of the Manchu custom of "assigned marriages" (*zhihun*). The marriages between upper-class Manchu families was not left to the machinations of the families concerned, but was the responsibility of the Eight Banners administration.[48] In one of her poems Mengyue proudly refers to her marriage "by imperial decree." Although such marriages were prestigious, families could not predict in what kind of family their daughter would end up, which was a matter of great concern to Lady Tongjia at the end of the eighteenth century. One should also keep in mind that the Qing government pursued an active policy of intermarriage of Manchu and Mongol elites through this system.[49] Wanyan Jinchi's collection contains a set of poems in which she worries about her daughter's future now she has been married to a Mongol nobleman and will have to leave the capital for distant Kulun (Ulan Bator).[50]

Lady Tongjia provided a more detailed treatise on the moral and intellectual education of girls as part of her *Family Instructions from the Hall for Cherishing Goodness* (Baoshantang jiaxun), which she had printed some years after her son had been raised to the highest princely rank. Following a long preamble on the different social roles for men and women that are cosmically grounded in the mutual complementarity and relative position of yang and yin, Lady Tongjia provides an educational program for girls. This starts with the selection of proper nurses and nannies, who were to model proper speech by their own proper usage, teach young girls their first characters, and instruct them (from age four or five) in the proper way to eat and other rules of behavior. Girls were taught their first text on female education from the age of ten, and a female tutor was engaged when they turned fifteen to teach them the Four Books. From the following text it becomes clear that Lady Tongjia is thinking of the *Four Books for Women* (*Nü sishu*), a well-known set of texts on female education in Ming and Qing China. This is not only because of the intrinsic value of these texts, but also in order to prepare girls for marriage into families that insist on a strict practice of the norms. Such a strict practice certainly was not common—Lady Tongjia allows herself a long diatribe against the neglect of female education and the resulting moral laxity she observes around her: many parents (in her view) pamper their daughters and many families honor the rules on the segregation of the sexes only in the breach. Girls who grow up in such liberal households should be well prepared for the eventuality of marrying into families that live quite differently so they will not sink into depression or worse. Lady Tongjia also left us a detailed description of her own education by her mother and tutors in one of her prefaces.[51]

There is no indication that Sibo and Lady Tongjia see the virtues and behavioral norms they teach as specifically Chinese, and their adoption as a process of positive sinification. For them, the discourse on the different duties of men and women is universal. At the end of the nineteenth century, Lady Husihali wrote a set of twelve songs addressed to the women of Yuanzhou instructing them in their duties. The Manchu women would appear to have embraced these values and norms for female behavior with enthusiasm, the more so as many may have shared Lady Tongjia's argument that their talent should not be seen in opposition to virtue, but in support of virtue. A number of them embraced the devotion to their husband and his family to such an extent that they committed *gegu* (cutting off a slice of flesh from one's body and feeding it to a diseased relative). In Ming and Qing times *gegu* was on one hand widely condemned as unfilial—because one damaged the body one had received from one's parents—but on the other hand highly praised as the ultimate expression of sincere devotion.[52] Lady Tongjia is known to have committed *gegu* to save the life of her husband, but to no avail. In a long autobiographical poem, Xiguang provided a grisly description of her act of *gegu* to (unsuccessfully) save her husband.[53] The only efficacious act of *gegu* by a Manchu woman poet on record was Baibao Youlan's for her gravely ill father-in-law Gui-liang (1785–1862)—he recovered from his disease and pursued his career, living long enough to sign the Treaty of Tianjin and to assist Prince Gong in a coup d'état that opened the way for the ascendancy of Empress Dowager Cixi. Baibao Youlan's collection also contains a poem in praise of another woman who committed *gegu*. *Gegu* was not without its dangers: both the Hangzhou poet and painter Hualiang and her younger brother Wenliang committed *gegu* for the sake of their mother, but Wenliang died when he tried to slice a piece of his heart.[54]

All of the poets in this volume were married, with the exception of Miss Nalan who apparently died before she reached marriageable age (or suffered from a disease that precluded marriage).[55] Some appear to have had long and happy marriages, even though explicit evidence on the topic is rare. Not all husbands wrote poetry, but those who did rarely were explicit about affections for their wives.[56] One rare exception is Song-shan, who following his release from prison is said to have often exchanged poems with his wife Orchid Pavilion. He remembered her fondly on numerous occasions during the decades he survived her. Tie-bao and Yingchuan had a companionate marriage as we learn from the poem he wrote on the occasion of her sixtieth birthday, but that marriage included one or more concubine(s) who bore the couple's children.

We hear little about the relation of daughters-in-law and mothers-in-law. Poems by both Wenhuang Xianghua and Guizhen Daoren addressed to their mothers-in-law testify to their affections, and Lady Tongjia and Lady Husihali have left poems in memory of their mothers-in-law. Lady Husihali lost her mother-in-law when she had been married for four years. Having lost her own mother rather early, Lady Husihali had been taken in by her maternal grandparents and thanked her mother-in-law for her deep affection and instruction. Lady Tongjia is, as usual, effusive in the expression of her grief, but she too thanks her mother-in-law for treating her like a daughter.[57]

A considerable number of women poets became widows at an early age: Sibo, Xiguang, Lady Zhoujia, Lady Tongjia, Bingyue, Mengyue, Guizhen Daoren, Baibao Youlan, and Zhuyou. None remarried as they all embraced the "bitter ambition" of chaste widowhood, serving their parents-in-law (if still alive) and taking care of the children. Some of these widows appear to have been their husband's second (or third) wife, so might have been left in care of both their own children and children from his earlier marriage(s) and concubines. If they had already given birth to a son, they might, like Mengyue and Baibao Youlan, continue to live with their parents-in-law for some time, but many widows eventually chose (or were forced) to live on their own with their children in Beijing. Several sources hint at a "disharmony" in Gui-liang's large household that resulted in Baibao Youlan's decision to settle with her son in Beijing. Even if these widows would continue to receive a government subvention of some kind, their circumstances would be much reduced.[58] Responsible for the ancestral sacrifices and the education of the children, many widows may well have shared Lady Tongjia's feelings when she wrote:

> The many responsibilities of rules and norms
> Come all down on a single woman's shoulders.[59]

It will come as no surprise that Lady Tongjia starts one of her prefaces with the statement that she regrets not having been born a boy. Some women strongly express their resentment at the limitations imposed on them by their gender by lamenting the fact that their talent and learning will be of no use to the world. The embrace of traditional morality by these women in no way precluded their awareness of gender inequality.

Many collections by widows contain poems lamenting their loneliness and poverty as they supervise the education of their children. The love and devotion for their husbands, which could not be publicly expressed in print during their lifetimes, now often inspired the widowed poets to moving poems. In quantitative terms Lady Tongjia is the undisputed champion: she published a volume of 170 quatrains lamenting her husband—in her preface she informs us that these were selected from more than two hundred compositions. Vindication came for these chaste widows when a son was married, passed the examinations, and was appointed to a post in the imperial bureaucracy. When Baibao Youlan's son was appointed as prefect in the troubled Jiangnan region in the 1850s, she accompanied him there, and when a few years later the Hangzhou Manchu garrison was overrun by Taiping Tianguo rebels in late 1861, she completed her son's education by urging him to fight till the end while she committed suicide by drowning.

In poems dedicated to their deceased husbands, some women lamented that they had lacked the decisiveness to commit suicide upon their spouse's death, even though such behavior was officially condemned. The Yongzheng emperor had already emphasized that a chaste widow was a living widow who continued to serve her husband's parents and raised his children. Once she had done so, she was entitled to the joys of old age and to a certain degree of liberty in widowhood, including a room of her own. It was mostly widows who developed intense ties of friendship with fellow women, often widows themselves. The widow Xiguang, who committed suicide the day after her daughter was married, leaving behind a long poem in which she explained her decision, was an exception.

The women who saw their children grow to adulthood were of course lucky compared to the many who lost their children in infancy. Lady Tongjia lost three of her four sons in quick succession in the early 1760s. In her poems, Wenhuang Xianghua laments the loss of a daughter in 1813 shortly after birth, of another daughter in 1814 shortly after birth, and of twin boys in 1815 also shortly after birth. In the first collection of Bingyue there are also a number of poems lamenting young children. Guizhen Daoren lost her children soon after her husband had passed away.

For all the insistence on the importance of female-authored tracts on women's education by Lady Tongjia, we know very little about the actual reading practices of women.[60] We find many general references to the moral benefits of readings in the Classics and the Histories, and we may assume that biographies of virtuous women may also have been read avidly. But Lady Tongjia in her chapter on the education of girls already mentions that many preferred to read drum ballads and novels, without condemning that practice outright. Among the women poets in this collection, Mengyue wrote a poem inspired by her reading of *Peach Blossom Fan* (Taohua shan), Kong Shangren's (1648–1718) famous play on the collapse of the Southern Ming regime. The earliest poet in this collection to leave poems on the subject of *Dream of the Red Chamber* as a novel is Lady Husihali, who wrote these poems when only thirteen. It is difficult to imagine, however, that the other women poets of the nineteenth century had not read this novel.[61] Women all over China were avid readers of *Dream of the Red Chamber* from the moment it appeared in print.[62]

When widowed, many women turned to the reading and reciting of Buddhist sutras in order to find solace, as part of a larger program of devotional exercises such as practicing mediation. In one of the quatrains in memory of her husband, Lady Tongjia denies the power of buddhas and gods to grant wishes, but elsewhere in the same set she describes herself as reciting the *Diamond Sutra*, which is well-known for teaching the ephemerality and emptiness of all existence. In other poems she describes herself reciting sutras without specifying any title. Mengyue explained in a lengthy preface to a pithy quatrain that she read sutras, yet avoided monks. But two-day trips to the Buddhist monasteries in the Western Hills outside the capital definitely were part of the lifestyle of Manchu ladies of the eighteenth and nineteenth centuries and are often mentioned in their poems.[63] Lady Zhoujia is exceptional in mentioning the name (Dongwu) of the Buddhist nun with whom she was in frequent contact. Some Manchu women may have been more attracted to Daoist-inspired teachings of Inner Alchemy that were associated with the famous Daoist temple Baiyunguan and the veneration of Bixia Yuanjun, the widely-venerated goddess of Mount Tai. Yun Zhu's family appear to have belonged to the major patrons of Baiyunguan.[64]

ISSUES OF ETHNICITY

The Manchu women poets of the eighteenth and nineteenth centuries lived in a segregated world.[65] From the early years of the Qing dynasty the banner population lived in special quarters with their own walls, separate from the general Chinese population, in each city that housed a Manchu garrison. In Beijing, the Chinese were ordered in 1648 to move to the southern suburbs, reserving the quarters surrounding the Palace City for the banner population. Within the Inner City, each banner had its own districts. The families these Manchu women poets belonged to were a hereditary military and administrative caste that lived on government stipends and maintained certain customs that were typical to Manchus.[66] Manchu men of elite families were in daily and extensive contact with non-banner Chinese in the context of their official activities, but upper-class Manchu women were, like all upper-class women in late-imperial society, excluded from public life and expected to spend their days in the inner quarters. If these women's proud awareness of belonging to the privileged clans of the conquest elite needed any further reminder, there was their distinctive headdress and clothing style that set them apart from Chinese women.[67] Even the shape of their bodies was different because they did not bind their feet (though they imitated the gait of Chinese women by wearing high-soled shoes).[68] More specifically, several of the women poets in this volume were born into the imperial Aisin Gioro clan, and others were descendants of commanders who had joined Nurhaci early in his career, while those surnamed Wanyan claimed descent from the ruling family of the Jürched Jin dynasty (1115–1234), which the Qing saw as its predecessor.

Whereas Manchu men were subject to periodic government campaigns to reinvigorate their sense of the Manchu tradition, such as revitalizing the use of Manchu as a language or demanding improved riding and shooting skills, no such campaigns seem to have been directed at Manchu women. Actually, the reverse may have been the case. While the Qianlong emperor exhorted Manchu men to maintain the Manchu Way, his reign witnessed an explosive growth in the number of Chinese-style chaste Manchu widows honored by the authorities.[69] Traditionally, Manchu society had had no objections against widow remarriage, but it also had known a tradition requiring that one or more of the wives and servants of powerful men follow their master in death. This tradition may have been rejected as "barbarian" by the Manchu rulers of the eighteenth century as has been argued by recent scholars, but it was not forgotten in society at large. For instance, when the Manchu general Ming-rui died in battle in Burma in 1768, his Manchu wife, Lady Chang, committed suicide by hanging herself.[70] She earlier had sent him a poem, reading:

> Do not concern yourself about the many household matters;
> The bond that I have tied with you is based on prior karma.
> I do not seek to be like birds that briefly roost in couples:
> Let's be two lotus flowers on one stem that wilt as one.[71]

This may help to explain why many Manchu widows who survived to raise their children displayed in their poems a strong feeling of guilt over their failure to immediately follow their husband in death.

When Manchu women, inspired by their experiences, wrote poetry, they unavoidably from time to time also reflected on aspects of their life that were typical for their status as Manchu. Housing in Beijing, for instance, was assigned by the government, and families moved as the career of the head of the household went up or down. While the descendants of Ming-zhu continued to live in the same palatial establishment until 1790, other families were forced to move faster. Several Manchu women poets have left poems on their emotions on passing the mansions where they had lived in earlier, more glorious days. Mengyue proudly noted her marriage "by imperial decree," while Wanyan Jinchi voiced her concerns when her daughter was married to a Mongol prince—and her joy when that young man was later reassigned to Beijing. Some of the Manchu men who served in the military or in the administration followed the emperor to Chengde (Luanyang) for the autumn hunts in the years of the Qianlong emperor—or to flee the British and French troops in 1860. Lady Tongjia's father and husband followed the Qianlong emperor on some of his eastern and southern tours. We hear about appointments to "the old homeland" of Manchuria—but while Shenyang was a hardship posting for those who had been raised in Beijing, it was a grand capital in the eyes of Lady Husihali, who grew up on the Liaodong Peninsula. As the Manchu empire expanded into Inner Asia, we first hear about fathers taking part in campaigns and later about the postings of brothers to Xining and Urumchi—Lady Tongjia's husband spent nine months on the road escorting a party of Uighurs from Beijing to Aksu (and then returning); Yingchuan's husband Tie-bao sent her a poem on the occasion of her sixtieth birthday while he was on his way back to Beijing from faraway Kashgar. In her long autobiographical poem, Lady Tongjia expressed her pride in her son's horsemanship and shooting skills—defined by the Qianlong emperor as the quintessential skills of the true Manchu.

Mostly living in Beijing, the Manchu women poets were to a certain degree sheltered from the direct impact of major historical developments. The Taiping Tianguo rebellion did not reach Beijing, but Lingwen Zhuyou lamented the Taiping rebels' capture of Nanjing and Yangzhou, cities she had visited as a teenager during her journey from Hengyang to Beijing. Baibao Youlan, however, who had followed her son to the Jiangnan area, died in the massacre of the Hangzhou Manchu garrison. The impact of the West also had its more positive side: Naxun Lanbao enjoyed the fresh lychees that were brought by steamboat from the south in the 1860s. Lady Husihali even traveled by steamboat from Niuzhuang to Shanghai and marveled at the Western-style buildings there, but once in Yuanzhou, Jiangxi, was alarmed by the news of the activities of Japanese troops in Manchuria during the Sino-Japanese War (1894–95).

As members of prominent political clans, however, several of the Manchu women poets in this collection were quite directly impacted by court politics. The vicious factional struggles that preceded the Yongzheng accession, and the vindictive actions of the Yongzheng emperor once he occupied the throne against some of his brothers and their supporters, greatly impacted the Nalan family, and resulted in a complete change of fortune for Nurturing Simplicity and Orchid Pavilion when the latter's husband Song-shan was imprisoned and banished. The Yongzheng emperor's actions against his former supporter Nian Gengyao (d. 1726) still affected the circumstance of Bingyue several decades later. The Qianlong emperor's quick reversal of many of the policies of his father undid the consequences of some of his actions, but not all. The Qianlong emperor's own redefinition of the nature of the Manchus and their role in the conquest greatly enhanced the position of Lady Tongjia, first when her husband was unexpectedly raised to princely rank, and then again when her son was suddenly raised to an even higher princely rank. Baibao Youlan witnessed her father-in-law's rise to power when one of her sisters-in-law married Prince Gong, and Lingwen Zhuyou closely followed the career of her former tutor Peng Yulin.

While Manchu women writers at times express great pride in their individual descent from major personalities of the founding generations, they rarely if ever problematize their own ethnicity. They seem to have enjoyed their privileged status as a given. The woman poet who shows the strongest ethnic awareness in her work is Naxun Lanbao. When she provides a detailed description of the heroic suicide of her good friend Baibao Youlan, she explains her behavior first of all in terms of loyalty but ends by exclaiming that her friend had been born in order to "bring glory to us women in the banners." Though born as a Mongol herself, she identified with her Manchu family to the extent that she could refer to Manchuria as "our old homeland" in a poem to see off a trusted maid servant who had been selected to accompany her elder sister-in-law on a trip to Shenyang. But the clearest expression of her contradictory ethnic self-awareness is found in a poem (ca. 1858) for her elder brother Yingjun when he was reassigned from Beijing to their old hometown Kulun (Ulan Bator). In this poem she proudly recalls her family's descent from Chinggis Khan, sketches the warlike nature of her forefathers, and urges her brother to continue the family tradition. No wonder this poem has often been quoted in studies emerging from Inner Mongolia that claim Naxun Lanbao as a Mongol poet. However, in this same poem she admits that she has not been back to her "old hometown" for thirty years since she moved to the Beijing at the age of four, does not know Mongolian anymore, and follows the capital fashion and loves Chinese literature. One cannot escape the feeling that she was only too happy she didn't have to accompany her brother to those faraway regions she now considered a "foreign land."[72] According to her son Sheng-yu, he was at one time indirectly attacked by a political opponent who quoted his mother's poem to prove to what extent she had forgotten her origins. It is probably this same heightened ethnic awareness that spurred Naxun Lanbao on to conceive of an anthology strictly devoted to Manchu women poets. As she conceived of this anthology, she also constructed a Manchu genealogy of women poets under the patronage of the famous Manchu scholar Tie-bao by making him the northern rival to Yuan Mei. But when she started her *Anthology of Poetry by Manchu Women*, she still identified herself as a "female scribe of a foreign fief" (*waifan nüshi*).

MANCHU WOMEN AND WOMEN'S LITERATURE

Recent decades have seen an upsurge in the study of Chinese women's literature of the Ming and Qing dynasties. This has not only resulted in a number of fine monographs and conference volumes, but also in two extensive anthologies of women's poetry and other writings. Most of these studies and anthologies focus on women authors of the Jiangnan region, as the greatest number of female authors hailed from Jiangsu and Zhejiang, where they lived in a society in which print was easily available. As a result, our primary sources are overwhelmingly from that area. This applies not only to the seventeenth century, when the Qing replaced the Ming, but also to the eighteenth and nineteenth centuries when the Manchus were the ruling elite. It is therefore not surprising that the women writers of the Jiangnan region have attracted most scholarly attention.[73] Only recently have scholars started to focus on the female authors of other regions.[74]

The poetry of the Manchu women in this volume is in many aspects similar to the poetry produced by women of the Jiangnan area in its contrast to male-authored poetry of the same period. In women's poetry there is an even greater stress on the principle that poetry should be the direct expression of spontaneous emotion. While Manchu women may have enjoyed a somewhat less restricted lifestyle than upper-class Chinese women, they too were excluded from the public life of academies, examinations, class-mate networks, and, most importantly, the bureaucratic career in the civil administration or the military, in the provinces or at court. Whereas the overwhelming amount of poetry authored by men in the late imperial period is linked to their social experiences in this public realm, women poets, with the exception of those few who traveled extensively, were primarily dependent on their experiences and their emotions within the private sphere of family and gardens, friendship, and short trips. This places strict limitations on their subject matter, but at the same time frees it from the allusion-ridden obsequious verbiage that makes so much of male social poetry of the late imperial period nowadays indigestible. What happens when social poetry becomes more dominant in a woman's work can be observed in the collection of Guizhen Daoren: when writing to her male and female patrons she tends to be more formal and flattering than in her other poems.

But because of its more private character and its stress on the direct expression of spontaneous emotion, late imperial women's poetry has the potential to appeal more directly to modern readers. No poem is ever the direct expression of spontaneous emotion, of course, and the women poets of late imperial

China, including the Manchu women poets of the Qing, wasted no effort to find the right word and the perfect line, but the belief in the direct expression of spontaneous emotion made them prefer short forms and avoid the learned display of allusions. Whereas male poets at the time might have competed in the competitive display of obscure quotations, the few allusions we find in the poetry of these Manchu women poets tend to be commonplace and can be immediately understood by contemporary readers. Some of the Manchu women poets were evidently highly educated, but none (if we exclude Yun Zhu) displayed a clear interest in scholarship, in contrast to some of their contemporary Chinese sisters. While Miss Nalan wrote a number of poems on historical characters, such poems are rarely found in the collections of later Manchu women poets. Manchu women poets also did not involve themselves in the debates between literary schools of the times—whether one should model one's poetry on that of the High Tang or on that of the Song dynasty.[75] When Duomin Huiru allows herself to write on the topic, she does so by denying the value of such critical discussions to women poets.

Discussing Poetry with My Female Disciple Sufang

What is the need to talk of Tang or Song?
A poem gives expression to one's nature.
If your emotions are as bright as moonlight,
Your writings too will sparkle like the stars.
  Your words will rob the green of mountain ranges,
Your thoughts will turn the river's blue all clear.
It's of no use for poets of today
To cling to norms and models of the past.[76]

The private character of this poetry not only allows for the expression of strong personal emotions such as those following the loss of parents, husbands, or children, but also allows for the display of wit and playfulness. For men, poetry tends to be serious business; for women, poetry can be pure entertainment and fun. And whereas the completed works of male authors usually are printed as a massive public monument, the small collections of women authors more likely were published only for relatives and close friends. The latter scenario allows for the inclusion of personal materials that in the case of a male author's collection would probably be edited out.

For all the similarity to the poetry of the Jiangnan women, however, the poetry of the Manchu women also had its own characteristics. These are not due to expression of a Manchu ethnic identity. When some PRC scholars appeal to such an essentialized ethnic identity in their discussion of the poetry of Manchu and Mongol women, they usually end up praising these women for qualities of moral fortitude and perseverance that may be laudable enough but not necessarily exclusively Manchu or Mongol. That the poetry in this volume displays shared characteristics is due to shared experiences. The Manchu women poets lived mostly in a specific region of China, and very much in a world apart. Their special status resulted in many events that were unique to their lives. But for all the shared characteristics, the poetry of each of these Manchu women is also highly individual as they coped with their personal experiences very much in their own way. One widow published a collection of 170 quatrains to lament her late husband, another asked her recently deceased dog to take a message to her partner in the underworld.

Scholarship on Manchu women is still limited in scope. While we have several detailed descriptions of Manchu customs and family life, they rarely discuss women's literary and artistic activities. The most detailed studies focus on those topics for which abundant archival source materials is available, such as the government policy of Manchu-Mongol intermarriage. Recent years have seen a growing interest in Manchu literature, both in texts composed in Manchu and texts composed in Chinese by Manchu men. But even the most comprehensive surveys up until the present at most touch only briefly upon a few Manchu women authors.[77] There have been a few short general survey articles on poetry by Manchu and Mongol women, but their coverage is very superficial and incomplete. Whereas there have been a number of articles that hail Naxun Lanbao as a Mongol woman poet, no Manchu woman writer has attracted the same kind of attention. Most Manchu women writers have only attracted a few short articles at most. The two exceptions here are, of course, Yun Zhu and Gu Taiqing. Yun Zhu's editorial activities in publishing *Correct Beginnings* have been scrutinized repeatedly, while Gu Taiqing is hailed as the finest (female) lyricist of the nineteenth century. The whiff of scandal that surrounds her life continues to attract both serious and less serious scholars. Studies on Yun Zhu and Gu Taiqing, however, rarely treat them as Manchu authors; they treat them instead as women authors of the Qing.

The poetry of the Manchu women in this volume is overwhelmingly lyrical in nature, the patterned expression of emotions as stimulated by sights and events. These sights and events are at times described in great detail in the titles of the poems, or in prefaces attached to the titles. Background information needed for a better understanding of the poem may also be provided by the authors in interlinear notes. This poetry therefore very much reflects the lives and times of these women poets. Of course, this is not a reflection that answers all our questions on their lives and thoughts. Strong conventions govern the suitable topics for poetry as well as the suitable language for these topics. In that sense, many poems do not strive to be creations, but rather to be subtle variations on well-established themes. But new experiences call for new topics and conventions. Miss Nalan explored descriptions of the often cold and bleak landscapes of northern China; two centuries later Lady Husihali traveled by steamboat and was amazed by the modern city of Shanghai. Like new experiences, strong emotions, whether of friendship or of loss, also found their way into these women's poetry. Few men wrote about the pain of losing their children, but women did as they struggled to make sense of their experiences. Orchid Pavilion wrote about her life as the wife of an imprisoned husband, Mengyue expressed her anger at being forced to wear female dress. By reflecting their experiences in poetry and by reflecting on their experiences in the same poetry they created a record of their lives. Even if not all of these women poets published their own collections during their lifetime and some of them demanded that their poems be destroyed upon their death, I am convinced that the male relatives who published their works understood that these women wanted to be remembered in their own words. Because of this, I too want them to speak as much as possible in their own words, and include large selections from their works in translation. I believe that this is the best way to come to know them in all their diversity and individuality.

All poetry is patterned language, and I have tried to reflect the formal features of these poems in translation as well as the differences between Chinese and English allow. I have labored to bring out the structure of the parallel couplets on which these poets worked so hard. In many cases I have rendered their poems in a strictly metrical fashion, but I have never tried to reproduce rhyme. As far as possible I have translated complete texts, but in dealing with long sets of poems I have often made a selection.

In order to avoid clutter, I have not referenced the source page of individual poems in the poetry selections. The poems are found in relatively small collections and are presented here in the sequence in which they appear in the original collections. Readers who know Chinese and have access to the original collections should have no problem in locating the Chinese originals.

1

The Women of the Nalan Family

Miss Nalan, Sibo, and Madam Zhaojia

MISS NALAN WAS NOT THE EARLIEST MANCHU WOMAN POET. We know the names of several others of the Kangxi period (1662–1722), and in some cases we also know the titles of their collections, but usually only one or two poems have been preserved. This makes Miss Nalan the earliest Manchu woman poet whose collection has survived in its entirety. Its title, *Poetry Drafts from Leisure after Needlework* (Xiuyu shigao), echoes the titles of many other collections by women poets and stresses that poetry was only an avocation—she would turn to the writing of verse after she had finished her work for the day.

As the youngest daughter of Nalan Ming-zhu (b. 1635–1708), one of the richest Manchu officials of the late seventeenth century, Miss Nalan was a younger sister of the well-known male poet Nalan Xing-de (1655–1685). Her slim collection of poetry was published following her death with a preface by her nephew Yong-shou (1702–1731), the adopted son of her elder brother Kui-xu (1674?–1717). Yong-shou's wife Sibo would, as a widow, also author a modest collection of poetry titled *Preserved Together: Selected Poems* (Hecun shichao). *Preserved Together* contained not only her own poems, but also those of Gong Danting, the woman she had hired as teacher of her daughters. In the small collection of prose essays that Sibo published some years later, we also find an essay by one of her daughters.

Ming-zhu was a close confidant of the Kangxi emperor. He was one of the few officials who supported the emperor in his confrontational policy toward Wu Sangui (1612–1678), the Ming general who in 1644 had admitted the Manchus inside the Great Wall and had been rewarded for his role in the Qing conquest of the empire with a semi-independent kingdom in Yunnan and Guizhou. When the confrontation resulted in the so-called Rebellion of the Three Feudatories (1673–1681), Ming-zhu rose to become grand secretary in 1677 and used his position to greatly enrich himself. In 1688 he and his clique were accused of corruption and Ming-zhu was forced to step down, but he continued to enjoy the emperor's favor and increased his possessions by investing in the government-controlled salt trade.[1] His descendants enjoyed great wealth until in 1790 Kui-xu's great-grandson Cheng-an was stripped of all his positions at the instigation of He-shen (1750–1799), at that time the all-powerful favorite of the Qianlong emperor, after which all family property was confiscated. The family's mansion too was confiscated at that time and redesigned for use as a princely palace. Known as the Chunqinwang Fu, it is presently one of the best preserved princely palaces of the Qing. When Cao Xueqin's novel *Dream of the Red Chamber* (Honglou meng) became widely popular in the nineteenth century, one theory, claiming no less an authority than the Qianlong emperor himself, held that the novel's descriptions were based on life in the Ming-zhu household.[2]

Ming-zhu patronized Chinese officials and scholars and saw to it that his sons received an excellent education.[3] His eldest son, Xing-de, served the emperor as a personal attendant and quickly rose through the ranks, but died at a relatively early age. He is known to this day as the finest lyricist of the Qing dynasty.[4] Some of Xing-de's sons and grandsons would continue to serve the dynasty in high positions. Ming-zhu's youngest son, Kui-fang, died at a relatively early age too. He was married to the eighth daughter of Giyesu, Prince Kang (1645–1697), a great-grandson of Nurhaci, who was in charge of the southeastern front in Fujian during the Rebellion of the Three Feudatories. When the princess quickly followed Kui-fang in death, the couple's two young sons (Yong-shou and Yong-fu) were entrusted to Kui-xu, who had no sons of his own. (From a poem by Sibo we learn that the grandparents, though now officially granduncle and grandaunt, remained in close contact with their grandsons and their wives.) Kui-xu had started out in his career as a member of the emperor's bodyguard, but because of his conspicuous literary talents, he was quickly moved to the Hanlin Secretariat, and served as its chancellor from 1703 till his death, on occasion also concurrently holding other high positions. Kui-xu not only left a large collection of his own poetry, but at the emperor's behest also compiled a small anthology of women's poetry titled *Fine Poems by Women of Successive Dynasties* (Lichao guiya).[5]

This collection in twelve *juan* is a highly selective anthology of *shi* poetry from the Tang to the Ming dynasties. The poems are divided by genre (five-syllable old style poetry; seven-syllable old style poetry; five-syllable regulated poems; seven-syllable regulated poems; five-syllable quatrains; seven-syllable quatrains; and miscellaneous forms). Within each genre the poems are arranged by dynasty, and for each dynasty the poets included are arranged in the order of empresses and imperial concubines, well-born ladies and concubines, nuns and courtesans, foreigners and the spouses of local rulers. The collection carries no preface in its 1703 edition, but includes a detailed set of "editorial principles" (*fanli*). Kui-xu stresses for instance that he has omitted all poems of questionable authorship. The final item of these editorial principles reads:

> The rise of literature is related to orderly administration. Our Sovereign the Emperor has scrutinized the past: if one completes the wide world by the privileging of transformation through culture one will not only see a proliferation of human talents but also witness of a multitude of masters because of mutual competition. And those who wield the brush to compose their texts in the inner chambers will often be able to compete with men of letters. It is therefore our intention to collect the poems of well-born ladies of the present age and to compile a matching volume to record that the transformation by civilization of this Sagely Era even among women is capable of proclaiming the glory of this dynasty![6]

Unfortunately, such a second collection, in which Kui-xu could have included a fair sample of the poems by his younger sister, never saw the light of day, because Kui-xu died the year *Fine Poems* was published. The project to compile an anthology of women's poetry that manifested the universal civilizational mission of the Manchu Qing dynasty was only undertaken one century later by Yun Zhu.

Kui-xu may well have been motivated to consider the compilation of a collection of poetry by women of the Qing because he was surrounded by highly literate women in his own family. These included not only his younger sister but also his mother and his wife. Ming-zhu's wife (1637–1694) was a daughter of Ajige (1605–1651), one of the major Manchu generals in the conquest of China.[7] She married her husband at the age of fifteen, when her husband was only seventeen. From her grave inscription we learn that she was literate both in Manchu and Chinese.

> In her youth, her ladyship learned the national script and was not yet acquainted with Chinese characters. But when she later made up her mind to study them, she could completely understand [a text] on first reading. She loved to read works such as the *Comprehensive Mirror* and *A History of Women*, and when practicing calligraphy she excelled in the regular script.[8]

The grave inscription proceeds with a description of the excellent care she took of the scholars her husband hired for the instruction of their sons, mentioning that she would attend the lectures on occasion from behind a screen. She is also highly praised for her philological acumen, and was a pious Buddhist:

> In her daily life she had taken refuge with the Buddha, and each morning on rising she would burn incense, make her devotions, and recite one roll of scripture. When she once had copied out the *Diamond Sutra*, her handwriting was so perfect that it was distributed in print, and both clerics and laypeople revered these copies as exceptional treasures.[9]

Despite this piety we learn from another source that she was a jealous woman. When her husband took a fancy to a serving girl and praised her eyes, she had those eyes gouged out and presented them to her husband in a box. At least one modern scholar is willing to give credence to the account that she died because of the wounds she suffered when the girl's father tried to take revenge.[10]

Kui-xu's own wife Lady Geng (1671–1719) was a daughter of Geng Juzhong (d. 1687), a younger brother of Geng Jingzhong (d. 1682). When his older brother rebelled as one of the Three Feudatories, Geng Juzhong stayed loyal to the Qing and informed on his brother even after the latter had submitted. Lady Geng's mother was an imperial princess, and throughout her life she would continue to frequent the imperial palace; the Kangxi emperor was quite fond of her. Her grave inscription praises her for her moral seriousness from an early age:

> From birth she displayed a preternatural intelligence, and her sharp understanding was beyond compare. From her infant years her behavior was correct and composed like an adult. In her youth and once an adult she read books such as *Inner Rules*, and she needed only to read them quickly to memorize these completely. In her calligraphy she practiced the regular script, and she was also conversant with the national script.[11]

Elsewhere in the grave inscription we learn that she and her husband discussed the Classics and poetry like fellow students. But when he asked her why she did not engage in the writing of verse, she is said to have replied: "The study of books serves to elucidate the Great Meaning, so making poems is not the business of women."[12] Such a statement, of course, does not mean that she never indulged in versifying, only that she did not want to be considered a female poet.

Kui-xu's younger sister lived during the days of the family's greatest wealth and prosperity, but a generation later Sibo was confronted with a quite different situation. As one of the richest and most powerful families of the land, the Nalans could not avoid involvement in the issue of the dynastic succession even if they had wanted to. The Kangxi emperor had many sons. He originally had appointed the second, Yin-reng (1654–1725), as crown prince, but Yin-reng suffered from bouts of insanity.[13] When in 1708 he was incarcerated and the emperor convened a meeting of high officials to discuss the succession, these officials, including Kui-xu, all proposed the name of the emperor's eighth son, Yin-si (1681–1726), much to the emperor's displeasure.[14] The emperor suspected a cabal and many officials involved were punished.[15] When eventually the emperor's fourth son, the highly capable but also extremely jealous and suspicious Yin-zhen, succeeded him as the Yongzheng emperor (r. 1723–1735), he accused Kui-xu of having financed a campaign in favor of Yin-si, and in 1724 ordered that Kui-xu's grave should be inscribed with the following words:[16] "Grave of the disloyal, unfilial, underhanded, and treacherous Kui-xu."[17]

The Yongzheng emperor viciously persecuted those brothers whom he considered a threat to his position, including not only Yin-si, but also Yin-tang (1683–1726), the ninth son of the Kangxi emperor. Yin-si and Yin-tang were seen as forming one clique. Yin-tang was known for his great wealth, which to a large extent derived from support from Ming-zhu. The ties between the two families had been further cemented by a marriage between Yong-shou's younger brother Yong-fu and Yin-tang's third daughter (Yong-shou's wife was a goddaughter of Yin-tang). Yong-fu was stripped of all his functions by the Yongzheng emperor following his ascension to the throne, but Yong-shou's own career would appear to have suffered little impact as he continuously advanced in rank until his untimely death. When the Yongzheng emperor passed away in 1735 and was succeeded by his fourth son, Hong-li, as the Qianlong emperor (r. 1736–1795), Yong-fu was one of the many cashiered officials whose career had a second start. However, he died in 1739, and his two sons and two daughters were raised by Yong-shou's widow, Sibo, as her own (Yong-fu's second son Ning-xiu was formally adopted as the heir of Yong-shou).[18] One of Yong-shou's daughters later became the imperial concubine Consort Shu (1728–1777).[19]

Miss Nalan lived from circa 1680 to circa 1705. She probably was born later than Kui-xu. In one poem she suggests that in their youth they studied together. Another of her poems, which harmonizes with the rhymes "used by my elder brother," would appear to match a poem encountered in his collection. Her own poems were printed in the early eighteenth century, but the undated preface (unfortunately damaged in the only known preserved copy) by her nephew Yong-shou is so uninformative about her life that one wonders whether he had ever known his aunt in person. Yong-shou hardly moves beyond the commonplace of wondering why someone so talented had to die at such an early age.

Miss Nalan's collection consists of 120 quatrains and eight-line "regulated poems." We have no information on the principles that account for the sequence of the poems. Most likely the poems are arranged according to date of composition. If that is true, and if the sequence of poems is reliable, the poems would appear to date from an eight-year period. But whereas many poems contain in their title a direct or indirect reference to one of the four seasons (most often spring, less often fall, and on occasion summer and winter), none of the poems are dated to a specific year.

Most of the poems in Miss Nalan's collection are nature observations. Contemporary critics love to quote her poem "The Eagle" as a reflection of the fierce nature of the Manchus in their early days of power, but that poem is rather atypical of her collection as a whole, in which freezing crows and sparrows are more numerous.[20] Many of the poems in her collection stand out because of their description of the cold and bleak landscape of northern China. Starting halfway through the collection we also encounter a handful of poems on historical subjects.[21] Whereas the collections of many later Manchu women show that they interacted frequently with other Manchu women poets, we find no such evidence in the collection of Miss Nalan (the only two social poems in her collection are both addressed to her elder brother, presumably Kui-xu).

Sibo (b. ca. 1702) was the wife of Yong-shou. When Yong-shou, then a vice minister, died at the age of thirty, he left her in care of one (adopted) son (Ning-xiu) and six girls (four daughters and two nieces).[22] She thereupon engaged the services of another widow, the sixty-year old Gong Danting, as a governess for her children. Gong Danting came from a well-established family, and one of her elder brothers rose to the rank of provincial governor.[23] She and Sibo became closest friends. When Gong Danting after nine years expressed a desire to return to her hometown of Yangzhou once one of her sons had passed the metropolitan examinations in 1736, Sibo in 1738 had a small collection printed of the poems they had written during their years together. The collection consists of four scrolls and arranges the poems by genre: the first scroll is dedicated to five-syllable regulated poems; the second to five-syllable quatrains; the third to seven-syllable regulated poems; and the fourth and final scroll to seven-syllable quatrains. In each section poems of the two women alternate, but only poems by Sibo are included here. Both Danting and Sibo provided a preface for the collection. Sibo's preface is mostly taken up by fulsome praise of Gong Danting, while the preface of the latter is mostly given over to a lengthy survey of her own family background. After Danting has described her decision to accept the invitation to serve as tutor and her pleasure in teaching her charges, she devotes the following words to her and Sibo's versifying:

> Thereupon we would share out the sheets and prepare the ink, and grieved by our husbands' deaths we each would write words of lament; with clouded eyes and aching hearts we would sadly comfort the infants and together chant of our bitter ambition. From time to time there also were stanzas on gratitude for presents and lines that described objects. Basically we made use of brush and ink to dispel our worries as we did not want to be overcome by gloom.

Danting then concluded her preface by praising Sibo for the way she managed her large household.

Sibo's father, A-han-tai, is described as a vice commander-in-chief of the Chinese Plain Yellow Banner and appears to have served in the Central Asian campaigns of the early eighteenth century.[24] The name Sibo ("thinking of the cypress") most likely is not her original name but a sobriquet she assumed when she became a widow and took to writing. The cypress, an evergreen that keeps its foliage even in winter, is a common symbol for fidelity and chastity. The name may also contain a reference to the poem "The Cypress Boat" in *The Book of Odes*. According to the canonical Mao Commentary to this classic, "The Cypress Boat" is an oath sworn by Gong Jiang: "When Gong Bo, the crown prince of Wei, died, his wife remained loyal to him. When her parents wanted to marry her off against her will, she refused, swearing an oath, and that is why she wrote this poem to break with them."[25] The sobriquet of the author also serves as an indication of the content of her collection as many of her poems voice her continuing devotion to her husband and her sufferings as a widow. We will encounter many of the themes she explores (dreams of the deceased, visiting the grave, supervising her son's education) in the later collections of widowed poets. Sibo's collection contains a small number of poems relating to her Buddhist piety and practice of mediation, but we do not yet find any poems narrating visits to Buddhist shrines in the Western Hills. The copy of *Preserved Together* in the National Library in Beijing comes with handwritten comments by a later reader. On the title page this reader wrote: "A pure spirit and fine bones, without the slightest trace of dust or vulgarity. I was very much impressed to find this among women."

Three years after the printing of *Preserved Together*, Sibo also printed a short collection of prose pieces titled *Beyond Poetry: Combined Explanations* (Shiyu hejie). Five of the seven texts in this collection are by Sibo; the opening piece is by Gong Danting, and the final piece ("On Gratitude") by one of her pupils, Yuxuan. The first of the two essays by Sibo included here is on the education of daughters in view of their future as wives in other families. The tradition of writing such motherly advice can be traced back to the first century when Ban Zhao (ca. 48–ca. 118) wrote her *Precepts for My Daughters* (Nüjie), which by the Ming dynasty (1368–1644) had become one of the most authoritative moral handbooks for women.[26] Sibo's essay may also be compared to the chapter on the education of daughters by Lady Tongjia. More original is the second essay in which Sibo argues that good friends should write funerary laments for each other while both are still alive, so they can read the heartfelt emotions of their partner. Perhaps inspired by this piece, Bingyue and Guizhen Daoren would go on and write such poems for each other.

Sibo was perhaps not the only daughter-in-law of the Nalan family to write poetry. Fashishan tells the story of a Madam Zhaojia who married into the Nalan family, was widowed from an early date, and lived a life of poverty:

> Madam Zhaojia was a Manchu. She wrote *Xiyuan shi* [Poems of the Western Garden]. From her earliest youth she loved to read books; she was conversant with the instructions for women and also skilled in chanting and singing. When she grew up, she married into the Nalan family, but was soon widowed. Living in poverty, she instructed her son like a strict teacher. Her poems are filled by sounds of sorrow and suffering. Whenever she met with falling flowers or a waning moon, a chilly wind or bitter rain, she would grasp her brush and moisten the ink stick for short songs and long chants. Her pure resolve and bitter virtue can be easily imagined by the reader.[27]

The references to poverty seems out of place for the widow of any of Mingzhu's descendants and suggests that Miss Zhaojia married into a different branch of the Nalan clan, but of course it may also be a pious trope to stress her sufferings as a virtuous widow. But in *Elegant Chants,* which contains no less than seventeen poems by Madam Zhaojia, Tie-bao limits himself to the information that she was a Manchu and makes no reference to her marriage to a member of the Nalan family.[28] Apart from her poems on the bitter sufferings of a widow's life, the selection of poems in the *Elegant Chants* also include some poems of contentment; it further contains four of her *Songs of Roaming with Immortals* (Youxianci), a genre we will reencounter in the collections of Guizhen Daoren and Baibao Youlan.[29]

MISS NALAN

Freezing Crows

They're waiting for return of spring, this flock of evening crows;
Lingering in the trees they fly about without a pattern.
When spring is back, there is no need for you to stay around:
There will be yellow orioles to grab the finest flowers!

A Peasant Family

Where in this spring breeze will I find Peach Blossom fairyland?[30]
Here in this mountain village where the little birds are chirping.
Now when the peasant has come home, the sun is setting fast—
As darkness falls, a lonely moon shines on the simple door.

Spring Breeze

Oh soft so soft, it blows through flower lanes;
Oh light so light, it enters willow clusters.
But most I love it when it after dusk
Leads rain to penetrate the paper window.

Watching the Moon following a Shower

Now clouds have left, the hills are once as black;
As mists have cleared, the moon is once as bright.
The night lasts long and I become frustrated—
The roosting crows are startled on their branches.

Boating in the Final Month of Spring

The oars speed forward, following the breeze;
Our boat makes headway on a winding stream.
The pond is fully filled by the bright moon—
The thousand petals drifting down so red!

Late in Spring

With flowers gone, the willows soon will wither,
Now springtime splendor is about to fade.
The song of orioles is getting scarcer,
But butterflies I still have failed to see.

Autumn Day

It's only me who loves the pure crisp air
As in square ponds the autumn waters rise.
The sun that passes through the screen is cold,
And chilly is the draft inside the curtains.
  On the long dike the wutong drops its leaves;
Osmanthus fragrance fills the little yard.
I sit and savor this fine scenery—
This is an unforgettable excursion!

A Strong Gale

In this Eighth Month a chilly storm starts blowing,
It has arisen in some distant desert:
It urges the migrating geese to hurry;
You'd think to hear the angry roar of thunder!
  Here in the courtyard, dust and sand swirl upward,
And on the steps the tree leaves levitate.
Throughout the day the painted screens stay down,
And all alone I hear the autumn sounds.

A Song of the Han Palace

Oh deep so deep in autumn nights the scent of the osmanthus—
The Palace of Eternal Trust: the moon resembles frost.
The Phoenix Carriage does not arrive—how long each hour now lasts
While from afar one hears the song and dance in Zhaoyang Hall.[31]

Remembering the Past at the End of the Year; for My Elder Brother

The little room is cozy in this sunlight—
I still remember how we read our books:
While outside the gauze windows birds were singing,
The flowers bloomed in front of the pavilion.
  How I admire your great and lofty talent!
My studies were, alas, to no avail.
Again I feel the warmth is bringing back
Another year with all its springtime splendor.

The Eagle

Fierce winds that chill you to the bone: release the autumn eagle!
Pupils of gold and claws of jade, it roams the skies at will.
When grass starts wilting on the plains its eyes are once as sharp—
Where it descends in one fell swoop it terrifies all birds.

Freezing Sparrows

Madly they dash across the empty courtyard,
Unable to find peace on swaying branches.
Weak as they are, they fear the blustering wind;
Afraid of snow and frost they twitter softly.
  Without a mate they follow painted beams,
For love of warmth they hug the balustrade.
Just wait until the springtime sun returns
And you can test your wings amidst the flowers!

Northern Winds

How strong these freezing gales on level plains:
They blow the bitter fleabane from its roots.
With their great noise they shake the brightest sun;
Deliberately they stir up gloomy dusk.
  The falling leaves drift through the door in front;
The startled sand disturbs the distant village.
And I recall how standing under flowers
My sleeves once whisked away the warmth of spring.

SIBO

Five-Syllable Regulated Verse from *Preserved Together: Selected Poems*

After the Rain

The clear skies following the rain are great:
The wind is pure, the scenery is quiet—
Below the hedge early chrysanthemums;
Above the rivers gulls both white and light.
A lucid dew, as streams and brooks are cold,
And chilly clouds, as plants and trees all wither.
There is no need to add to my emotion:
For all eternity that single grave!

The New Autumn

The air is crisp as coolness first arrives;
The sky is high now humid air retreats.
The autumn window hears the early geese;
The wutong leaves drift lightly as they fall.
At night I listen to the first cicadas;
Trees start to rustle in the evening breeze.
Delighted that the sultry heat receded,
I read a book and love this lucid quiet.

Written on the Spur of the Moment

Dispirited, I love this autumn scene—
What can I do about this orphaned heart?
Thin clouds stretch out to the horizon,
And weeds and tares are covering the road.
The shape of hills has turned to pure and slender;
A tipsy blush shows on the face of maples.
As I dispassionately watch this landscape,
Transparent waves cleanse sorrow from my heart.

Five-Syllable Quatrains from *Preserved Together: Selected Poems*

Practicing Stillness

Loudly or softly—let the birds but sing;
Allow the flowers each to bloom in time.
When I sat down, the moon was not invited—
It came all by itself to shine on me.[32]

On a Picture of Manjusri Practicing Meditation by the Light of the Moon[33]

His mind forever fixed in meditation:
Freed from all guile, the night is oh so pure.
Too bad that in the world of men our dreams
Turn brightest day into a midnight darkness!

Listening to My Son Reciting His Books at Nighttime

The hour is late, none stirs outside the window:
I listen as my son recites his books.
When his voice slows, I think he's growing lazy—
Loudly or softly, he is quite at ease!

Strange Grief

The strangest grief rips my small heart to pieces,
And brush and ink replace my moaning sorrow.
When comes an end to all these tears of blood?
The grave goes down beyond a thousand miles!

Seven-Syllable Regulated Verse from *Preserved Together: Selected Poems*

Emotions on New Year's Day

All celebrate Ascending Peace, enjoy the new year's splendor,
I am the only one whose eyes are filled with ample tears.
My husband passed away, became a dream of former ages;
My father serves the emperor ten thousand miles away.
  His features in that distant clime—a goose beyond the frost;
The tidings from that cloudy realm—a flower in a haze.
My darling son and little daughters all have no idea
And do their best despite all this to laugh and talk and shout.

Rustic Lines Respectfully Mourning Her Royal Highness, the Wife of My Great Uncle-by-Marriage, the Prince Kang

1.

In tears I think how often you have taught me while alive:
Your character was stern and sober but your words were kind.
A scion of the ruling house, you were of noble birth,
But how you loved the proper norms, the rules for inner chambers!
Day in, day out uncle and aunt bestowed on us their favors;
For many years nephew and wife enjoyed your ample grace.
Alas, I am a widow now, just like a vine or creeper—
To whom can I entrust myself as this high tree has crashed?

2.

Over the years my little heart had slowly turned to ashes
And now it is again my aunt who sinks into the grave.
New tears succeed old tears that still have not yet dried;
The suffering, already full, is doubled by this pain.
I learned how to behave by watching your comportment;
The norms and the ideals I cherish come from your instruction.
If on the roads of Yellow Springs[34] you run into your nephew,
Please tell him of the sadness of his widow's dreaming soul.

On the First Day of Winter I Made a Sacrifice at His Grave, and upon My Return I Expressed My Emotions

The waxing moon is like a hook, the night right now lasts long;
The wind blows on the graveyard road, and stirs up grief and pain.
Accompanied by frost and snow I cried where you lay buried,
But with your soul and spirit gone, the cold had taken over.
As long as we can never be united in this life,
Each festival that I encounter brings me chilly gloom.
The separation that remains, alas, will be forever:
The tears of blood, still coursing down, soak this white mourning skirt.

In the Xinchou Year [1729] My Late Husband Sent a Western Box[35] Back from the Border, Which I Had Never Opened. After He Passed Away, I Looked Inside while I Was Going through His Curios and I Found a Small Version of His Portrait in an Informal Pose. The Face Was a Perfect Likeness and His Attitude Was as if He Were Alive. The Only Difference Was That the Portrait Kept Silent, Not Saying a Word! As I Held It in My Hands, I Was Filled by Emotions of

Sorrow, and My Innards Were Torn to Pieces. While Shedding Tears I Ground the Ink and Wrote a Poem to Express My Pain.

Of course I'm happy now I reencounter thus my husband!
How is it possible for him to be here in this picture?
He seems to jest and joke with me—but I don't hear his voice;
This is the image of his face—it only lacks his breath.
It would appear to have a soul, so I could cling to him;
It does not have a heartbeat that can fuse with that of mine.
Only last night I saw my husband in a dream. Today
The wound I suffer in my heart is once again the same.

Seven-Syllable Quatrains from *Preserved Together: Selected Poems*

From *Lamenting My Husband: Various Episodes*

1.

Appointed as emissary to venerate Zhenwu:[36]
In gown and cap after his bath he looked as good as new.
Alas, when he reported on his mission and returned
He had become a person in an everlasting dream.

3.

Soughing and sighing, windy rains invade my lonely sorrow;
Departing for the realm of shade you left me all alone.
Oh, could my body but be like the trees and grasses
That keep your grave here company in spring and autumn too.

Essays from *Beyond Poetry: Combined Explanations*

On the Instruction of Daughters

We all have to study the ancients, whether we are male or female, and whether we are poor or rich, noble or base. When a son is born, one teaches him the proper manner of walking, standing, sitting, and lying down as soon as he can speak, and once he is ten, he will have a teacher on the outside. Girls also will receive their mothers' instruction in the Classics and traditions. It is all found in chapters such as "Minor rituals" (Quli) and "Inside Rules" (Neize). Their norms are very detailed and complete, and one will understand them by imitation.

Our family has enjoyed the Imperial Grace for several generations, and official appointments have followed one upon the other. Our family status can be called grand indeed! I joined this family at the age of fifteen when I married your father. I served the elder generations and assigned the servants their tasks, so all family affairs were well ordered. But unfortunately your father abandoned us in his middle years and he did not live to see you reach adulthood. Whenever you are all assembled before me or side by side gather around me at the beginning of the seasons and the other annual sacrifices, I cannot but be overcome by emotions, lamenting your father's poor luck.

At present your younger brother Ning-xiu already has completed his studies and he also very much follows my teachings.[37] Moreover, His Majesty the Emperor, filled with loving care and concern, has entrusted him with an important post, yet I still do not dare allow him to follow his inclinations and constantly remind him [of his duties]. You, sisters, grew up in the inner apartments and have little experience, so how can I not instruct you? You have to realize that as long as you as daughters live with your parents, you may be forgiven and not punished even if your character is not yet transformed and your behavior nor yet perfect. But once you have a husband and become a wife, you will have to prepare the dishes for the ancestral sacrifices and provide for the succeeding generations. In between you will have to serve your parents-in-law, assist your lord and master, raise your sons and daughters, and command servants and slaves. It will not be one person or one task anymore. If you slacken your attention but a little, the family's welfare will suffer. You have to remember at this time that in case you commit a mistake, your parents cannot help you out of your problems however much they may love you. You have to carefully stick to the main guidelines and detailed norms that I explained to you in the past, such as the threefold obedience and the fourfold virtue, and each and every word and action of famous ladies and pure maidens from past and present.[38] Don't think that when you later have a husband it will be just like when you were pampered by your parents!

As for the daily necessities in your household you have to consider the origin of each and every thread of silk and kernel of rice to make sure there will be a continuous supply. Make sure to be diligent and thrifty and don't indulge in wanton luxury. Since ancient times even royal queens personally participate in all aspects of sericulture, so how much more so should this apply to those of lower status! Is it permissible not to personally engage in spinning and weaving? Since ancient times the ladies of lords took care of their clothes and their laundry, so how much more does this apply to those of lower status! Is it permissible not to take care of silks and linen? By extension you should not shrink from physical labor and not disdain bran and chaff.[39] Whenever you have a surplus you have to provide for times of lack, so you will not have to long back to the days of plenty once you are confronted with poverty. You should not only be thrifty in your personal expenses, but you should also act in the same way when managing the family capital. The way to care for wealth also should be the same.

As a woman I live in the inner apartments so how can I understand the ways of the world? But fortunately I have a rudimentary understanding of the books and histories, so I have been somewhat enlightened. Day and night I am filled with anxiety. You girls cannot because you come from a noble family adopt a grand and haughty manner. You will then waste goods and people because you slight money, or you will look down on your husband's family because you pride yourself on your birth. One misspoken word and one wrong action will be enough to occasion hatred and resentment and your parents will be blamed too. That is not the intention of my earnest instructions to you all along, and it is also not the way to comfort your father in his grave. Be warned!

Funeral Prayers for the Living, Written in Jest

The ancients said: "Life and death are great indeed!" They also said: "Life is a temporary stay; death is a return." That is why I always laugh at those stalwart heroes who are mightily pleased whenever someone wishes them a longevity of a hundred years, but get visibly angry as soon as one mentions death and will say: "Why would someone utter such an inauspicious word?" So wouldn't we upset people even more when they hear or see that we, healthy and hale, all of a sudden have come up with the idea of a funeral prayer for the living? The two of us may be living in the inner apartments and may not have grasped even a little bit of the hidden mysteries of the subtle purport of [the discourse on] nature and fate of the sages and scholars of the ancient past, but we do feel that death is unavoidable. Once one dies, there will be a funeral with sacrificial prayers. As there will be a funeral with sacrificial prayers anyway, why not each write one's life story and honestly express her innermost feelings before our death, so you can be happy on hearing my words and I too can be happy on hearing your words, rather than compose some phony words and false phrases upon the other's death and pronounce a prayer that will neither be heard or read?

Moreover, the two of us are not people who were born in the same region and live in the same village. But we are not people whose nature and feelings, passions and preferences are somewhat dissimilar. We are even less people who have shared the same couch for less than a day. Actually, originally one of us is from one edge of heaven and the other is from another corner of the earth, from north to south several thousands of miles apart! Even if we could guarantee that in life we will live together, could we guarantee that we will be together when we die? Such is the unpredictability of the affairs of this world. When fate brought us together in this house, you were the teacher of my daughters, but we felt an immediate affinity, and even though the common name was host and guest, we were in fact like elder and younger sisters. Whenever it rained or stormed, whether it was dark or bright, on flowery mornings and on moonlit nights, we would exhort each other: "Don't slacken, don't get lazy, don't act pampered." You would say: "Right!" and I would say: "Right!" And we would encourage each other: "Be diligent! Be thrifty! Be kind! Be compassionate!" I would say: "Right!" And you would say: "Right!" You loved the *Odes* and *Documents* and I was devoted to literature; you honored wise ladies and I loved chaste women; you were diligent at embroidery and I engaged in physical labor.[40] Even more remarkable was that I was a widow and you also were a widow. It seemed as if Heaven had taken pity on the loneliness of the two of us and brought us together in one house. Our natures and feelings, passions and preferences and also our life experiences were exactly the same! And it has been like this for almost ten years.

In the course of these ten years we almost did not know anymore who's the guest and who's the host; we have completely forgotten such things beyond shape and body. If for the duration of one night you do not appear before my face or I do not appear before yours, it is even worse than losing one's left and right arms. Such is the endurance and tenacity of our friendship. And during these ten years our love has not diminished. The more years this has endured, the more our energies have been united. The more our energies have been united, the more our solidarity has deepened. Now if Heaven would continue to take pity on us two lonely widows because we are like flesh and blood even though we have different surnames, and have the one from the south not return to the south and the one from the north continue to stay in the north, then it would not betray our love and affection over several decades if I would pass away before you or you would depart before me, because we still would be able to open the bed curtain in person, inform ourselves about the other's illness, and lament and libate to her soul. But if Heaven shows no compassion with the two of us and future developments are unpredictable, with the result that the one from the south will go to the south and the one from the north will stay in the north, and, at the end, we do not know the day of death and cannot be present at the funeral, then having this love and affection of decades will become the same as not having this love and affection of decades. Moreover, if longing and longing for each other, we still don't see each other despite our longing, you will perhaps grow depressed because of me and I may well end up wounded because of you. And then we would regret this love and affection of decades! This would mean that those who would have no chagrin at staying together while alive have to feel chagrin at being separated by death.

Therefore the two of us, not avoiding silly foolishness and ignoring taboo and prohibition, in jest write funeral prayers for each other and call them funeral prayers for the living, so you may know my intent and I will understand your heart. We hope that so our children and grandchildren may read these texts and be moved by our friendship, we who will never forget each other, for all eternity. Even if in the future we may be separated and each end up at another corner of the earth, we will have no regrets whether in life or in death.

MADAM ZHAOJIA

A Short-Line Song[41]

Alas, how empty is this room!
But empty it is still my home.
The gate and door are dark and still:
The dwelling of a Madam Meng![42]
  The clear candle casts its wavering light
While my son recites his books:
From dusk till night full diligence,
An ambition large in its design.
  May August Heaven look down on us
So my son will be able to become a scholar,
And I, when I eventually will pass away,
Can face my husband without shame.

A Winter Night

All plants and trees have lost their leaves completely:
A piercing chill is champion in this season.
One lonely goose honks through the freezing night;
Bare branches bend under the weight of snow.
  The room is small—I move the candle closer;
The window cold—the moon is slow to rise.
Because it knows I sit here all alone
A cup of wine provides me company.

An Autumn Day

The dew drips down and drenches the red orchid,
The blowing wind disturbs the verdant leaves.
Poetic talents far below Song Yu;
Emaciated bones just like Shen Yue.[43]
The mirror case locks remnant jet away,
In bags for cloths old fragrance has turned cold.
There is no need to warn me with a nightmare
As all I see are only passing clouds.

A Flying Goose

How still and lonely the late autumn night!
Lost and forlorn that one migrating goose.
Its freezing call is flooding the wide fields;
Its tears so clear enter the farthest skies.
The lofty pinions wide like river mists;
The single body blocking out the moonlight:
It mostly causes grieving ears to listen—
My feelings are identical to yours!

Visiting My Late Husband's Grave

Inscrutable is Heaven's Way—beyond our comprehension;
A greening spring that lost its leaves—alas, you did not live.
Still a young man you had not yet achieved your high ambition;
A wisp of air is what remains of your returning soul.
A chilly dew and freezing mist cover the fields with gloom
And dying shrubs and dried-out grasses fill the barren plain.
The netherworld must lack a place where one can bury grief:
A broken heart and orphan boy here bow before your grave.

Contentment

I have a son so I refuse to hope for people's pity;
For twenty years of miseries I've always coped alone.
In this great age I did my best to teach to him the Classics;
Because of Heaven's grace we had no worry about food.
He may not wear a golden seal of office like Su Qin
But he will make a fortune selling poems like Xiangru.[44]
He tries to please me in all ways, from early on till late—
My tears course down when hearing him recite his father's writings.

From *Songs of Roaming among the Immortals*

On leaving Yingzhou,[45] mists and clouds convene to see me off;
Riding a crane I play the panpipes as I roam the seas.
When I return to my abode after a single tune,
I find the peaches without leaves, the purple orchids wilting.

The tinkling sounds of belt ornaments descend from jade towers;
Fragrant clouds cover the ground and osmanthus flowers bloom.
Shuangcheng pulls Feiqiong by her sleeve with a naughty smile:
By the light of the magic moon they throw the embroidered ball.[46]

2

A Prisoner's Mother and Wife

The Mistress of the Study for Nurturing Simplicity and the Mistress of the Orchid Pavilion

WHEN TIE-BAO COMPILED HIS ANTHOLOGY OF POETRY BY MEMbers of the banners, he devoted the two final scrolls of this extensive selection to poetry written by women. The first of these is devoted mostly to the work of Cai Wan and Gao Jingfang, both of whom belonged to one of the Han banners. Cai Wan is represented by a selection of twenty-two poems, while Gao Jingfang by no less than forty-two. The same scroll also contains nine poems by Sibo and seventeen by Madam Zhaojia, both of whom we encountered in the preceding chapter. The most prominent Manchu women in the second scroll are the Female Scribe of the Study for Nurturing Simplicity (Yangyizhai Nüshi), the Female Scribe of Orchid Pavilion (Lanxuan Nüshi), and Xiguang (discussed in the next chapter). The first of these is represented with thirteen poems, the second with ten, and the third with twenty. These three women represent three generations: Orchid Pavilion (d. 1750) was the daughter-in-law of Nurturing Simplicity (d. 1738), while Xiguang lived during the second half of the eighteenth century.

These three women earned their inclusion in *Elegant Chants* with such a large number of poems probably in part because of their moral stature. Nurturing Simplicity, who was widowed at a young age when her husband Zhu-liang passed away at the age of twenty-eight, saw to the education of her sons, of whom the eldest were Song-shan and Tong-shan. Orchid Pavilion showed remarkable composure when in 1726 her husband Song-shan was imprisoned, and she displayed great filial piety toward her mother-in-law during the twelve years of his absence. Xiguang was yet another exemplary widow who upon the death of her husband saw to the education of their daughters and made arrangements for their weddings. But in her self-sacrificing devotion to her husband, she outperformed the two women in this chapter: when her husband fell ill, she committed *gegu* (described in detail in a long autobiographical poem), and once her daughters were married, she committed suicide as she had sworn to do on her husband's death.

Printed collections of the poetry of both Nurturing Simplicity and Orchid Pavilion exist. These collections were included in the *Poetry Drafts of the Donggo Family* (Dong'e shi yijia shigao), together with the works of Zhu-liang, Song-shan, and Tong-shan. This collection was printed in 1789, when Song-shan's eldest son Neng-tai had restored the family's fortune.[1] Tie-bao, however, may well have had access to the manuscript editions of these two women's collections, which had not yet been edited and trimmed for printing—titles of poems are often different, the number of textual variants is considerable, and some of the poems he includes are not found in the present collections.

The poems of Nurturing Simplicity, a granddaughter of the State-Protecting Duke A-gong, were printed as an appendix to her husband Zhu-liang's collection. Zhu-liang was a son of Supreme Commander Qi-shi (d. 1724). As such, he was a descendant of Hohori (1561–1624), who with his Donggo tribe had joined Nurhaci at an early date. Zhu-liang inherited the title of baron but never achieved a higher rank because he died at the early age of twenty-eight. His poems were printed as *Collected Poems of the Cold Moon Mountain Hall* (Lengyue shantang shiji).[2] Despite the limited size of his collection Zhu-liang is rated as one of the finest Manchu poets of the early Qing.

Zhu-liang's eldest son, Song-shan, hoped to follow in the footsteps of his illustrious ancestors and pursue a career in the military, and had started to serve by the early years of the Yongzheng reign. Disaster struck, however, in 1726 when he was arrested and expected to be executed. Eventually he and his younger brother Tong-shan were incarcerated and banished to Wula. The year 1726 is also when the Yongzheng emperor not only turned against the high officials Nian Gengyao and Lungkodo (who had earlier assisted him in seizing the throne), but also did away with his younger brothers Yin-si and Yin-tang. When several decades later an extensive selection of Song-shan's verse was published as *Poems of Yulian Hall* (Yulian tang shi), several prefaces mention his ordeal and his stoic reaction to his sufferings, but they remain silent regarding the cause of the emperor's wrath. The most forthcoming comment is found in a postface to the collection by He Fu, a hereditary servant of the family, who writes: "Alas, in the *bingwu* year [1726] he was out of the blue caught up in the posthumous implicating case of his grandfather, His Excellency Qi." As Yin-tang's father-in-law, Qi-shi was considered by the Yongzheng emperor as the evil genius of the "faction" that supported Yin-si. On the twentieth day of the fifth lunar month of 1724 [July 10], Qi-shi was relieved of his functions and banished with his wife to northeastern Heilongjiang, where he died later that year. In the summer of 1726, Qi-shi was condemned once again (this time alongside Su-nu)[3] as one of the ringleaders in the clique of Yin-si and Yin-tang (by this time officially renamed Cur and Pig).[4] Qi-shi's corpse was ordered to be exhumed and destroyed, its ashes to be scattered to the winds, the most extreme punishment for traitors. Qi-shi's and Su-nu's sons and grandsons were all incarcerated.[5]

Song-shan is said to have been in his early twenties in 1726, which means that his mother must have been born in the 1680s if not earlier. Song-shan and Tong-shan were pardoned with many others in the earliest years of the reign of the Qianlong emperor. While Tong-shan took to farming in the countryside, his elder brother Song-shan (who returned from banishment suffering from an unspecified disease) continued to live in Beijing but never served in office. Their mother died one year after they had returned in 1738. When Neng-tai in 1787 took concrete steps to have the family's poetry collections printed, Song-shan contributed the following brief postface to his mother's collected poems:

> Throughout her life our late mother loved to read the Classics and other books. She also liked meditation and the Buddhist scriptures. She did not particularly like to write poems or lyrics, and if she did by any chance write some poetry, she would immediately burn or destroy most of it. That is why very little was preserved upon her death. We only have several scores of poems that she used to recite in her old age and that were impressed in our hearts. We have respectfully recorded them, but it is hardly enough to make a collection. I discussed this matter with my brother and we decided to attach them as an appendix to the surviving drafts of our late father as a single collection.
>
> Now it may not accord with my mother's intention in earlier years that I expose her past traces and publish them to the world; while she was alive she did not preserve a single word and effaced her presence, but how could I, as her son, not act in this way? I hope that those who know me will understand.
>
> In the *jiyou* year [1789] of the Qianlong reign, on the auspicious Double Ninth day

In Tie-bao's bibliographic entry on Nurturing Simplicity's collection in the *Comprehensive Treatise on the Eight Banners*, he characterized her works as follows: "Her poems mostly consist of lines on loyalty and filial piety, chastity and duty."[6] While her collection indeed contains a fair number of moralistic poems, it also includes poems on other topics. Most of preserved works would appear to date from the final year of her life when the family had been reunited, but one poem in which she voices her determination to fulfill her duties as a widow probably dates from shortly after the death of her husband, Zhu-liang.[7]

Song-shan's wife Orchid Pavilion belonged, like his mother, to the Aisin Gioro clan. She married Song-shan at the age of seventeen and studied poetry writing with her husband, whom she addresses in her poems as the Master of Quietude. When her poems were collected upon her death, Song-shan contributed a short colophon:

Postface to *Orchid Pavilion*

> My late wife, the Mistress of Orchid Pavilion, became my spouse when we both were young. She shared my troubles and adversities and for over thirty years never enjoyed a life of ease as she desired. She excelled both in serving my parents and raising my children. Alas, we do not all enjoy the same long life. In her middle years she fell ill and died. To her son Neng-tai it was unbearable that the memory of his mother's lifelong virtue would disappear from the world, and so he collected her surviving poems and asked me to write a preface.
>
> Alas, when overcome by emotion, sadness and happiness combine at one time. Wiping away my tears I write this colophon.
>
> On a lucky day of the Second Month of summer of the year *yihai* [1755] of the Qianlong reign period
> By Song-shan of Dong'e, the Quiet Greybeard

This short piece may well strike many readers as rather cold, but it should be noted that Song-shan's poetry collection contains several poems that are addressed to his wife or were written in her memory. The number of such poems is actually rather high if one bears in mind that Song-shan claims that he only truly took to writing poetry in his fifties, which must mean that the overwhelming majority of the poems in his collection were written in the later decades of his life. Through these poems one can follow the couple's evolving relationship as experienced by the husband. The following stern admonishment would appear to have been written by Song-shan when he was deported from the capital:

An Exhortation to My Wife

Serve mother well, and comfort our dependents;
Instruct our son, and cultivate your virtue.
Don't be afraid of bitter toil and pain
But aim to be a model for the ages.[8]

A quite different mood, however, can be perceived in the following poem, which Song-shan most likely wrote during his years of banishment to Wula:

Thinking of Orchid Pavilion

The moon of then is like the present moon—
Now she is thinking of her man in prison:
A honking goose calls up a dream of absence,
And chirping insects move to lonely sighs.
  The night is long, her cotton blanket thin;
The candle fades, her brow is deeply furrowed:
"When will it shine again on both of us
As each tells how he missed the other?"[9]

The following poem by Song-shan appears to date from shortly after his pardon:

Talking at Night with Orchid Pavilion

The north wind rattles through the little courtyard;
Refusing to flare up the fire grows dark.
How to express one's feelings in one's words?
Time and again I have to stop and stutter.
  I caused you an unending chain of sorrow,
Which fills my bones with sadness to the marrow.
A prisoner, I lacked a fixed direction
As if I was but drifting on a raft.
  My dear old mother had to suffer greatly—
How could one bear to offer her wild greens?
My children were exposed to cold and hunger
Because all our possessions were exhausted.
  When fortune fails, each move will not succeed,
And all I won were only these grey hairs.
Our life on earth may only be a dream,
But practicalities can still not be neglected.

Winters and summers took each other's place
But when would come an end to grief and pain?
The night but deepens as the bell-sound fades
To shared emotions at the moonlit window.[10]

The couple's life in later years may have served as the inspiration for Songshan's following poem:

Sitting Outside at Night with Orchid Pavilion

The place secluded, free from any trouble;
The scene so pure it fills us with contentment:
The clouds are idling now the wind died down;
The sky is clear because the rains are gone.
The wine-stand is supported by the flowers;
The zither table moved into the moonlight.
Inspired by this my wife requests that I
Write matching poems to her "Orchid Dew."[11]

And when his wife passed away, Songshan wrote the following elegy:

Lamenting Orchid Pavilion in the Year Gengwu *[1750]*

You shared in my adversities for a full thirty years
But as of now love and affection has been torn in two.
As I observe my weeping sons, my heart feels as if pierced;
When comforting my grieving daughters, even tears run dry.
Whom did you have when still alive to help you in your illness?
Before you died you lacked a mate to overcome misfortune.
Oh dearest soul, make sure to go to the ancestral graves
And wait for me to die and to renew our destined bond.[12]

A somewhat more detailed prose record of the life of Orchid Pavilion was written by He Fu:

Postface to *Poems of Orchid Pavilion*

Her Ladyship my master's wife was by nature and character poised and elegant. She loved to read the *Odes* and other writings. At the age of seventeen she married my master, with whom she studied poetry. Practicing with pleasure she exhausted within a few years all of the most refined and subtle aspects of his art.

In the autumn of the year *bingwu* [1726], my master was suddenly thrown in jail because of some issue. The whole family was in an uproar, but Her Ladyship chatted and bantered as before. Unruffled, she composed two poems on virtuous women that she had sent to him in prison, in this way promising him she would follow him in death. After a few days my master was spared the death penalty. While he was incarcerated Her Ladyship exerted herself in serving on and caring for Her Old Ladyship, his mother. She did so through winter cold and summer heat for more than twelve years, and the fame of her filial piety reverberated throughout the community.

Only in the year *dingsi* [1737] was my master pardoned so he could come back home. In the following year Her Old Ladyship, his mother, passed away. Her Ladyship supported him fully in the way of lamenting the departed. For more than ten years thereafter she accompanied my master in his elegant pastimes of the zither and calligraphy, and she excelled in the education of her sons and daughters. Her bright perspicacity in her choices could neither be understood nor imitated by the vulgar crowd. She died at the age of forty-eight.

Her second-born son, Jianfu, studied with me at the behest of my master. In the spring of the year *jiaxu* [1754], he brought me a manuscript that he handed to me with these words: "These are the surviving works of my late mother. I have asked permission from my father to order you, my teacher, to edit these." Surprised, I said in admiration: "This is an expression of your undiluted filial piety. Moreover, you also obey your father's orders. Of course I will exhaust my humble abilities." Selecting and comparing the poems I completed this book, and I respectfully made a full record of events.

Alas! The ancients said: "When one leaves one's writing one will never die; when one has a son and heir, one will not perish." Now these two conditions are both met. Isn't this the happiest affair in the world? How could I disregard my lowly position and dare to rashly compose a preface, ignoring my allotment? Respectfully I have recorded these few words as I hand this collection back to her son.

> Written in the *taizu* month of the *jiaxu* year [1754] of the Qianlong reign period
> By your humble servant He Fu

The two poems on virtuous women that He Fu mentioned can probably be identified with the two poems at end of the collection, following the poem that contains her deathbed exhortation to her son Neng-tai to see to the publication of her work ("the rarest passion since creation in a hundred poems"). The first of these poems on virtuous women is "A Song on Wenjun," which criticizes the young widow Zhuo Wenjun for allowing herself to be seduced by the dashing young poet Sima Xiangru (172–117 BCE), and contrasts her lack of resolve with that of Green Pearl (Lüzhu) who committed suicide when she learned that her master Shi Chong (249–300) had been forced to cede her to a political rival. The second poem, "A Short Song to Mourn the Chaste Women Suhui [White Flower] and Qiuyan [Autumn Mist]," is written in praise of two women who committed suicide when their master had died. The poems in the collection Orchid Study do not seem to follow any systematic order, but it should be obvious that the poems addressed to her imprisoned husband should date to the period from 1726 to 1738, while the remaining poems most likely date from the later years.[13]

The collection of Orchid Pavilion is prefixed by three prefaces. The first of these, from 1758, describes the collection as consisting of hundreds of poems, which the author had read in one breath. It also provides an alternative title, *Remnant Poems from a Boudoir Jug* (Guihu yishi). Perhaps the author saw a more complete collection of Orchid Pavilion's poetry, which was later trimmed to size when printing became a real possibility. The second preface was written in 1769 by her nephew Yehe Zao-wang-bao and mostly consists of a selection of couplets that are seen as illustrative of the moral fortitude of his aunt. The third preface dates from 1769 and was written by her son-in-law Duo-fu and provides a somewhat fuller portrait of his remarkable mother-in-law:

> Master Kong[14] once said: "Those who have virtue also will have a talent for words." So, when well-blended harmony is stored up inside, brilliant flowers will become manifest outside—often they will express themselves as poems. Such texts are able to lead the current age and provide a model for later times. How could one consider such poems as superficial chatter!
>
> My late mother-in-law was a third-generation granddaughter of Prince of the Blood Zhuang [Surhaci; 1564–1611], a full brother of our Great Ancestor the High Emperor [Nurhaci].[15] From birth she was gentle and serene;

by nature she was chaste and filial. She was well-versed in the six styles of calligraphy, but also excelled in playing the seven strings of the zither; she was well-trained in needlework, but also had a marvelous aptitude for riding and shooting. Alas, she met with a Creator who reversed her fate and so she ran into a disaster that caused storm and rain! She suffered bitter troubles and adversities and only after thirteen years could she restore her old inheritance. Living to a ripe old age she passed away peacefully, with a smile on her face.

Once I had become one of her closest relatives, I often had an opportunity to peruse her surviving writings. It was as if I saw the sun surrounded by the colored clouds of early morning, as if I stood in front of fragrant lotuses on an autumn pond. Their torrential energy even shook the Five Marchmounts; their noble tune rose above all eternity. If you compared them to ancient and modern productions from the inner chambers, the difference between divine and human showed clearly upon analysis.

In those days she only spontaneously chanted these poems to herself as an extempore pleasure. Today there are people who will publish her surviving works through printing. How could that ever have been her intention? Now, when the world produces exceptional vessels, these may initially be famous or unknown, but it is rare for these vessels to completely annihilate their traces forever. This situation is brought about by the Heavenly Principle. From this it is clear that this collection is not some idle private pleasure, but that it belongs to those who cry out in their poetry.

Written in the Grain Dawn of the year *yiyou* [1765] of the Qianlong period
By her humble son-in-law Duo-fu

According to the *Correct Beginnings*, the collection was printed at the same time as the collection of her mother-in-law, so not earlier than 1789.[16] Yun Zhu's biographical notice on Orchid Pavilion does not mention her husband's period of imprisonment, but stresses how she comforted her husband during his years of illness (upon his return from jail) by composing poetry together with him:

Song-shan was the son of the Female Scribe of the Study for Nurturing Simplicity and used the style Boren. He was famous for his poetry. In his middle years he was disabled by a disease. Orchid Pavilion was by nature kind. She knew many arts. She would often dispel his gloom by composing matching poems with him. Boren would then immediately forget his illness. . . . She died before she reached the age of fifty. Neng-tai collected her surviving poems in a collection of one scroll, for which Boren himself composed a preface. It was printed at the same time as *Collection of the Study for Nurturing Simplicity*.[17]

THE FEMALE SCRIBE OF THE STUDY FOR NURTURING SIMPLICITY

My Deepest Feelings

The cosmos can't contain a loyal man:
He risks his life repaying heaven's favors,
And through the ages women of fierce virtue
Have followed that same Way in their behavior.
  I will not swerve from principle and nature,
But life or death depends on circumstances.
How could I shirk from a survivor's pain?
I'll only seek the weal of the deceased.
  I choose my neighbors and destroy my weaving:
Earlier generations praised such wisdom.[18]

Improvised while Traveling at Dawn When Going with My Sons to Dingzhou

We silently pass through the daybreak fields;
In this slow cart at peace now with myself.
The sun above the hills breaks up the clouds;
A freezing goose descends on misty banks.
  The dust is soft now drizzle has stopped falling;
The wind feels gentle—autumn's yet to come.
There is no need to sigh about past sorrows:
Today is different from other years.

Gazing Out over the Wilds from a Mountain Pavilion

At leisure I look far into the distance:
The fields stretch wide, stilled by a gentle breeze.
Below a freezing sky all trees are bare;
By the horizon flies one mourning goose.[19]
  The dew is clear, the rapids' waves are white;
The sun descends, the clouds on hills turn red.
This autumn scenery is short in nothing—
But who will share my loneliness with me?

Composed in Leisure during an Autumn Evening Staying Together with My Sons and Their Wives at the Villa in the Northern Hills

Dwelling in simplicity I love this realm of wonder:
Keeping to the Classics, I seek the source of the Way.
We're sitting at ease by the light of the autumn moon
And in the frosty evening migrating geese are calling.
The reservoir water multiplies the shadows of pines,
The mountain flowers add to the scars on bamboos.
The little boys have just finished their schoolwork
And chanting and joking we lock the gate early.

Hearing the Spring at Night at the Dragon-Spring Convent

A chilly dew falls on the Buddhist convent
And gentle breezes stir the chimes to sound.
I sit and hear how Heaven's Pipes[20] fall silent,
And find at night the spring is purer still.
Pond water deepens colors of the pines,
The high skies catch the feelings of the moon.
So why should I devote myself to doctrine
And study no-birth meditating blindly?

Watching the Clouds

The wind falls still and clouds assemble widely;
The wind arises and those clouds disperse.
But then the cloud that hugs the mountaintop!
It seems like nothing will disturb its shape.

Gazing from a Tower

The men, resembling colonies of ants, rush to the markets;
The oxen, like a flock of crows, disperse to plow the fields.
The only ones not in a hurry are two fishermen—
Sharing one straw cape in spring rain and angling in the mist.

Emotions

Why follow one in death if not for being fully chaste?
It's easy to enjoy his favors, hard to pay them back.
The pine and plum have long endured the sufferings of winter[21]
But do not know how biting cold the eastern breeze can be.

To My Sons

For twenty years I've suffered bitter poverty and want;
I imitated in my teaching the exemplars from the past.
I will not have to be ashamed down in the underworld;[22]
Your wisdom or stupidity will all depend on Heaven.

THE FEMALE SCRIBE OF ORCHID PAVILION

Idly Chanting with the Master of Quietude

To cleanse our eyes we have the pure, cool night;
To awaken our heart we have the crisp autumn.
Misfortune is all part of Principle
And scary dreams are based on idle sorrows.

Below the flowers crickets chirp so softly;
Beyond the clouds a goose calls out, forlorn.
A single candle shares these lofty pleasures;
The waiting brush scoffs at the murky wine.

Passing by the Grave of the Loyal and Concerned Duke Yang while Visiting Dingzhou with the Master of Quietude[23]

How could his fame be due to his report?
His actions never swerved from Heaven's rule.
His lofty rage reached to the highest clouds;
His noble heart determined good and bad.
 The toppled walls are curtained off by mists;
The grave is overgrown and clothed by grass.
But high up in the sky there is the sun
That shines as brightly as his name and surname.

He loved his lord and followed the straight road,
Cared for the state and acted on his worries.
His mind made up, he was like Long and Bi;[24]
His feelings could not stand a Mang or Cao.[25]
 The sun weighs on the cold and broken stele;
The wind howls through the bare and dying trees.
But how I laugh at all those cunning heroes:
Their bones too are accompanied by weeds.

On an Autumn Night I Receive a Prison Letter from the Master of Quietude

Your letter from afar I read once more
And my reply I hesitate to seal.
The house is cold as chilly breezes whisper;
The silent courtyard is suffused by moonlight.
  The autumn candle slims my figure's shadow[26]
And sadder than the crickets sounds my poem.
In truth, the many savors of this world—
One should not taste them all too strongly.

To the Master of Quietude in Prison

This pleasant season stirs so many yearnings;
In this fine night I am the one to sorrow.
The Seventh Night:[27] the moon shows its bright ears;
Ten thousand miles: one gorgeous autumn sky.
  The yard is still, the fulling blocks resound;
The screen is sparse, the stars flow of themselves.
I force a smile beside your loving mother,
Who dares to talk once more about her sorrow?
  The moon of then is like the moon of now,
But now today is different from then:
My ailing husband is a thousand miles away;
Your darling children haven't seen you for six years.

Sitting at Night with the Master of Quietude in the Garden of Venerating Leisure

There is no need to talk of things bygone—
How great it is today to share this leisure!
Our minds and bodies still beset by worries;
The hair of beard and temples turns to gray.
  The moon and flowers are for us enough,
But tea and poetry don't yet allow us leisure.
And so we spend the night together here
Somewhere between old sorrow and no sorrow.

Written at the End of the Manuscript

Some scenes describing plums, bamboos, hilltops, and springs;
Feelings inspired by colored clouds, moonlight, and snow:
In need of polishing for lack of formal schooling,
Completed by reliance on spontaneous emotion.

Ideas on life and death, on rise and fall
And thoughts on happy joy and sad dispersal:
What I experienced throughout my life
Should find a later reader who will sigh.

To My Son

The water steams the rice till it is cooked;
The rocks turn into lime by force of fire.
Things have to suffer an unending pain
Before they turn into some useful stuff.

About to Say Adieu Forever to the Master of Quietude

These thirty years of love and of devotion
Will only gain me one small earthen mount.
I leave you now with an abiding longing;
Throughout the night I'll walk alone in sadness.
　Our children can rely on their wise father,
And so my heart will not be choked by sobs.
Once buried I will wait on your dear mother:
That you're alive is bound to be of comfort.

Sent on the Day of the Double-Fifth Festival to the Master of Quietude in Prison

So far apart with sorrow filled, but without dream connections:
To whom will I, this festive day, now raise the foremost cup?
But for your mother' sake I cannot but adhere to custom—
I'll force myself to find a charm and wear a smiling hairpin.

Fatally Ill, I Lay My Brush Aside; for Neng-tai

After a life of bitter toil I've come to Threefold Peace—[28]
The rarest passion since creation in one hundred poems.
The book now done, I lay aside my brush—but filled with fear
That narrow-minded vulgar types will fail to hand it down.

A Song on Wenjun

A loyal vassal serves no second lord,
And a chaste woman will not wed again;
She does not advertise herself for gain,
Nor does she choose a partner on her own.
　Now when one comes to think of Zhuo Wenjun,[29]

She was both praised for talent and for beauty.
And when she thought of serving her first husband,
They were united by a deep and lasting love.
  Of course she knew the zither song's intention!
She wrote herself the Song of the White Heads.
But once she was misled by her desire,
The ice and frost turned into flowing water.
  Below the banner of that Linqiong wine shop,
Tending the stove, she must have felt ashamed:
To please the heart of a romantic rake
She was abused by gazing eyes of men.
  Now Sima Xiangru was no common poet
But he disgraced his wife for times eternal.
Then there was Shi Chong's concubine Green Pearl:
She saved her name by leaping to her death.

A Short Song to Mourn the Chaste Women Suhui [White Flower] and Qiuyan [Autumn Mist]

White Flower is bound to be pure,
Autumn Mist is bound to be clear:
How admirable that single death that preserved the honor of both—
For thousands of autumns, for myriads of years their names will survive!
  Don't say that their faces resembled the blossoming trumpet creeper—
Beauties, they did not prize to be those who topple cities and states.
So delicately—for whom did they make up their red cheeks?
Ever so lightly—for whom did they brush on their eyebrows?
  When confronted with their great duty, they were not spineless:
A white silk noose—hanging by their neck, they showed their will.

Alas,
This fleeting life is a short stay of not even a hundred years;
Why is such great longevity necessary for achieving fame?
It's hard to meet your opportunity,
But your hair quickly turns grey.
    Don't you see how often
Conspicuously exceptional men are born in this world
To die of old age without any credit, without any fame!

3

Chastity and Suicide

Xiguang

IN THE CHAPTERS OF *ELEGANT CHANTS*, DEVOTED TO POETRY by women of the Eight Banners, Tie-bao prefaced his selection of Xiguang's (d. 1781) poems with a brief biographical notice:

> Xiguang was a Manchu woman. She was the wife of Vice Director Yi-song-a. She followed him in death and was awarded official recognition for her virtuous behavior.[1]

But the story of her life is more complicated than suggested in these few bare lines. Xiguang was the daughter of the Manchu official Ai-bi-da (d. 1771), who was a grandson of Ebilun (d. 1673), one of the great Manchu generals in the conquest of China.[2] Rising through the ranks, Ai-bi-da was appointed in 1744 to the position of provincial administration commissioner for Jiangsu, concurrently in charge of the imperial silk factories in Nanjing and the tax office at Hushuguan. In 1755 he became governor-general of Yunnan and Guizhou. He served in that position (with one small interruption) until 1761, when he was appointed governor-general of Guangdong and Guangxi. But in 1763 he was relieved of his post for shielding corrupt underlings and banished to Yili to redeem himself. In one of her poems, Xiguang fondly remembers that she was her father's favorite.

Xiguang's husband Yi-song-a, a poet in his own right, was related to another high official of the time.[3] Some sources call him a son of Yong-gui, others (more likely) a nephew. Yong-gui (1706–1783) had already been appointed as governor of Jiangxi during the reign of the Yongzheng emperor. During the reign of the Qianlong emperor, Yong-gui would continue to serve in high positions, and for the last twenty years of his life he served in the capital, as the Manchu president of one of the ministries and a member of the Grand Secretariat. Yi-song-a reached the rank of vice bureau director, but he died suddenly before he reached the age of thirty. At that time the couple had only been married for two years. Fashishan characterizes him as "complete, circumspect, alert, and serious," and mentions that following his death his poems were collected and printed by Xiguang.

Tie-bao provided a more detailed account of the circumstances of Xiguang's death in his updated version of the *Comprehensive Treatise on the Eight Banners*. This history of the banners had originally been published in 1739, but an update was commissioned in 1786 and completed in 1799. It lists Xiguang's collection of poetry in its bibliographic section, and adds the following information:

> When Xiguang's husband fell ill, she cut flesh from her thigh to cure him but to no avail. Because her tender daughter had no one to rely on, she forced herself to stay alive and live the life of a widow, suffering great poverty for ten years. The day after her daughter was married, she composed two regulated poems in seven-syllable lines to declare her ambition, and then committed suicide by hanging herself. Her father-in-law, Assistant Grand Secretary and President of the Ministry of Personnel Yong-gui [1706–1783], collected her poems and presented them to the emperor, who commiserated with her and awarded her official recognition. Her poems are mostly filled with sad and mournful sounds. Her "Lament for a Loyal Wife" was written on behalf of Lady Dong'e [Donggo], the wife of a son of Grand Secretary Shu-he-de [1711–1777]; it shows her feelings of sympathy for a person who shared her ambition.[4]

Yun Zhu, in her *Precious Records from the Maidens' Chambers* (Langui baolu), provides a slightly different account of Xiguang's life:

> She belonged to the Niohoru clan. Xiguang was a Manchu. She married Vice Bureau Director Yi-song-a, a son of the minister Yong-gui. When her husband fell ill, she sliced flesh from her thigh to heal him, but without any result. She swore to follow him in death. On his deathbed Yi-song-a said to her: "My father is already old but my younger brother and younger sister are still quite young and my daughters have not yet been married, so I leave you with unfinished business." Shedding tears, Xiguang promised to live on as a widow until she had finished these tasks. Over the course of ten years she arranged for the marriages of their daughters. On the day following the marriage she composed an old-style poem in seven-syllable lines to explain her ambition and then committed suicide by hanging herself. Yong-gui collected her poems, which he presented to the court, upon which she was publicly recognized for her virtue.[5]

In the early years of the twentieth century, Zhen-jun's account of Xiguang's life in his *Anecdotes from Close to Heaven,* which otherwise would appear to be based on the notice in the *Comprehensive Treatise on the Eight Banners,* adds the detail that upon reading Yong-gui's report, the Qianlong emperor commented in red: "Have her family provide her with a lavish funeral."[6]

Zhen-jun also explains that Xiguang did not immediately commit suicide, because she did not want to burden her parents-in-law with the care for her daughters. The short account of Xiguang in the "Biographies of Virtuous Women" in the *Draft History of the Qing* (Qingshi gao), "Liezhuan" 298 (Lienü 4), probably basing itself on the original report, provides yet another variant. Yong-gui is now described as an uncle of Xiguang's husband, who together with her own father urged her to stay alive in order to take care of the wedding arrangements for her daughters.

> Yi-song-a belonged to the Baidu clan and was a Manchu of the Bordered Yellow Banner. His wife Xiguang belonged to the Niohoru clan and the Plain White Banner; she was a daughter of Governor-General Ai-bi-da. Yi-song-a was a nephew of Grand Secretary Yong-gui and died at an early age. When he was ill, Xiguang sliced a lump of flesh from her thigh and had him eat it. When he did not recover in the end, she promised to die with him. Ai-bi-da and Yong-gui both tried to change her mind. She then swore that she would join her husband in death once their daughters had been married off. She brought home a bride for Yi-song-a's younger brother and married off his younger sister and her two daughters. The day after her second daughter had left the house, she committed suicide by hanging herself. She left a poem posted on the wall that said, in short: "On the oath of ten years ago I will report today." This happened in the Third Month of the forty-sixth year of the Qianlong reign [1781]. Yonggui brought this case to the notice of the emperor. The Qianlong emperor devoted a poem to her, and awarded her official recognition of her virtue.[7]

In her long autobiographical poem "My Ambition," Xiguang not only provided a grisly description of her act of *gegu,* but she also stressed that she had not immediately followed her husband in death because he had asked her on his deathbed to take care of their daughters and see them properly married.[8] If Xiguang married her husband in 1771 and committed suicide in 1781, this must mean that these two girls were not her own but the children of an earlier wife.

XIGUANG

Ever Since You Have Departed, Two Poems

1.

Ever since you have departed,
I haven't faced the bronze mirror
Because I pity this face of today
That is so unlike its former self.

2.

Ever since you have departed,
I don't love flowers anymore.
Everyone gapes at fine flowers—
Fading flowers are left alone.

Visiting the Grave on New Year's Day

The eastern wind disturbs my chilly dreams;
Still dark, the chirping birds tell me to hurry.
I force myself to rise, sad at the season;
Riding a cart I'm moved by evening dust.
  Down in the grave you too must now shed tears;
Here in this world we are bereft of spring.
This long succession of heartbreaking business
Can only wound the spirit with its grief.

Remembering My Father, Two Poems

A pampered daughter of the Xies,[9] I was my father's darling;
From early morning until late I followed him around.
He favored me—I always feared the envy of my sisters;
He loved me most, so I at times usurped my brothers' place.
  All that remains are some old drafts that sadden me at present;
Bereft now of that brilliant pearl, I long for those past years.
Unable to pay back his care I often feel like crying
But how can these red tears of mine get to the Yellow Springs?[10]

Two years into my wedded life I suffered desolation
And I've become a widowed wife, a woman not yet dead.
For consolation in the past I turned to my old father

But at my natal home today I only find my mother.
　A bond of blood of twenty years became a midnight dream
And at the grave outside the walls emotions crowd my heart.
I cannot serve my father and I cannot serve my husband—
Let's for the karmic cause consult the King of Emptiness.[11]

From *Emotions after Moving House, Two Poems*

The iris charred, the orchid wilted: cause of many tears;
The painted pillars and carved beams: a source of greater grief.
Since this grand mansion brought about the end of my old partner,
It's fitting that I now should cede this house to other owners.
　Opulent splendor is no place to seek a chaste existence;
"Out of the way" accords much better with my sorry fate.
When at a later date I will report to my late husband,
He'll understand the measure of my filial devotion.

Using the Rhyme Words of "Moving House" by My Fifth Younger Brother

I cannot stand the noise and bustle of my present place,
But there's no need when moving house to move into the mountains.
A hidden dragon should seek out a far and secret valley,
But moving birds do not despise the woods they know so well.
　A splendid house has never been the choice of widowed women;
This quiet corner fits perfectly with my loyal aim.
His grave is far away but if his faculties survive,
He'll hear my feet as I approach the tablet for his soul.

Written while Filled with Emotion upon Reading Poems by My Late Husband on a Winter Night

All alone I intone his pure lines and marvelous words—
Who knows my intense desolation as midnight nears?
I try to recall his face but still don't see him before me:
Shadows of snowflakes on the window by moonlight.

Two Poems at the Shrine of the Loyal Wife

1.

A champion among women, you followed your husband in death:
All through the world your fragrant fame is spread by all people.
I want to throw away my life but have not yet been able to do so,
And so envy you for having already set an example ahead of me.

2.
My husband entrusted me with a charge that I diligently perform
And ready to die I keep this present body alive for the moment.
Inform the heroic soul of this woman she should not laugh at me:
She must know that I, too, am one who will arrive in her wake.

New Year's Eve

To the noise of firecrackers the old year is sent off;
By the light of a lonely lamp new sorrows congeal.
Like the wax candle my heart is shedding red tears
That drop on this paper, turning into flowing blood.

My Ambition[12]

Like clinging vine and rising pine, such was our marriage;
My husband of such eminence, he was beyond compare.
Forget about the hundred carriages that thronged the gate;
I loved how entering the room you startled all those thousands!

Received into your house as bride and married in all style:
In bright and gilded house and hall a pair of pearl and jade.
In springtime breeze and moonlit nights you showed me your affection;
I was allowed to serve Qin Jia—my wishes were fulfilled.[13]

Once you had played the jasper zither in the vestal hall,
We were united by a bond of diligence and love:
You understood my mind as white as jade, as pure as ice;
I knew your heart to be like lofty hills and flowing streams.

But then when we, "like guests, like friends,"[14] were happy as could be,
Misfortune struck out of the blue in that disastrous year.
You had been ill for thirty days and still had not been cured,
When you accompanied the court and trekked a thousand miles.

Away from home while gravely ill, your illness but increased;
In letters home you said "I'm well," but that was but a lie.
Since you had left, my heart was constantly beset by sorrow;
When you returned, your body had become a bag of bones.

You took to bed and did not rise: your situation worsened—

Who had the skill to send away the "urchins deep inside"?[15]
"A single hour of relaxation" was an idle claim;
One hundred dosages of ginseng were prescribed in vain.

It soon was clear that all our efforts were to no avail
But still my only thought was how to save my husband.
I once had heard that my own flesh perhaps might move the gods—
So how could I in times like these still care about the pain?
The knife shone bright, as white as frost: I bit my lips and sliced,
And took the lump and secretly I cooked it in a soup.

With silly piety and loyalty my heart was filled,
Hoping that Heaven would respond to my sincerity.
Even today my feeble body clearly shows the scar;
At that time all my clothes were splattered by my blood.

"Man's mind, made up, can conquer fate" is only idle talk;
My burning zeal made in the end no difference at all.
The jasper zither, brocade lute, alas, were thrown aside,
As on that day, o bitter grief, you passed away forever.

My heart was broken now my life had been destroyed completely;
Your younger brothers, younger sister were still young of years.
Like Bodao once, you had no son and sadly lacked an heir,[16]
But like Cai Yong you had a daughter as your only child.[17]

How could your wife desire to stay behind here in this world?
I had decided early on to join you in the grave.
It's not because I want to live that I am still alive:
I kept my own desire in check and followed your command.

About to die you held my hand and asked me urgently
To take care of the matter of the weddings of our daughters.
You spoke in tears, then gave the ghost, but still this task remained:
You trusted it would be the same if you were here or I.

You, husband, left this task to me because you knew my worth,
So how could I have failed today to meet your expectations?

For me it is an easy thing to die and join my husband,
But I would have no peace in death had I not met my promise.
A day will come when we will meet there in the underworld,
And, earlier or later, you would know it anyway.

The weddings of our daughters now at last have all been settled;
The oath I swore ten years ago today has been fulfilled,
And in the grave I will report, my master, on my mission—
My innards filled with bran and chaff may serve as proof.[18]

4

Mourning Royalty

Lady Zhoujia, Lady Tongjia, and Lady Fucha

LADY TONGJIA (1737–1809) WAS BORN INTO AN ARISTOCRATIC Manchu family. Her father, Na-mu-tu (Namtu), was the eldest son and heir of Kua-dai, who had inherited the dukedom that had been bestowed on his father, Tong Guogang (d.1690). This transpired in 1726, when Tong Guogang's elder brother E-lun-dai (Olondai) was executed on the orders of Yongzheng for criticizing the emperor's treatment of his bothers.[1] Lady Tongjia provided a detailed account of her education in the preface to her collection of poems, *Preserved Drafts of Crow-Like Attachment* (Wusi cuncao), written to lament the death of her parents.[2]

> I have always thought that it was a misfortune I was not born a boy; I might have accomplished some great deeds for the state that would have benefited morality and could be transmitted to later ages. But it was still my good fortune to be born in the inner apartments of a noble house, where I received teaching concerning the sages of the past and acquired some understanding of principle, so I would not waste my life on "brocade gowns and jade food."
>
> We were four children, as I had one younger brother and two younger sisters—I was the oldest child. I remember how when I had barely turned five, my dear mother started to teach me my characters. When I turned seven or eight, she instructed me in classical texts such as the Four Books and *Earliest Studies*.[3] I also remember that my mother once personally instructed me: "When one is a noble lady, one is not allowed to neglect needlework and wifely tasks, but one also needs duty and principle to broaden one's understanding, and the *Odes* and *Documents* to mold one's nature and feeling. Only then can one perfect the virtue of modest grace and correct stillness. But I am old and sickly and burdened by household responsibilities, and to my regret I do not have the time and background to instruct you all." Thereupon she had people search far and wide for an educated woman who, because of her learn-

ing, would be fit to be our teacher, and she truly did not stint on the salary to hire such a person.

When I had just turned ten, she hired a certain Lady Feng from eastern Zhejiang. Her personal name was Fan, and her literary name was the Elder of Cypress Fragrance [Boxiang Laoren]. She lived with us in our mansion in the Paulownia Loft for a number of seasons. She instructed us in the careful collation of classics and histories, and in the time left she combined that with poetry. She expounded these matters in great detail. For five years there never was an end to our chanting and humming from early in the morning till late at night! My two sisters and I all greatly benefited from her teaching.[4]

Later I was married and my sisters too left our parental home, and so I was overcome by the emotions caused by scattering clouds and flowing rivers. Soon we experienced the death of our stern father, and then we suffered the passing away of our dear mother. Unfortunately, a few years later my younger brother also died. Alas, our family suffered many misfortunes, and my whole life was very much like the many tears of Duling.[5]

Going through my old cases I reencountered the poems lamenting my father and the poems lamenting my mother, thirty poems all together.[6] I have now arranged them as one collection, and I have written this preface to explain the circumstances.

Written by the Mistress of Heaven's Suchness in the month of the osmanthus in the *bingshen* year [1776] of the Qianlong reign period

When Lady Tongjia wrote this preface she had already been a widow for six years. At the age of seventeen she had married Ru-song (1737–1770), a great-grandson of Dorbo. Dorbo was the fifth son of Dodo (d. 1649), a Manchu prince who played a major role in the conquest of the Ming dynasty. Later, Dorbo was adopted as son and heir by his uncle Dorgon (1612–1650), the regent for the Shunzhi emperor and the leading architect of the conquest. Dorgon's great power created suspicions, however, and following his sudden death, he was stripped of all his ranks, whereupon Dorbo was disinherited, while the rank of his own father was also reduced posthumously.

Dodo's descendants, however, had not lost their status as members of the imperial clan. Ru-song distinguished himself through his riding and archery skills, to the extent that the imperial prince, who in 1789 prefaced his poetry collection, devoted most of his space to praise of his equestrian qualities.[7] He occupied a series of high offices, and in 1762 was selected by the Qianlong emperor as the fifth-generation heir of Dodo to become a prince of the blood of the second rank.[8] Ru-song died in 1770, when Lady Tongjia was only thirty-four. Her husband's princely rank, however, was not assigned to her only surviving son, Chun-ying (1761–1800), who inherited a lower title, and the family's circumstances were much reduced.

The situation of the family improved spectacularly in 1778, when the Qianlong emperor reversed the verdict on Dorgon.[9] This reversal was only one aspect of the ongoing revision of early Manchu history during the Qianlong reign period, which culminated in the 1770s and 1780s.[10] This imperial decision meant that the heirs of Dorbo once again were recognized as such: Chun-ying, still only a boy, was now ennobled as a prince of the blood of the first rank, becoming as Prince Rui one of the "Eight Great Princes," who, as a special mark of imperial favor, could, in perpetuity, bequeath their title without reduction in rank to their heir.[11] The family received an estate of 300,000 *mu* and was given a palace with 360 servants.[12] Chun-ying further strengthened his family's position when he assisted the Jiaqing emperor in toppling Qianlong's favorite, He-shen, once the former emperor had passed away.[13] When Chun-ying died in 1800, he was succeeded by his eldest son, Bao-en, and when the latter passed away in 1802, he was succeeded by Chun-ying's fourth son, Duan-en.[14]

Lady Tongjia had assiduously preserved her poems from the moment she started composing them at age of thirteen, under the guidance of the Elder of Cypress Fragrance. By 1770 she had collected the poems of the first twenty years of writing as *Green Window Chanting Drafts* (Lüchuang yingao), in two scrolls. The first scroll contains by her own count 204 poems from 1749 until 1757, while the second scroll contains 106 poems from 1758 until 1767. The second scroll also includes four short lyrics (all to the same tune), and is concluded by a "continuation" (*xuji*), which consists of the poems mourning her father and mother that were later printed as *Preserved Drafts of Crow-Like Attachment*. In contrast to her other works, *Green Window Chanting Drafts* was never printed and only survived in manuscript form.[15]

Many of Lady Tongjia's earliest poems are observations of the changing seasons and compositions on assigned topics. One of the rare exceptions is a poem occasioned by the grand celebration of the sixtieth birthday of the empress dowager. Some poems express her troubled feelings following her marriage, culminating in the exclamation: "Which situation in this world can truly be called bitter? / That only is that of a girl who lives in inner chambers."[16] But before we interpret such statements as forerunners of modern feminism, we should perhaps read them as an expression of her frustration over the impossibility to fulfill both her filial duties to her own parents and to her parents-in-law at the same time. Later statements lamenting the unfair distribution of responsibilities between men and women from her days as a widow come perhaps closer to prefiguring a feminist awareness.

When she married, Lady Tongjia found that both her mother-in-law and her husband were practicing poets. Her mother-in-law, Lady Zhoujia (ca. 1715-ca. 1773), was orphaned at an early age and raised by an aunt (she would later take care of orphaned nieces herself). She became a widow after only a dozen years of marriage. When her son Ru-song in 1762 was raised to princely rank, her husband posthumously received the same rank, so from that moment on she was addressed as a consort-dowager. Before his death in 1770, Ru-song had a collection of his mother's poetry printed as *Rue Window Chanting Drafts* (Yunchuang yingao).[17] This collection of nearly two hundred pieces includes an undated preface by Ru-song's brother-in-law Kui-qing and another undated postface by Ru-song. Kui-qing praises his mother-in-law's exemplary behavior as a widow, and Ru-song thanks his widowed mother for his stern upbringing. Ru-song briefly mentions her devotion to Buddhism and to poetry, and praises her poetry for its sincerity and simplicity. All poems in *Rue Window Chanting Drafts* date from her life as a widow; many of them appear to have been written in the 1760s.

Rue Window Chanting Drafts opens with three sets of eight poems each in which Lady Zhoujia expresses her undying love for her husband and laments her life as a widow, respectively titled "Lamenting my Fate," "Sad Musings," and "Emotions." Most of the followings poems are devoted to descriptions of the changing seasons and their typical flowers. Her Buddhist devotion is reflected in the many poems written following the rhymes of works by the female Chan master Dongwu.[18] Lady Zhoujia also wrote several poems following the rhymes of poems of the Female Scribe of Practiced Seclusion (Xiyou Nüshi), a daughter of Gong Danting who worked as a tutor in her son's household from the mid-1760s. While *Rue Window Chanting Drafts* contains several poems by Lady Zhoujia that were written following the rhymes of poems by her children, I have found no poems that follow the rhymes of poems by her daughter-in-law. *Green Window Chanting Drafts,* however, contains in its second scroll a number of poems written by Lady Tongjia "following the rhymes" of works by her mother-in-law. Judging from several poems in Lady Tongjia's collections, the relationship between the two women must have been quite friendly. Lady Zhoujia would survive her son, and several decades later, when the elderly Lady Tongjia lost her only remaining son, Chun-ying, she often referred to her mother-in-law and spoke of their shared fate as a "family tradition."[19]

The first scroll of Lady Tongjia's *Green Window Chanting Drafts* includes a sizable number of works that follow the rhymes of poems written by her husband Ru-song (designated by his sobriquet Person of the Plain Heart [Suxinren]). As a member of the court, Ru-song was often away from home for extended periods of time: in 1756 he followed the Qianlong emperor on an eastern tour, and in 1757 he followed him on a southern tour. During the latter tour, Ru-song wrote for instance the following poem:

Hearing a Bell during a Sleepless Night

I'm scared by this night scenery that enters chilly curtains:
A candle dripping crimson tears shines on my lonely blanket
And late at night the frequent bell-sounds from an unknown place
Shatter so far away from home this heart here on its cushion.[20]

This inspired his young wife to write the following quatrain:

Following the Original Rhyme Words of "Hearing a Bell during a Sleepless Night" by the Person of the Plain Heart

The bell-sounds from a far-off temple partner with your chanting
While sleepless in the quiet night you huddle under blankets.
Where in these inner chambers do I find such rousing peals
To shatter night on night this heart that sorrows in your absence?[21]

In Ru-song's original poem, the rhyme words (at the end of the second and fourth lines) were "blanket" and "heart"; in her matching poem Lady Tongjia used the same words in the same position.

In 1760 Ru-song was away from home for over nine months as he was ordered to escort a group of newly subjected Uighurs on their return from the capital to Aksu, "a journey of over thirty thousand miles." But when Ru-song in 1761was appointed as general of the Manchu garrison at Suiyuan, Lady Tongjia followed her husband to his new posting, and she also accompanied him when he was posted to Xi'an in the same position in 1762, which caused her to lament her separation from her parents and parents-in-law. During these years Lady Tongjia also had to mourn the loss of her eldest, second, and fourth sons.[22] During the late 1760s she also lost her parents.

Following her husband's death in 1770, Lady Tongjia wrote over two hundred quatrains lamenting him. Eventually she would have 170 of these printed as *Tearful Drafts from Beside the Coffin* (Suiwei leicao). As funerary writings had a very public character in traditional China, women only on rare occasions composed public texts lamenting their grief over the loss of their husband. And while there existed a long tradition of men remembering their spouses in *shi* poetry, women had started to do so only in the early Ming dynasty. The model, a long set of quatrains, was "One Hundred Poems Lamenting My Husband" by the late Ming poet Bo Shaojun (d. 1627).[23] Her set (of which eighty-one poems survive) enjoyed considerable popularity in the seventeenth century and thereafter. But whereas Bo Shaojun felt free to describe the life she shared with her husband in considerable detail, Lady Tongjia was more restrained. While we have no reason to doubt the depth of her emotions, her quatrains lamenting her husband do not achieve the liveliness and variety of Bo Shaojun's. In many later poems, too, Lady Tongjia would continue to testify to her desolate widowhood. In a number of her later works she also testifies to the comfort she derived from her Buddhist faith.

By 1792, when she published her *A Combined Selection from the Poetry-Instruction Loft* (Wenshilou hexuan), Lady Tongjia's opinion of her earlier poetry had changed drastically. As late as 1776, in the preface to *Preserved Drafts of Crow-Like Attachment*, the Elder of Cypress Fragrance is given pride of place as her poetry teacher. In the following collection, however, that position was now granted to the Female Scribe of Practiced Seclusion, and she now also claims that she found no "poet" in her new home when she married. The preface to *A Combined Selection* may be rendered as follows:

> I grew up in the inner quarters. From my earliest years my father and mother doted on me. But because they loved me so much, they instructed me in an all-round fashion, and they never treated me differently because I was a girl. From the age of nine I read the books with a teacher surnamed Lin. After a year she was replaced by a teacher surnamed Yang. These two people were both incapable of poetry. Only when I studied at the age of thirteen with the Female Scribe of Practiced Seclusion, and later when I studied with the Instructrix of the Snowy Loft [Xuelou Jiangshou], did I advance to a rudimentary understanding of tones and rhymes, and from that moment on I indulged in chanting.[24]
>
> Once I had married into the princely mansion, my love for paper and brush was not less than that in earlier days, but even though I sought everywhere for a poet, I could find no such person. Only when I occasionally exchanged verses with the late Prince did I try to write lines on "the crowing cock warning of the dawn," but I was always ashamed that these poems were not yet accomplished.[25]
>
> Later, in the *bingshen* year [1776] of the Qianlong reign period I hired the Female Scribe from South of the Range, Plum Kiosk [Lingnan Nüshi Meixuan], for teaching my daughter. As we were together from early in the morning till late at night, the old habit revived again. We stimulated each

other mutually, and the works we composed all gave expression to the joys of the moment.

Now some decades have passed in the blink of an eye. Snowy Loft and Practiced Seclusion passed away one after another. Even Plum Kiosk has left me for good to become a person of the past. These three people were all unhappy in their marriages, and their poems also were not able to imitate the famous women of the Tang and Song dynasties. But the manuscripts of these old friends, which I kept in my boxes, are quite capable of moving me when thinking about past and present, leaving and coming.

Therefore I have selected some of my own works for printing, and at the end I have appended works by these three women. I hope that at least some of their compositions may be preserved in this world and that their names will be transmitted. In this way I want to give expression to my abiding nostalgia for the past, so this is not the place to discuss the quality and ranking of their poems.

Practiced Seclusion's mother's surname was Yang. Her mother's literary name was Bland Pavilion [(Gong) Danting]. She hailed from Yangzhou in Jiangnan, and also was experienced in poetry. For a while she stayed at the house of Grand Secretary Ming-zhu. Her *Preserved Together: Selected Poems* [Hecun shichao] circulates in the world. Snowy Loft was surnamed Shen. She married a Mr. Feng and hailed from Suzhou. For a while she taught in the mansion of Prince Shen of the second rank.[26] Plum Kiosk's surname was Xu. She hailed from Guangdong.[27] Later she met Stone Orchid [Shilan], whose surname was Hu. She was originally the wife of an official. They met in the mansion of Grand Secretary Fu. She also was experienced in poetry and often exchanged poetry with me in recent years.[28] Here I have made a selection from her manuscripts, and added them to the collection in order to document our friendship.

Written by the Mistress of Heaven's Suchness on the "First *Si*" of the *renzi* year [1792] of the Qianlong reign period

As a widow, Lady Tongjia continued to be a productive poet. The poems from the 1770s onward were printed in the early years of the nineteenth century as yet another two-scroll collection titled *Elegant Exercises by the Empty Window* (Xuchuang yake). This collection carries an undated preface by the Manchu grand councilor Qing-gui (1735–1816)[29] and an 1805 postface by Ying-he (1771–1840), who at that time served on the Grand Council.[30] In many poems in this collection she expresses her abiding devotion to her husband and expresses her sufferings as a widow. In other poems she describes the progress of her son's studies, including his advances in poetry.[31] In his preface to Chun-ying's collected poetry, Ying-he stressed Lady Tongjia's emphasis on poetry in her son's education in the following words:

> The Prince lost his father in his youth. His consort, Lady Tongjia, a chaste widow and well-versed in literature, raised him in an exemplary fashion, serving both as his mother and his teacher. In the spare time left after his practice of riding and archery she would always discourse on the study of poetry, going into great detail on its source and development. Whenever she wrote a poem, she would order the Prince to write a matching composition, and if he showed but the slightest improvement she would show her pleasure. Once, when the Prince followed His Imperial Majesty on a trip beyond the Wall, she still personally inscribed a white fan and send it to him as an admonishment.[32]

Throughout his life, Chun-ying would continue to write matching poems to his mother's compositions.

The most conspicuous work in Lady Tongjia's *Elegant Exercises by the Empty Window* is her long "An Autobiographical Song" (Zishu ge), in which she recorded the reversals in fortune in her husband's family during her lifetime, up to Chun-ying's appointment as Prince Rui.[33] This poem, which concludes the first volume of *Elegant Exercises*, may be exceptional for its length, but not necessarily for its literary brilliance, and at the end the author confesses that "many of the lines . . . are quite prosaic." It is also a rather one-sided account of the family's history. Lady Tongjia does not mention, for instance, that her husband Ru-song in 1765 was about to be stripped of his princely rank because of corruption and was only allowed to keep his title once the Qianlong emperor personally intervened and allowed him to get off the hook by paying a hefty fine, after which Ru-song's bureaucratic career had come to an end.[34]

The poems in the second volume of Lady Tongjia's *Elegant Exercises*, dating from the last two decades of the eighteenth century, are somewhat lighter in tone than the gloomy poems of the first volume up to the "Autobiographical Song."[35] One also finds here the poems she exchanged with other Manchu women poets such as Bingyue.

The poems Lady Tongjia wrote during the year following her son Chun-ying's death in 1800 were collected and printed as *A Heart Ripped Apart* (Liexin ji).[36] This collection opens with two short poems in the *sao* mode, followed by twenty-three seven-syllable quatrains all entitled "Lamenting My Son" (Kuzi).[37] The series continues with five-syllable regulated poems for the one hundredth day following death, and then one poem for each month until a full year is reached. The collection is concluded by eight more five-syllable regulated poems. In this collection Lady Tongjia not only expresses her distress over the loss of her child, but also states her regret that she had not followed her husband in death but had herself allowed to be "led astray" by her son to stay alive in order to see to his education.

As the matriarch of a new princely house, Lady Tongjia also composed a set of family instructions, the *Family Instructions from the Hall for Treasuring Goodness* (Baoshantang jiaxun; 1800). Despite its general title, this work is primarily a moral tract for women, as will be immediately clear from the chapter titles: "Serving One's Parents," "Serving One's Mother-in-Law," "Serving One's Husband," "Managing the Household," "The Teaching of Sons," and "The Instruction of Daughters." A translation of this last chapter is included here. As may be expected, Lady Tongjia stresses the importance of filial piety and subservience to parents and parents-in-law, and flexibility and modesty toward the husband. Women once married should not return too often to their natal home and complain about their new surroundings. Remarkable is her repeated insistence on frugality; lavish spending by the wife is condemned as the cause of corruption by the husband in his official career. She also urges wives to accept her husband's concubines: an accommodating attitude will be the best means to maintain their own position, while loud complaints to relatives will only make them a laughingstock. Throughout her *Family Instructions*, Lady Tongjia criticizes the moral laxity of her contemporaries, accusing them of spoiling their daughters.

While Chun-ying was instructed in poetry by his mother, he himself served as the poetry teacher for his wife Lady Fucha (Fuca), the Mistress of Bland Fragrance (Danxiang Zhuren).[38] We learn this from a small pamphlet in the National Library in Beijing, listed as *Selected Poems of Bland Fragrance* (Danxing yingao).[39] This small collection comes without a preface or postface that would explain the reasons of publication. It consists of poems exchanged by Chun-ying and his young wife during one year in the early 1780s, when Chun-ying was away from home on a trip to the region north of the Wall (possibly accompanying the Qianlong emperor on a trip to Chengde for the autumn hunt at Mulan?). The second title of the poems contributed by Chun-ying reads:

> Yesterday I saw the poems that had arrived. Your inner feelings are tactfully expressed and the construction of your lines is very beautiful. They amply show that you have not only quietly stayed in the inner chambers since my

> departure, but that you also have made quite some progress in your studies. But as these are the lines of a beginner they unavoidably cannot yet be effortlessly elegant, so I have now corrected them, and I also have written two poems using the same rhymes.[40]

Apart from the ten poems by Lady Fucha included in this small collection, which properly give expression to her longing for her absent husband, none of her other poems are known.

LADY ZHOUJIA

Lamenting My Fate

1.

I lost my parents' counsel early on,
And first was educated by an aunt.
An orphan, I felt pity for myself
Because I lacked the tender love of siblings.

2.

When I was given to my lord in marriage,
Our harmony resembled drum and zither:
Before the window with you when you studied—
And when the lamp was lit we talked of love.

3.

Only a dozen years of such attachment—
The pain of your demise will last my life.
Before you were a guest in noble houses
But now you are a figure in my dreams.

4.

Two years have now already quickly passed
And dust has settled on my rouge and powder.
Before the mirror I am filled with pain;
As I think back my tears will dye my clothes.

5.

Cold and forlorn the empty heavy curtains;
My toilet table covered all by grime:
This little heart is overcome by sadness
And scattered books are lying all around.

6.

I sit alone here in this quiet study,
Remembering our love of former days.
The endless sufferings of desolation—
There is no way that I can tell you all.

7.

I humbly bow my head and ask Blue Heaven:
What was your purpose giving life to me?
Not destined to become a phoenix couple—
You could have made us intertwining branches!

8.

A honking goose and lonely lamp at night:
I sit here idly as I think of you in pain.
I want to visit you in dreams, but where?
Roads to the Yellow Springs are far and vague.

From *Sad Musings*

2.

The moon when autumn comes is always once as bright:
I long for you but see you not, and so my heart is flustered.
The chirping crickets are bereft of any sense of feeling
And make most noise next to the ears of people filled with sorrow.

7.

Outside cloud-covered window gauze the flowers are ablaze,
But I was never led astray by any vulgar feelings.
Let flowers bloom, let flowers fall, it is of no importance:
The moon shone on a heart of ice for these last twenty years.

From *Emotions*

4.

While leaning at the window I recall your former features
And in my silliness I seem at times to see your face.
How often I did want to speak, but speak I never could;
The pent-up pain that fills my breast now festers even more.
  Although I know that you have gone to regions of illusion,
All that is left for me today is seeking you in dreams.
And if by any chance this night our souls can find each other
The watchman shall on no account announce the break of dawn.

7.

Before it's even Clear and Bright[41] I do not eat or sleep;
Turning and tossing in my bed I shed a thousand tears.
When I by chance look in the mirror, I feel dazed and dizzy;
My tender guts, tied into knots, cause a still greater pain.
  With now some rain and now some sun the flowers age so quickly;
One moment sad, and then depressed: the days last once as long.
Could I become a butterfly and trail behind you,
I would for all eternity roam through transcendent realms.

Emotions on Waking Up from a Dream

A floating cloud that's drifting all day long:
I longed for you but long you did not come.
Last night at last I dreamed you spoke to me
And your kind feelings showed me your intention.
  You pitied me as I have little knowledge
And told me I should stick to my ambition.[42]
Now you have left, it's hard to meet again:
I'm grateful for your everlasting love.

A Poem on the Chaste Woman

A bright-red heart like rock or iron reaching to blue heaven;
A chastity that can't be moved, as strong as pine or cypress.
For centuries the gods and ghosts admire her self-denial:
Heaven is bound to love the ones who die for virtue's sake.

The Lantern Festival, an Impromptu Poem[43]

The streets here in the capital are filled with song and music;
Fine steeds and perfumed carts speed by as fast as shuttles.
The people blame this night of spring for being way too short:
The light of all these lanterns pales the brightness of the moon.

On the Elegant Pastimes of Dongwu's Convent

The incense burner has grown cold, the night is at its end:
By meditating on one's couch, one's nature is set free.
The bamboo path is softened by red rains from apricots
And on the single pine tree hangs the rounded moon of fall.

Regretting My Lack of Study

I force myself to hold the brush and try to write a poem:
Searching through all my barren guts I hardly find one line.
Now I regret that in my youth I did not study harder
And to my shame I must confess that I am "rotten wood."[44]

Instructions for My Daughter

While they are young the girls in inner chambers
Must learn to follow all the rites and norms,
So listen to instructions by your teachers
And stick to the example of your mother.
  Avoid close contact with your husband's brothers
And do not join the games of little children.
If you distinguish between wise and foolish,
You'll understand which things are most important.

The Goldfish in Its Bowl on My Desk, Written in Jest

You're living in translucent waves but still you are deluded:
You hurry on and take some inches for a distant journey.
A silly fool, you do not know the marvels of the mystic—
How I admire the giant Kun fish out there in the lakes![45]

From *Sending My Daughter Off in Marriage*

1.

I did not stint the heavy labor of these eighteen years,
I polished on throughout the night until the early hours.

And even though you were a niece, I loved you only better,
As much as your dear mother did—my care for you sincere.
But now alas you're married off and I must let you go;
You find it hard to leave my side—you cannot serve your mother.
As long as you are able to not disobey my teachings
You still will always be the pearl I treasure on my palm.

LADY TONGJIA

Poems from *Green Window Chanting Drafts*

On Crabs

We eat our fill of "frost of the Ninth Month":[46]
The fat is pure, the marrow full of fragrance.
Their sideways movement[47] has, it seems, its purpose:
Don't chide these animals for lack of guts!

In a Village

A bluish green fills open fields and grasses spread their flowers;
The mountain villages lack trees: no oriole that sings.
My lessons done, I idly watch the plowing of the plain
And hear across the stream the shouts that hurry on the oxen.

On My Fourteenth Birthday My Teacher the Elder of Cypress Fragrance Gifted Me a Poem, So I Respectfully Followed the Original Rhyme Words

I pass these fleeting years in vain: again another spring!
Atop the ridge I suddenly espy a new jade plum.
To no avail you gift me with your lofty mountain tune:
I imitate it day and night, but still don't get it right.

My Ambition[48]

The slightest error in the rites will be my lifelong shame;
"No fault against the Inner Rules" may be my fame in death.
I will alert my mind and body at all times
As I refuse to spend my days like mediocre types.

Longing to Return to My Parental Home[49]

Like threads of silk the rain resembles tears of homeward longing:
Ever so light, tossed by the breeze, they soak my patterned jacket.
My mother's virtue like warm spring I never could repay—
Can I allow my younger siblings to gain all her pleasure?

A Sudden Thought

Since I arrived here at your house, it now has been two months
And without cause my trains of thought are tangled all like silk.
Whenever I take up my pen I only write down "longing";
As soon as I put down the brush I only talk of sighs.
  It's only now I understand the taste of sweet and sour;
As of today I've come to know the flavors of vexation.
Which situation in this world can truly be called bitter?
That only is that of a girl who lives in inner chambers.

In the Spring of the Year Bingzi *[1756], the Person of the Plain Heart*[50] *Followed His Majesty on His Eastern Tour, So I Improvised Two Quatrains to See Him Off*

1.

We rise at dawn: the heavy mist has suddenly cleared up,
The scenery outside the window now is pure and quiet.
The freshest reds and palest greens are all of no avail:
They can't tie down the traveler, they only tie down sorrow.

2.

Those precious birds that share their wings will always fly together;
When separated for a moment they feel still attached.
Before the parting meal is set, my heart feels drunk and dazed;
Afraid to cause your parents pain, I wipe away my tears.

From *Spring Day Inner Chamber Longing, Eight Poems*

1.

I still remember last year's song of west wind separation,
Now spring has come and once again I set out parting cups.
This mansion may be made of gold, but who sings carefree songs?
My longings for the one who left outnumber willow strands.

2.

Gauze windows on a cloudless day: the grass grows lush, so lush,
But when I watch the blooming twig, who's there to hold my hand?
The days of spring all last so long, the nights are really endless—
I cannot bear to sit alone, I cannot bear to sleep!

3.

The peach trees seem to be on fire, like silk[51] are all the willows:
These springtime colors have a woman dream long noontime dreams.
Could we but soar and flutter like that pair of butterflies—
On peonies they rest together, each and every day!

5.

O still, so still, the late spring day—I face the setting sun.
The flowers bloom, the flowers fade, it's all one blurry mess.
In idle moments I would like to find solace by chanting
But overcome by sorrow not a single word will work.

In the Spring of the Year Dingchou *[1757], the Person of the Plain Heart Followed His Majesty on His Southern Tour and Sent Me a Poem. Respectfully I Follow the Original Rhymes to Substitute for a Letter*

By feelings filled I'm leaning on the balustrade all day;
I pity how this short-lived splendor is about to go to ruin.
How could I bear to sweep away those many fallen flowers?
I battle sorrow when I watch the moon that's full and bright.
At dusk I lower screen and blind to keep the springtime warmth;
At night I pace the steps of stone and fear the chilly dew.
I have no way to ease my mind and fall to silent weeping
When stamping boots deliver me your letter, "All is well."

In the Year Renwu *[1762], I Followed the Person of the Plain Heart to His New Posting as General at Xi'an, and I Completed This Poem on the Spur of the Moment When Saying Goodbye to My Mother-in-Law*

These ten years long at dawn and dusk I asked about your health
But now I leave for distant parts I'll fail to do your bidding.
The hills will stir up homeward longings, tangled in their hundreds;
The streams will carry sobs of parting, twisted many times.
I'd like to sing a "blackfoal song"[52] but feel too much depressed;
Before I set out on the road, I wipe away my tears,

But dimly visible my soul will with the midnight moon
Arrive at mother's bedside, there to learn how you've been doing.

Two Poems Respectfully Harmonizing with My Mother-in-Law's Chants on the Heart of the Chaste Woman

1.

Ambition like the autumn frost that far transcends the crowd:
Such chastity in inner chambers equals stellar service.
The lasting fame by a red brush transmitted to green records[53]
Will make her story still renowned after a thousand ages.

2.

The pine tree is her skeleton and jade will be her heart:
She wants to be like gold that is a hundred times refined.
Her strict behavior does not seek the praise of other people;
The lonely goose that honks at night will be her only friend.

Poems from *Preserved Drafts of Crow-Like Attachment*

From *Lamenting My Father, Eight Poems*

1.

Suddenly a messenger arrived who has rushed through the dust,
Startling us with the news that our father had died on the steppe.
His good deeds had already filled the number of three hundred,[54]
But the years of his life did not yet add up to seven times ten.
Earlier we wondered why he had failed to send letters home,
Now the portending dreams of many nights turned out to be true.
Even though we'd have a statue carved, imitating Ding Lan,[55]
This ends the days of repaying him, while alive, for his care.

3.

Your unlimited sincere grace was as capacious as the ocean,
Teaching me all kinds of books, you loved me more than a son.
I was unable to fully please you while you were still alive,
Weeping blood I vainly must carry this with me after your death.
Your portrait can be delineated with the aid of powder and ink,
We'll sacrifice to you in your shrine as if you banter and smile.
Summoning your soul, the roads of darkness, I find, are boundless,
So I collapse from grief and revive again—twice, thrice each day.

4.
A bitter rain and chilly wind: a breast that's filled with grief,
The sad notes of migrating geese pass over the cold window.
Apart while alive—no poem could dispel that tangled pain,
Separated by death—words cannot tame this wrecked heart.
Guiding our tender parent with a banner, wearing the white rope,
My younger brother, supported by a staff, guards the soul's pennant.
When I stroke the coffin I am overcome by a thousand sorrows,
And tears pour down in streams, as copiously as the river.

From *Lamenting My Mother, Ten Poems*

9.
One has a child to guard against old age,
But this son died before the mother did.[56]
And even though some daughters are around,
They are not equal to a single male.
A grandson—what good fortune—does remain,
Who will continue the ancestral line,
A little baby in his swaddling-clothes
Still unaware of sorrow and of pain.

Poems from *Tearful Drafts from Beside the Coffin*

From *Poems Lamenting My Husband; with Preface*

From my earliest youth I practiced gentle grace and strictly observed the teachings of my female instructors. When I grew up I was addicted to the *Odes* and the *Rites*, and became the partner of a scion of the imperial family. I only expected that the phoenix-mirror would always remain complete—how could I have expected that the swallow-hairpin would be broken halfway? Even if one would exhaust all the bamboo on the southern hills,[57] it would be impossible to give expression to my feelings of sadness, and even if you would raise the waves of the northern ocean, they would fail to provide a comparison for my tears of blood. And so, cherishing the seasons I am moved by events, and encountering scenes my feelings are mournful. All together I wrote more than two hundred pieces, but now I have pared away and rejected more than half.

Alas, if fate is like this, why should one indulge in writing? I have always admired Xie Daoyun's single line on the willow floss,[58] so why should I on this occasion brag about quantity? But I compare myself to the soul of Shu who cried tears of blood,[59] so I preserve them and fittingly make a selection. It is not that this will in any way limit my pain or ease my sorrow—I just choose them for the search for the mean by discarding prolixity.

1.

Your love for me while still alive was larger than a mountain,
I held your hand to make you stay, but found it hard to speak.
You had my innards break to pieces, tied them up in knots,
I had to cry—my shirt was stained with tears I wiped away.

4.

The mother's old, the wife alone, the son not yet a man—
So how can heaven watch the death of such a splendid hero?
Husband and wife should not be separated here on earth:
Resting together in one grave is better than surviving.

7.

Your love for me when still alive was boundless like the sea,
So now I feel it's easier to die than go on living.
Oh, hand in hand there in the grave we'd sing a song of joy,
As there's no pleasure left for me while staying here behind.

10.

"They share a grave who shared a blanket" is the ancient maxim,
And all my life I never wanted to betray that lesson.
But even though I want to die, I lack a proper method,
And cannot match the spontaneity of simple folks.

72.

The law of Buddha has no power I have come to know,
Ridiculous were all my prayers to those gods and ghosts!
It was the teachings of the sages that were not deluded,
So may all people learn a lesson from my silly faith.

86.

The glories of this floating world have all come to an end,
The fleeting waters, without feeling, just flow to the east.
The fancy scenes of former times here still remain today,
But fortune fled and husband gone now fill the place with sorrow.

104.

There is no road that can connect the heavens to this world,
And, all alone, I'm at a loss here in my empty chamber.
Right now I'd like to sign a contract with the winds of spring,
Forbidding them to let the flowers riot like last year.

121.

Most painful is that stupid question of our silly boy:
"Where is my daddy living now that he has left this world?"
With lowered head, eyes filled with tears, I have no ready answer,
As endlessly the yellow clouds confront the graveyard site.

124.

Watching the actors play, we whiled away the pleasant seasons,
Seated before a mica screen, together, side by side.
But now I know that scenes of joy are not my share while living,
So I devote myself to a regime of meditation.

162.

Each day I again recite the *Diamond-Wisdom Sutra,*
Hoping to benefit your well-being in the world below.
This illusion told in an illusion is truly hard to trust,
But if only my feelings were true, the Buddha may help.

170.

The piercing cold of early spring—a heart that's filled with grief:
I do not want to watch the sun that's rising in the window.
I must confess I failed and did not follow you in death—
A couple while you were alive, but since you died not yet.

Poems from *Elegant Exercises by the Empty Window*

From *Accidental Outpourings*

1.

Seeing this sea of suffering I'm moved by Jambudvipa:[60]
The empty glories of this world—I'm done with them for good.
My sorrow-line was lengthened by a thousand feet of trouble
When twenty year of happiness burst like a water bubble.

My passion is the greatest hindrance to enlightenment—
I can't forget my duty to repay him with my death.
Send word please to the Double Springs that he should wait for me,[61]
Would I be willing to stay here for profit and fame?

Deepest Feelings

1.
I'm slow to fix my mourning white: it shows my recent tears,
I'm facing the chrysanthemums—a chilly evening glow.
You talk about "an understanding friend," but don't you know
I'm filled with longings for my parents, longings for my lord?

2.
Why scribble on this little note a "broken-hearted chant"?
"The phoenix parted forms its mate" evokes the deepest grief.
But then in this cold night, there is this clear and limpid moon
That through the window shines on me and on my suffering heart.

3.
The rustling western winds of autumn make my sleep last longer,
Awakened by the bells of dawn, I'm dumb, bereft of speech.
Those endless tender words which we exchanged while I was dreaming:
I want to write them down, but don't succeed and wrack my brain.

4.
Suffering frost, the maple woods mix red with green and yellow,
Filling my eyes this sorry scene increases grievous pain.
Freezing chrysanthemums, with understanding, even tarry
And wait to show their flowers until after Double Nine.

Emotions

1.
Back from a dream—the window-moon rising,
On my cushion I count the remaining watches.
In deepest stillness the lamp lowers its flame,
Chilly and cheerless, tears secretly come down.
Bereft of sleep: like ice and snow so pure,
I have a mirror: like the jade vase[62] so clear.

Since my enlightenment, body and mind are bland,
Not because I force myself to control my emotions.

2.

The occasion which most of all ruins the spirit
Is the heart as the bell rings out the fifth watch.[63]
When the cock crows and the cold moon sinks,
The blanket is too thin to keep the late cold out.
I've come to know the taste of chewing wax,
When eating *tu*, I fear the "bitter chanting."[64]
The many responsibilities of rules and norms
All come down on a single woman's shoulders.

The Night of Double Seven[65]

Since you departed for eternity, two autumns passed,
I've no desire tonight to watch the Weaving Maid and Oxherd.
In heaven "parted while alive" still brings one day of joy,
On earth "separated by death" means no occasion to meet.
The candle's tears here in the wind combine with human tears,
The clouds of sorrow in the sky increase to rains of sorrow.
Could I but cross the Yellow Springs like they the Silver River—
A broken heart in deepest silence in the Needle Loft.

Paper Kites

By making use of just a single thread in some boy's hands,
They freely roam on spring winds through green poplar skies.
Their scattered shadows in the sunlight look like those of geese,
The whirring sounds rise to the clouds, just as the notes from strings.
Their little tricks beguile the people, people all fly kites,
They follow fashion in their shape, a shape that lightly soars.
I have had for years a bellyful of grievances and complaints
I'd like to lay before High Heaven—please deliver them!

From *Lamenting My Mother-in-Law*

1.

I once said that the *tu* I ate was bitter,
But bitter was in truth my mother's lot:
For many years a mind of chaste resolve,
So all her life her brows were creased by sorrow.

She raised her son, but then she lost her son,
Her parents died before she knew them.
When my mother-in-law was three, her father passed away, and when she was five, her mother succumbed.
And at the end, she did not leave a word,
As phlegm hindered her to voice her grief.

2.

My "one-inch square" had since a year already turned to ashes,[66]
Today it is my mother who is lowered in her grave.
While past tears had not dried at all the current tears continue,
My heart was wrecked by suffering, now pain destroys my heart.
For twenty years she showed her love by her advice and words,
And all that time she treated me more kindly than a daughter.
If you below the earth are reunited with your son,
Be sure to pity this young widow and her mournful dreams.

Reading the Sutras, an Impromptu Poem

Throughout the day a thousand strands of sorrow,
So I read sutras to control my feelings:
A peaceful heart removes all silly thoughts,
A quiet mind forgets one's idle fame.
Glory and shame: my body's unconcerned,
Through tolerance my energy is calmed.
I strictly teach my children in the Classics,
In this way spending my remaining years.

When I Saw My Son Practicing Poetry, I Was Filled with Joy and Wrote the Following

I see that you are practicing your verses,
And therefore I feel very much relieved.
You have improved in literary studies,
Your martial skills you earlier perfected.
You must continue your late father's aim,
Please understand your mother's toil in teaching.
So I beseech you, give it all your effort,
As earnest study brings your parent joy.

Seeing My Son Grow Up, I Was Filled with Joy and Exhorted Him

Next year already you will be a lad,[67]
You'll know your duties toward your lord and parents.
The *Odes* and *Documents* will mold your mind,
You're fully trained in archery and riding.
  Reprove yourself for any evil thoughts,
Be more forgiving when it comes to others.
Be modest in your ways and also cautious,
So you maintain our family tradition!

For Years I Have Suffered from a Liver and Spleen Condition, Which Greatly Worries My Children, So I Wrote This Poem to Set Their Mind at Ease

That year when I was parted from your father,
That was the time at which my sorrow sprouted.
I forced myself to do the household chores,
And strictly checked the lessons of my sons.
  I did not care about our rank and status,
And life and death too left me unconcerned.
My fate depends on heaven's disposition:
Why do I need a treatment by some quack?

When Reading the Poems of Plum Kiosk I Encountered the Line "No Poem Came to Me, Alas, and Neither Did a Dream." I Loved This Line So Much That I Dashed Off the Following Four Quatrains.

1.

No poem came to me, alas, and neither did a dream—
Awake I counted the long watches by the freezing window.
The pleasures of my days of youth have all dissolved completely,
Like fleeting rivers years and beauty both betrayed this life.

2.

I sit and face a sprig of plum[68] throughout the many watches,
No poem came to me, alas, and neither did a dream.
I've realized that form is empty, emptiness is form,
Now *Master Zhuang* is clear to me as soon as I start reading.

3.

The wind howls through the many trees, the cold is almost piercing,
Lifting the curtain I see snow that's covering the plum trees.

No poem came to me, alas, and neither did a dream—
My tangled innards are all twisted, knotted like a thread.

4.
I could not serve my parents well, nor sacrifice myself,[69]
On top of that I fail to be an exemplary mother.
With wounded heart remembering events of long ago—
No poem came to me, alas, and neither did a dream.

An Autobiographical Song

In the year of *guiyou*,[70] when I had just turned seventeen,
Our two families, to mutual joy, tied the matrimonial bond.
My father instructed me, saying: "Adhere to respect and precepts."
My mother instructed me, saying: "Order his house and chamber."
My lord was eminent material, pure in his hundred actions,
I, to my shame, was often deficient in the four wifely virtues.

"Lifting the tray as high as my eyebrows," I learned from Liang Hong,[71]
"Treating me like a friend, like a guest," he exerted his influence.
Serving his parents to their pleasure, our life was filled with joy:
How could I have known my circumstances would be so accommodating?

In *jiaxu*,[72] when I was eighteen, my lord served at court,
"When the crowing cock announced dawn,"[73] he'd betray the spring night.
Spring nights' flowers and willows might increase their charms,
But year after year he'd be off on horseback to be at court.

From that time on he would run and race without a day of rest,
And His Majesty's favors would multiply to an amazing degree.
Golden seals and purple cords repeatedly were awarded to him,
Carrying the military tally of marshal he was a trusted minister.
Holding his court tablet he entered and waited on His Majesty—
The hooves of horses and dust of carts was beyond counting!

In the year *renwu*[74] he was ennobled as prince and given a fief,
From that moment on his brilliant status glorified our house.
Grateful above for His Majesty's favors and the ancestors' merits,
Below he comforted his loving parents for twenty years of worry.

Ascending the stair of five high steps he rose to the blue clouds,
Maintaining prosperity, holding on to fullness, he wrote on his sash.[75]
He stayed away from music and song, from strings and pipes,[76]
By nature hating conspicuous luxury, he loved the pure and simple.
Rank, status and power struggles were of no concern to him,
As he was happy enough to enjoy his riches and abide by the glory.

Who could know that at the height of happiness disaster would strike?
A clap of thunder ripped heaven apart, I awoke to a nightmare.

When the year reached *gengyin*,[77] when I just turned thirty-four,
My lord suffered a minor illness, which went from bad to worse.
The cures of those quacks brought no result, so what could I do?
I cut some flesh from my thigh, but to no avail: he never rose.

At this moment my wounded heart tossed and turned in agony,
I hated to have no miraculous plan that could reverse the heavens.
My body and soul had already for a long time turned to ashes:
If we could not live together in peace, death would bring us peace.[78]

When my lord knew his illness had "entered into his diaphragm,"[79]
His eyes filled with tears and he spoke to me after a long silence:
"You'll continue the sacrifices in my mother's waning years,
Please do not betray the worrisome task that I entrust to you!"

As soon as I heard these words, my soul and spirit were shocked,
In a sudden reversal I would not accomplish the aim of sad love.
I was shaken to such a degree that I found it impossible to speak,
But how could I refuse him my body—for my lord I would live.

Oh heaven, oh heaven, we were truly separated for all eternity,
If you do not want us to live together, you want us to share a grave!
His mother cried, his children wept—none could bear to listen,
Beating my breast I collapsed, then revived, then fainted again.

All day long I said not a word as tears of blood flowed down,
I didn't know about the other life, but this life here had ended.

Returning again to the red mansion, I discerned no road at all,
If I wished to see my lord, there were only the trees on the grave.

I did not know when I would see him in again in life or death,
When I saw the abandoned forest,[80] I seemed to have lost my wits.
At that time I could not bear to look back on glory and shame,
I only regretted that my body's experience was that of a woman.

When I returned again to the old mansion, the scene was desolate,
How sad it is to see that human feelings are as thin as paper![81]
Frittering away the years and months, I just followed my karma,
Never once shaming the pure and unblemished inherited style.

A floating cloud had destroyed the pleasures of twenty years,
I should have known when to wake up from the illusionary dream.
My body resembled a silkworm in spring, its thread unfinished[82]—
Even when the cold lamp had burned its wick, I still did not sleep.

In the still and empty courtyard the bamboo shades were heavy,
In the long, long watches, the clepsydra dripped in the urn's bronze.
Even though I was aware of the illusionary nature of my dreams,
The only place where I could vent my hidden grief was in dreams.

My heart resembled dead ashes, and my body resembled a tree,
Unconcerned whether the rivers ran dry or the mountains melted.
But moved by my lord's favors and his words before dying,
I made sure I would only be buried after vomiting all my blood.

From early till late I exerted myself, never slackening in purpose,
Whenever I visited his mother, she showed me her caring love.
Where did my lord go to that he had to abandon his dear mother?
Because of his childish affection he clearly appeared in her dreams.
Alas, alas! I would like to ask Heaven about the cause—
I should have known that the sea of suffering can never be filled!

On the thirteenth day of the Third Month of the year *guisi*,[83]
His mother fell ill, and all of sudden she was beyond any cure.
I cried to Heaven and stamped the Earth, but neither answered—
Was it true? Was it a dream? Had she abandoned me?

Personally I supported her weak body as my tears coursed down—
Grieving over my mother, longing for my lord, my innards on fire.
For twenty-two years her love and affection had known no limit,
Now I would never be able to repay this dear parent for her favors.

My tender innards, cut to pieces, could not be straightened out: before
My husband's mourning had ended, his mother's mourning followed.
Our house was reduced to four bare walls: all surrounded by worries,
My little heart, a thousand times and then ten thousand times.

At this moment even a man made of stone would have been moved.
Embracing my grief all day long, my feelings were most disconsolate.
How sad! All in vain are parents' effort and toil in raising their children:
Her care while alive and burial upon death were all on the simple side.

Ever since I was parted by that great divide from my mother's face,
I was filled by sadness all day long, dithering and at a loss what to do.
Her lasting, tender affection for her child had now come to an end,
Years and months passed in sorrow, the watches were indeed long.

From this moment on my body and mind were both without master,
My yearning for my mother even more painful than that for my husband.
Making bear-gall pills, writing with a reed,[84] I taught the fatherless child.
Suppressing my tears, I did my best to guide him, tenderly and strictly.

In the year of *yiwei*,[85] when my son had turned fourteen,
We fetched him as bride a daughter of a house known for its service.
By imperial grace he joined the guard, serving in the Qianning Hall:
He executed his job with great diligence, spoke with great earnestness.

Indeed, when misfortune is at its peak, prosperity comes, it's true:
His Majesty's boundless favors extend to His slightest servant.
The noble rank was that of a first-rank prince, above all others,
The inherited title of a hundred years was suddenly restored.

Deeply moved I grasped his hands and I said to my son:
"Never betray your Ruler's favors and your mother's love!
Carefully maintain modest harmony, respect and circumspection,
Never abuse your opulent riches and your lofty position!

Our family has been restored, your name will be known,
In the national history you'll leave a fine name for all eternity.
If your father in his grave has intelligence, he must be pleased:
The ancestral merit is repeated once more: his son is a prince!"

After a decade of bitter toil we have established our reputation,
Yet I will not dare take lightly the teaching and management.
The wall of sorrow of several years has now been broken down,
This time, as I record my joy, my heart is elated with pride.
 Both my husband and son were enfeoffed with a princedom,
A fine daughter-in-law and fine grandson serve me by my side.
The family is filled with a harmony which calls down blessings,
Enjoying the prosperity and good fortune of the Odes and Hymns.

For more than a year with nothing to do I force myself to make a song,
But as I lack literary skill, many of the lines, I know, are quite prosaic.
Yet this is far from the idle versifying of the inner quarters, as I try
To records my deepest feelings in my chanting and humming.

From *Moved upon Accidentally Seeing the Flowers of My Old Garden*

1.

The peach trees are still blooming like in springs of long ago,
Their reds reaching the forest's margin and the river's bank.
In vain I've cherished since I left a dream of ten long years,
Plucking some branches I just feel that some of them are new.
 Who is the host now in the Hall of Purity Retained?
In the Pavilion Bringing Freshness I am but a guest.
If flowers had the slightest feeling, they'd be lonesome too:
They would remember for all time the man who had them planted.

Impromptu

I sit before the mirror through the day,
So listless—not because I lack cosmetics.
For many years I have not sketched my brows,[86]
But it is this which shows me my true face.

Clear and Bright[87]

The willows start to turn yellow at the festival of Clear and Bright:
When today I think of my parents, I'm doubly wounded and pained.

There's only us, a few women, to conduct the ancestral sacrifices,
Pouring out a single cup to you from afar, I dither, at a loss what to do.

In Front of the Mirror

We've faced each other now for fifty springs,
Year after year my features have been changing.
Outer appearances are not the truth,
So even less this image of an image.

Rain in the Night of Double Seven

They say that in the night of Double Seven
Oxherd and Weaving Maiden cross the Silver River.
Each year again they are allowed to meet,
What is the need then for this rain of tears?

When the Late Prince Left This World, His Son Had Just Turned Ten. That Is Already Twenty-Eight Years Ago. Moved by the Past, I Am Overjoyed at the Present, and So I Wrote This as a Present for My Son.

Strictly and tenderly I taught the treasure in my palm,[88]
And now you are approaching forty as a famous man.
Not flattering, not arrogant: you trust the ancient Way,
A friend of virtue and of goodness, writing on your sash.
   With caring love you serve your mother, never disobedient,
You meet your task and please your parent, following your nature.
As I record this joy, there's nothing else that I can give you,
But wish you that your years and fortune may be doubled.

Discussing Meditation with My Son on an Autumn Night, I Was So Filled with Joy I Wrote the Following

The rustling western winds of fall, my mind unsure and doubting:
The shadows of bamboo on windows swaying back and forth.
Dreams of the past, bathing in moonlight, are deprived of meaning,
Chrysanthemums in front of me are blooming once again.
   My heart maintains its pure intent, though years increase my age,
My study turns away from poems as my brush grows dull.
Speaking with you on meditation I forget the hour,
It's true indeed, "The younger generation must be feared!"

On a Dilapidated Monastery

An ancient monastery of many years:
Bereft of monks, the gate is closed by silence.
The walls fell down—some cubits still are standing,
The tiles are broken but some beams remain.
  From sagging eaves the chimes are still seen hanging,
On fallen steles characters have been effaced.
Yes, solemn beauty may be an illusion,
But how can one discuss its rise and fall?

Monkey Show

Their crafty nature left ravine and mountain,
And, barely tamed, enters the marketplace.
They learned from man his arrogant behavior,
With feigned expression they play cute and meek
  Your coins and fruits: grasped by unbridled greed;
In no way shamed by dress of cap and gown.[89]
Because they proudly show their cunning tricks,
The watching public fills the city streets.

Poems from *A Heart Ripped Apart*

From *Lamenting my Son*

3.
"Curb your desires! Perfect yourself!" Such was my constant lesson;
Prohibiting the joys of vice I sought to guard your health.
Had I but known that you today would die an early death,
I would have let you have your fun and you'd be still alive.

9.
When suddenly I see your portrait,[90] I am struck by madness;
I beat my breast and cannot bear the thousand streams of tears.
How can you see your mother and still sit there stiffly,
Not turning to your dear own mommy with some words?

14.
My heart resembles a bright mirror, it is clear and empty
But waves and billows in their thousands overwhelm my bosom.
An earlier existence must have caused this hindrance
That has love and attachment lead to longing without end.

15.

Like floating clouds that go their way, so ends our former karma:
You were the first to wake up from this yellow-millet dream.
What is the reason it is me who keeps on dreaming, dreaming—
Despite all shouts and cudgel blows[91] I sleep and snore away.

21.

For thirty years, by day and night, I have been filled with worry:
Tradition here is that the son will die before his mother.
I never realized that this would happen now to me—
O how I hate that day I was led astray by you!

Selections from *Family Instructions from the Hall for Treasuring Goodness*

Chapter 6, "The Instruction of Daughters"

So the *Norms for Women* says: "*Qian* is imagined by yang, *kun* is imagined by yin: sun and moon spread the light of the two states; the man finds his correct place on the outside, the woman finds her correct place on the inside: husband and wife create the beginning of the myriad transformations. When the virtue of the Five Norms is manifest, the great root is thereby solidified; when the duties of the Three Rules are clear, human relations are thereby corrected. . . . The Way of the correct family starts from the observance of ritual by men and women; the principles of infant education are that teaching should start from food and drink. If one does not start teaching children in their infancy, they will be lacking in ritual when they grow up. In the case of boys, one can still complete their virtue by respected teachers and selected friends. But in the case of girls, how can one remedy their faults by following goodness and a sincere personality? This is why the way of teaching daughters is even more important than that of sons, and why correcting the inside should have priority over that of the outside."[92]

By turning bronze into a mirror, one can use it to correct one's dress; by using the ancients as our teachers, they can provide us with models. If one can take the ancients as her models, one no longer has to worry that virtue will not be accomplished and that the house will not be correct. So, on the third day after the birth of a daughter, one lays her down below the bed, gives her an earthen tile to play with, and fasts and announces her birth [to the ancestors]. If one lays her down below the bed, it is to clarify that she is lowly and weak; it symbolizes that she will be subservient to others. If one gives her an earthen tile to play with, it is to clarify that she will habitually do physical work; it symbolizes her diligent exertion. If one fasts and announces her birth to the ancestors, it clarifies that she will be the leading person in the continuation of the ancestral sacrifices. These three activities are the normal way of women, and the classical teaching of ritual and law.

What does it mean to be lowly and weak and subservient to others? It means one has to be modest and yielding, reverential and respectful, that one places the interests of others above those of oneself, that one's acts of goodness will not become known and that one will not shirk from any disagreeable task, that one suffers one's shame and patiently bears calumny, and that one always lives as in fear and dread. What is called diligent exertion? This means one will be the last to go to bed and the first to rise; that one will not slacken from early in the morning till late at night; that one will not shirk from any household task or private duty, whether extreme or easy; that one will accomplish whatever one undertakes, and that one's handiwork work be tidy and neat. What is implied in continuing the ancestral sacrifices? This implies that one will serve one's husband and master with a correct appearance and proper behavior; that one will maintain a pure and quiet lifestyle; that one will not indulge in light-hearted frivolities; and that one will prepare the food and wine to be presented to the ancestors in a clean and fasting manner. I have never yet seen a case of someone who was perfect in all these three aspects and had to worry that her fame was not broadcast or that she might suffer disgrace. But if one is deficient in these three aspects, what fame can be broadcast and how can disgrace be avoided?

As soon as a girl is born, one must select one or two pure and good-hearted, meek and obedient wet nurses to feed her, and one or two diligent and careful, proper and honest nannies to follow her around and to lead and guide her. When she learns to speak, they should teach her to know some numbers and recognize some characters. The nannies and nurses should under all circumstances speak correct words. They cannot be allowed to give free rein to their nonsense words and disorderly talk, because otherwise the little child might hear this and imitate them. When the child is four or five years old and can eat normal food, she has to be taught that she can only start eating once she has properly washed her face and her hands and has sat down in a proper way. Next, she has to be taught that she will not sit down when the mat is not correct, and that she will not eat the food if is it not correctly cut. It is inadmissible that she gulps down her food and drink in any manner she wishes.

Once she turns ten, she must be taught the *Instructions for Women*[93] and the *Classic of Filial Piety for Women*,[94] and those works should earnestly and tirelessly be explained. She should visit and greet her parents in the morning and before bedtime. When she meets with seniors and should rise and stand, she must indeed rise and stand. It is impermissible to act easygoing and perfunctorily. And one also cannot neglect the rituals because she is still so young. When she turns fourteen or fifteen, one must bring in a female teacher who excels in learning, who will teach her the Four Books.[95] She must indeed read these thoroughly and explore them to the full, as the Way of making one's intent sincere, rectifying the mind, cultivating the person, and ordering the house is of utmost importance. It is impermissible that she should continuously read ballads and novels just because she knows a few characters. Such "wild histories" all are tales without any foundation that have been concocted by later people, but they can most easily move a person's nature and feeling, and again and again people read them as if they were true, in this way abandoning the correct studies. One has to be cautious!

So the *Instructions for Women* say: "If a man has talent, this is a virtue—this still may be said. But in a woman it is a virtue to have no talent—such a pronouncement is completely wrong." This must be because they do not know the norm for talent and virtue and the distinction between heterodox and correct. Virtue serves as the basis of talent, and talent accomplishes virtue. So a girl who has virtue does not necessarily have to have talent, but those who have talent set great store by having virtue. Virtue is the root, and talent is the branch. This is indeed the proper principle. But if anyone commits a sin, it is not a crime caused by talent. And so even a wife's words may be of use if she has a talent for management and administration, but heterodox and outlandish skills are not fitting for a boy either. The *Rites* state: "Adulterous notes and lascivious beauty do not detain his hearing and sight; voluptuous music and secretive rites do not enslave his mind and intent—this is the way a gentleman teaches his sons." Can daughters be instructed in any other way? The *Classic of Filial Piety [for Women]* was written by the wife of Mr. Chen. The *Analects [for Women]* was written by Lady Song.[96] *Precepts for My Daughters* was composed by Ban Zhao.[97] *Instructions for the Inner Quarters* was produced by the Humane and Filial Empress, and truly provides the norms and rules for the Inner Palace.[98] These works provide indeed the fragrant guidelines for female studies.

When a daughter reaches the age of seventeen or eighteen, the day of her wedding approaches. Now she must even more strictly be controlled and instructed. At this time her mother must alert and warn her in most severe terms, and it is impermissible to be excessively tolerant. The daughter must be taught to display filial piety toward her mother-in-law, to show respect toward her husband and lord, and to maintain harmony with his elder and younger sisters, to be magnanimous and sincere, and to be diligent and frugal in managing the household. Needlework and such are of secondary concern. When it comes to a wife's virtue, appearance, speech, and skills, speech is the most important. As her mind reacts to the thousands of events, she will remain silent when she should not speak. When she speaks and hits the mark, she may thereby avoid regret, but if her words to do not conform to principle, disaster is bound to follow. The proverb goes: "Words that are few and wisely spoken: I am no stone that can be rolled; words that are wrong and loudly spoken: the fiery flames that burn the plains." And another proverb goes: "If your mouth remains locked, your words have value; if your words bubble forth like a spring, they are without foundation." One has to be extremely cautious when it comes to what one says.

So a girl must be chaste and quiet, gentle and serene, dignified and serious, sincere and constant—such is the virtuous nature of a girl. If she is filial, respectful, humane and understanding, tender, harmonious, meek and accommodating, her virtuous nature is complete. One's virtuous nature derives from one's innate qualities, but is transformed and completed by habit. It is not something which comes from outside, it truly originates with the person. The chaste maidens of ancient times ordered their feelings and nature, controlled the whiles of their heart, and venerated the Way and its virtue. So they were capable to be a partner to a gentleman in order to accomplish his teaching. So they dwelt in humaneness, acted according to righteousness, spread light with their wisdom, kept their word, and embodied ritual. They did not tread on that which did conform to ritual, and did not follow that which conflicted with righteousness. Each of their actions followed the Way, and each of their words was trustworthy. They did not speak when they should not have spoken, because that leads to disaster. If one acts in conflict with ritual, heterodox and weird behavior manifests itself. The door serves to limit her words, jade serves to regulate her actions, ritual serves to control her heart, and the Way serves to limit her desires. She nourishes her virtuous nature, and by that means decorates her person. One must be cautious!

So Tairen's eyes did not look on evil colors, her ears did not listen to voluptuous notes, and her mouth did not speak arrogant words.[99] Is such behavior the way to cultivate one's person? Yes, this was the way of the ancients. If one's eyes look upon evil colors, one is internally blinded by them. If one's ears listen to voluptuous notes, one undresses in one's mind. If one's mouth speaks arrogant words, then a proud mind flourishes. All these situations harm one's person. So while staying at home, a wife sticks to the correct way in order to guard against evil, and when walking, she will not stray from the path in order to accomplish her virtue. One even has to be more observant and cautious when it comes to the separation between inner and outer and the segregation of men and women.

You must have heard the principle that in ancient times men and women did not share the same mat, that outer and inner would not share the same well, that a sister-in-law and a brother-in-law would not directly address each other, and that aunts did not wash the gown [of a nephew]. One has to be cautious when it comes to the inner quarter instructions of a great family!

But the people of these times are not like this! Because a girl is not a boy, they refuse to teach her, and she does not have a clue what it means to be filial toward father and mother, to be sincere toward one's siblings, to respect one's seniors, and to maintain harmony between relatives. They have never heard about such things as reciprocity, the exchange of gifts, and ritual rules. They only indulge their belly and love their jewelry, and all they care for is their makeup. [The parents] take excessive tolerance for love, to the extent that they set no norm for leaving and entering, and men and women are not separated. [Their daughters] treat elder and younger uncles, and elder and younger brothers the same way as their own parents, and do not avoid suspicion. In all these matters they are not cautious at all. They meet equally with distant relatives and closest friends, and they call this "open-minded"! When it comes to watching a play or listening to songs such as the recent hexagonal-drum tunes,[100] they are allowed to listen and look with their faces publicly visible. That is really against all decency! When it comes to boisterous crowds, they visit temples to burn incense and have fun—that is even more ridiculous! Don't they know that such behavior is unseemly for men, so even more for girls from the inner chambers? If upon marriage their husband's family is a family that does not insist on ritual, this is all fine, but if their husband's families insist on ritual, they either fall ill or are filled with resentment. Moreover, if at home they do not know to show filial piety toward their father and mother, then how can they after their marriage know the way of serving their parents-in-law and respecting their husband? The lack of filial piety, the lack of respect, and the lack of common sense all originate from this. They have not the slightest idea that the husband and master has to be served and that ritual and righteousness have to be maintained.

So a beautiful jade without flaw can be considered the greatest treasure, and a chaste maiden's pure virtue can be a partner to a glorious spouse. By guarding her person and controlling the norms she will be able to be an exemplary mother, and because of her diligent frugality and lack of jealousy, she will serve as a model for the inner chambers. So I now urge all families who are raising daughters to teach and instruct them in the strictest manner—that is the only Way. May my sons and grandsons make every effort in this respect!

LADY FUCHA

Inner Chamber Laments

1.

The fading moon invades my windows and it stirs my longing,
But there's no way to catch these autumn colors in my lyrics.
By mountain passes separated I can't write these feelings
In still and lonely inner chambers known to me alone.

2.

The red osmanthus spreads its fragrance in the chilly moonlight;
The crickets chirp on all four sides, the nights are getting longer.
I think of you so far away beyond the mountain passes—
Alone I sit here in my room, so wounded by these thoughts.

Leisurely Chanting

The rain is gone, the sky has cleared, the sunset glow is fading;
The moonlight moves the bamboo shadows on the window gauze.
At leisure now I want to write a poem for amusement—
Alas, I lack poetic talent, am no Xie Daoyun![101]

Expressing My Emotions

1.

A lonely room: I sit alone—the night draws on and on,
And as my company I only have one silver candle.
I hear the mournful western storm that scatters falling leaves:
The wutong tree and golden well are shaking in the wind.

2.

The bamboo shadows move in wild profusion;
The moonlight makes the empty window chilly.
The crowing cock speeds up my daybreak dream:
Whoever called the nighttime watches long?

5

Sacrifice and Friendship

Bingyue

IN HER *CORRECT BEGINNINGS*, YUN ZHU PROVIDES A BRIEF account of the life of Bingyue, based, one assumes, on the contents of her first published collection of poetry and its prefaces:

> Bingyue's [Icy Moon] style name was Cold Study. She was a Manchu, and wrote *First Draft of Cold Study Chantings* [Lengzhaiyin chugao].
>
> Cold Study was widowed at an early age, and her children died while still young. She lived a virtuous life of pure chastity. Her husband's younger brother, Vice Minister Gui-pu, made a selection of the verse she had written and had it printed. Chancellor Tie Ye-ting [Tie-bao] provided a preface in which he praised the poems as "sincere and worthy of transmission." These are indeed no empty words![1]

This little notice unfortunately makes no mention at all of the curious background of the family into which Bingyue married. Her husband, Yi-sun, who died in 1777 as an assistant administrator of the Right Wing Clan School, was the second son of Heng-ren (1713–1747). Heng-ren is the author of a small collection of poetry titled *Moon Hill Poetry Collection* (Yueshan shiji), which was printed, together with his collection of poetry criticism *Moon Hill Poetry Talks* (Yueshan shihua), by his youngest son Yi-xing (also known as Gui-pu; 1747–1809) in 1796, when the family fortune had been somewhat restored. By that time Yi-xing held the rank of vice minister in the Ministry of Rites at Shengjing (Shenyang), and he was able to obtain prefaces to his father's collection from such luminaries as Ji Yun (1724–1805) and Weng Fanggang (1733–1818).[2] Yi-xing would go on to serve as governor of Shandong and Jiangsu.[3]

Heng-ren happened to be the son of Pu-zhao (d. 1724), a great-great-grandson of Nurharci and great-grandson of Ajige (Dorgon's elder brother).

But Pu-zhao had the bad luck of being an uncle of Nian Gengyao's (d. 1726) wife. When this once powerful official was stripped of his titles by the Yongzheng emperor and allowed to commit suicide, Pu-zhao's ducal title was posthumously retracted.[4] Heng-ren was consequently stripped of his inherited title within eleven months of receiving it. When he tried to revive his career by entering the newly established Clan School for members of the imperial clan, he was expelled after a mere twenty-five days precisely because he once had held noble rank. After that he lived at home, writing poetry and enjoying life in the company of an uncle who lived next door and also had lost his title.[5]

Heng-ren had three sons. The eldest, Zhuo-li, born to his first wife (d. 1735), died at the age of eleven, and both Yi-sun and Yi-xing were children of his second wife (d.1770) (Yi-xing was born to a concubine). She ran the family together with her mother-in-law, the wife of Pu-zhao (d. 1769). This woman, of the Guoluoluo clan, also wrote poetry.[6]

Bingyue mentions in her poems that her father-in-law had died more than twenty years before she entered the family, and that her mother-in-law had passed away by that time too. In her preface to her first collection of poetry, she mentions that her husband died one year following her marriage, which would mean that she had married him at the earliest in 1775. But in her poetry collections she mourns a son, a third daughter, and a fourth daughter, which would seem to suggest that she married her husband at least some four or five years earlier. Writing in 1796, Yi-xing (Gui-pu) states that Yi-sun had two surviving sons, Ming-sheng, then a secondary secretary in the Imperial Clan Court, and Ming-wan, then a student at the Imperial Clan School. In view of their age these men are unlikely to have been children of Bingyue. Most likely they were children of a first wife of Yi-sun, who may have married Bingyue shortly after the death of his mother and grandmother. As the preface to Bingyue's first collection is reprinted in a facsimile of her handwriting, it is not easy to dismiss her "one year" of marriage as a slip of the pen—perhaps we have to explain it away as a hyperbole. It is also possible to imagine that the third daughter and fourth daughter were the children of Yi-sun's first wife and were raised by Bingyue, while she herself only gave birth to a son.

Bingyue's poems were printed in two collections. The stimulus for the compilation of the first collection was the printing of Heng-ren's collected poetry.[7] The first collection was *First Collection of Cold Study Chantings* (Lengzhaiyin chubian) in three scrolls, containing 123 poems. It opens with a poem inspired by reading Heng-ren's *Moon Hill Poetry Collection,* and continues with some poems using the same rhyme words as Heng-ren's poems. Following more poems in which she laments her inability to properly serve her parents-in-law while they were still alive, two poems follow describing ancestral sacrifices. The remaining poems would appear to be presented in a roughly chronological order. In her own preface to the collection, Bingyue claims the women's songs in *The Book of Odes* as her inspiration, and includes a short description of her life, before turning to her admiration for her father-in-law:

Preface by the Author

Poetry is ambition. When one's ambition is stirred, it manifests itself in poetry. The poetry of the inner chambers is different from that of men of letters and professional writers. There is no system to be followed, and there are no purple patches to be anthologized.[8] Placid and calm [these poems] are the spontaneous sounds of the pipes of nature. The song "Mouse-ear" in the [Airs of] Southern Zhou set the tone at the beginning,[9] and the ode "Cypress Boat" in the Lesser Elegantiae later continued that beauty.[10] Modest, quiet, chaste, and still: as the airs arose they transformed the customs. These definitely are sufficient in many respects. But when it comes to physical features scorned in their own age but talent and beauty praised in later times, and the waiting for an engagement in a humble abode and heaving heavy sighs as spring grows old, or the dark candle in a run-down room as one swallows one's grief in the autumn wind—when hidden emotions and feelings of resentment manifest themselves as poems, there may be fine lines that are praiseworthy, but for all eternity the collector of airs will not choose from them, and I am different from those.

When still a child I followed, at the order of my father, my brothers to the family school. After I had been scented and formed by brush and ink for a long time, I achieved a rudimentary understanding of the *Odes* and the *Documents*. But when I grew up, I abandoned these studies and did not pursue them. When I had reached the age of twice twelve, I was married to [a member of] the imperial family. But after barely more than a year had passed, my husband left this world. At that time, I cried out to Heaven and stamped the Earth; I had no desire to go on living and neglected orphan and nephew. But then I forced myself to manage the household in order to comfort and care for them, and since then I have fully experienced bitter suffering. For these last twenty years I have crushed my body and mind, but this is what I had to do because of my fate, so it is not worth complaining about.

Now my husband's father and mother had already passed away before I was married, so as a daughter-in-law I have been unable to give expression to my feelings of filial piety for even one day. This inability to provide them with care truly fills me with sadness, and is a regret I will carry with me for the rest of my life. At the end of the year *bingchen* [1796], my husband's younger brother Gui-pu wanted to print my father-in-law's collection, and he asked me to read the manuscript for mistakes. As I was reading the manuscript, I was increasingly overcome by thoughts of sadness. My father-in-law's greatest joy throughout his life was his poetry. To my regret I never waited on him, so I could only obey each of my father-in-law's instructions and execute them, so as to replace my husband as his heir and prevent the tradition of collapsing. So whenever I would complete a poem, I would carefully keep a record, not so much because I wanted to cherish and preserve my poems, but because I made every effort to embody my father-in-law's ambition and continue it. When Gui-pu one day saw them, he urgently requested them so as to have them printed as a continuation of the earlier generation. I could not bring myself to refuse his intention, and so I made a small selection of over a hundred poems which I gave to him, both in appreciation of my cousin's virtue and as a stimulation to filial piety for the younger members of the family. It will be enough for me if sons and grandsons of later generations will understand the ambition of this widow. This is my preface.

On the first day of the Seventh Month of the third year of the Jiaqing reign, a *mouwu* year [1798]

Preface by Lengzhai

Bingyue's own preface is preceded by a preface by Tie-bao (1752–1824), one of the most celebrated men of letters of his time.

I have once argued that in poetry it is of utmost importance to free oneself from established conventions: a minister at court should not smell after gown and belt; a famous gentleman should not smell after mountain and forest; a priest or monk should not smell after vegetarian foods; and a female poet should not smell after handkerchief and head scarf. Once the established conventions are done away with, true nature and emotion will emerge and these poems will automatically be exceptionally different—they will not collect the purple patches of others, and will not follow the beaten track of others.

The Lady of the Cold Study, being the gifted child of a famous house, was married at an early age to [a member of] the imperial family, but unfortunately she lost "her Heaven"[11] quickly, and vowed herself to a life of chastity. She had nowhere to vent her frustrations over difficulties and her depression and unfulfilled ambition, but once she lodged these in her poems, she did not necessarily imitate the ancients, and she did not necessarily carve and chisel her words and verses. Her insuppressible emotions are directly expressed, and her innermost feelings are fully exposed. That is the reason why these poems should be valued and transmitted. Her work is truly in a completely different class from the trifling skills of putting on powder and applying rouge of the women and girls of this age.

When I selected and printed the *Selected Poems of the Eight Banners* and the *Preserved Drafts of Inner Chamber Ladies*, I did not include the writings of living poets. Because the lady did not meet the criteria of those compilations, she could not be included. But as she has carefully chosen those poems that merit to be recorded, and finalized a selection of over a hundred poems, I urged her to have them turned over to the printer so her basic characteristics may be preserved. Those who in later ages will collect songs are bound to record and store them, so they will be preserved for eternity—the Lady's frustrations over difficulties and depressions and unfulfilled ambition will be without regret. This is my preface.

The first day of the Seventh Month of the third year [1798] of the Jiaqing reign

By Yeting Tie-bao

The printing of her collection brought Bingyue to the notice of some other Manchu women poets of the day.[12] While her poetic contacts in her first collection would appear to be almost exclusively limited to her family, the second scroll of her second collection, *Cold Study Chantings, A Continuation* (Lengzhai yin xubian)—106 poems, published without any preface—contains a number of works written for or in remembrance of Lady Tongjia, as well as a number of poems for Guizhen Daoren. The second part of this *Continuation* also includes some lyrics, whereas all her other works are *shi* poems. The final page of *Cold Study Chantings, A Continuation* in the National Library of China was damaged at an early date, and the otherwise unknown Manchu woman Shanxi (also a member of the imperial clan) has filled out the missing characters of the final poem, as we learn from the little note she added to the text.

BINGYUE

Poems from *First Draft of Cold Study Chantings*

Reverentially Reading the Poetry Collection of My Late Father-in-Law I Was Filled with Regret at the Thought That I Had Been Unable to Wait on Him for Even One Day, and Deeply Moved I Wrote the Following Poem

My marriage was, alas, too late—a fate beset by troubles;
I never served my husband's parents food I had prepared.
Their boundless grace of love and care—a sadness without limit;
Their teachings I have kept till now—a heart that yearns and yearns.
  I see their portraits in the paintings—memories in vain;
I only have the sacrifices to display devotion.
The poems of my husband's father are so pure and broad:
These verses rise above the crowd—their model is Li Bai![13]
  My husband passed away, alas, when he was still so young;
A chilly mist rose from the tattered writings, broken strips.
His younger brother Gui-pu showed himself a worthy heir,
He carefully collated these to print them as a book.
  I open it while I burn incense but I cannot read—
His image as when still alive I vaguely seem to see.
With lowered head I am ashamed: no talent and no virtue;
I am a woman, would not dare establish my own fame.
  A wooden bowl and cap and gown: the duties of a son;
For stable norms and fine achievements I admire my elders.
How could I sketch in full detail the family's tradition?
Compilers of the nation's history here find his writings.
  Who will continue the ancestral merits and that virtue?
These remnant drafts, though but a few, transmit true understanding.
At present I am sick and weary, also absentminded,
And off and on I have my meetings at the Yellow Springs.[14]
  Time and again I now must ask for help to make my bows,
And I will not recover in the future from this illness.
I'll guard with care these remnant traces of our predecessor,
And wipe my eyes to see endless succeeding generations!
  The inkstone that he used one time I cherish without end;
The mirror's light on my behalf flies up into the sky.

With every heavy sigh I heave, I also break one gut—
There is no limit to the grief that fills my dying years!

Lamenting My Late Husband

The weeping rain and howling storm destroyed the line of geese:[15]
With tears that turned to blood I copy writings that you left.
I build and form expansive breath—are you perhaps aware?
I sit alone and through the screen point at the clouds so white.

Arriving in the Ancestral Hall

When offering sacrifice in the ancestral hall I arrive after purification,
To find that the gate to the shrine is already open to the morning sun.
When spring arrives, on whose behalf do the grasses turn deep green?
When dreams have left, the sounds of the wind strengthen my sadness.
For all eternity the gown and cap have been left to us in paintings;
Through a thousand years, sacrificial vessels resemble layered stages.
The achievements on the battlefield are recorded in the nation's chronicles,
And I look up in admiration to the wisdom, valor, and talent of the past.

Sacrificing in the Ancestral Hall

In absolute silence, cap and gown are penetrated by the chilly air;
As the smoke rises, the whole temple hopes the offerings are fine.
I never could serve them while alive in morning and evening;
Calling the absent to mind, I always want to imagine their image.
Below the temple portraits we again arrange the sacrificial vessels;
Before the wormwood bowl the dark notes are played as always.
Like Heaven they shade and protect us with a grace without limit;
In vain I gaze on the loving faces as I kneel down for a deep bow.

Teaching My Son

1.

By the light of the lamp I've selected the books for teaching my son,
Without knowing how his studies will turn out at some later date.
Too bad he has been without any instruction now for three years—
To my doting love he truly is like a pearl on the palm of one's hand.

2.

I stand alone by the idle steps dispelling my own depression;
For the sake of my son I have excerpted the *Odes* and the *Rites*.

In place of his father I provide him with courtyard instruction,
Not even noticing that the moon has risen above the balustrade.

Reverentially Written on an Informal Portrait of My Father and Mother

For sixty years you roamed at ease in the garden of learning,
In personal cultivation not lagging behind former worthies.
Pine and cypress of a thousand years, days of a thousand years;
Cedrela and daylily[16] that never age, a sky that never turns old.
Together portrayed in a single painting—longing without end,
So I respectfully complete eight lines to express my affection.
How moved the heart of your daughter who has married out—
Repeatedly I wish my parents a longevity that lasts forever.

From *Lamenting My Mother*

1.

When the news arrived of your crisis it was not yet midnight:
My soul dispersed beyond the clouds, my innards were on fire.
My heart was broken already when we learned of your death,
But vaguely I still seem to hear your voice calling me.

2.

Whenever I returned home for a visit, my mother was happy,
And filled with concern she'd continue to talk till late at night.
How can I bear to see from now on a daylily that is broken—
The pale light of half a moon fills the courtyard with its cold.

6.

Even if I might be as good as Song Yu in calling back your soul,[17]
I never would be able to expound your limitless parental grace.
Now I have written these few poems born from a broken heart,
I rub the inkstick in my ample tears as I copy them out at dusk.

From *Mourning My Son*

2.

My darling son entered the Yellow Springs,
This mother's heart is now an empty void.
My tears, amassed into a sea, an ocean,
Splatter, all mixed with blood, the frosty sky.

While Ill

1.

The night is still but gusts of wind are fierce;
As morning comes, the crows are huddling close.
Since the first week I suffer from this illness,
I haven't left my cloak now for three months.
  I often hear the herbs as they are pounded,
I taste the floating incense from the burner.
It's not for poverty I don't eat meat:
I will not add to grief because I'm ill.
  Bedridden long, there's none to help me out;
Worn down by care I don't reply to guests.
Open the window to refresh my eyes,
And what I see is adding to my sorrow.

2.

So still, knowing the haste of floating life,
I love in vain the scenery so dark.
Wishing to seek a dream beyond the dust
I find it hard to travel while I'm ill.
  Unsteady on my feet like with no staff;
A dizzy head as high atop a tower.
The western winds urge on the falling leaves,
And each of them increases idle sorrow.

Insomnia

While incense burns I think of past events:
At what time did these white hairs come about?
One quickly learns the cold of ice and frost—
To teach one's dream-soul to be pure is hard.
  A bluish candle shines now bright, then dim;
The brilliant moon that's waning will be full.
When one's awakened, life is lacking substance,
And this whole world as light as just one smile.
  The daybreak fog transmits the crowing rooster,
The end of night is told by sounding bells.
I sit and wait here till the window brightens,
Get dressed, and listen to the songs of birds.

My Simple House[18]

My simple house is in a dead-end alley,
But still and quiet it quite suits my mood.
Rejected by the crowd as hard to live in:
I see it as a temporary lodging.
The gate's deserted—you could net the sparrows;
The walls are crumbling—like a pile of pills.
The broken windows are repaired with string,
The rotten pillars are propped up by posts.
A row of geese—such steps can't be put in;
A fish's scales—the tiles show many missing.
I often move my bed because of drafts,
And doubly air the books for all the bookworms.
When guests arrive, the hall is far too small;
When flowers bloom, the courtyard is quite large.
I planted reeds that will replace bamboo,
And grow some herbs to serve here as my orchids.
The moonlight white at nighttime on the railings,
The sunshine red at daybreak on the eaves—
If this is what a high pavilion is about,
Why should I have a gilded balustrade?

Visiting the Western Hills

If one but sees a place fit for a poem,
What need is there to go and fetch a painter?
A precious pearl is frozen in the moon,
The realm of fragrance hidden by the clouds.
A living streamlet flows around the path;
A lonely pine tree pierces the blue sky.
As we go on, we find a rustic temple,
Admire the ancient look it has retained.
The rain has washed the multilayered green,
The frost sticks to the red of every leaf.
I never hear enough of soughing pines,
The number of the stone steps has no end.
Alone I rest—the north face of the hill,
And turn: the moon is shining in the east.
I linger on and cannot yet return,
And leisurely I watch the flying geese.

The Precept against Killing

It's not because of karma and it's not because of fame,
But all my life I've feared the sound of swishing butcher knives.
I pity the poor animal: what crime did it commit?
It just like us hopes to extend the days that it may live.

A Condemnation of Miscellaneous Writings

Throughout my life I've always been addicted to the Classics,
From dawn till dusk I spend my days with writings of the sages.
What truly is the benefit of all those other books?
Too bad, I say, they have not long ago been burned by fire![19]

The Ancient Battlefield

This place, they tell, served as a battlefield in ancient times:
Its barren sand and dried-up grasses truly break one's heart.
To the horizon the bleached bones are just as bright as snow;
The broken lances in the earth are piercing like the frost.
  On quiet nights in chilly winds one hears the howling ghosts;
Clouds covering a waning moon display the fireflies' light.
In vain the heroes' hatred buried for a thousand years—
Do not discuss with former dynasties their kingly power.

Realizing My Age

Moving about is getting difficult,
As youth and beauty turned to tattered dreams.
The maid now must remember all my questions,
And others have to check my things for me.
  The final month of autumn in the mirror,
But in my breast one flourishing bamboo:
This floating life slips gradually by,
Yet every instant still the scene is broad.

Poems from *Cold Study Chantings, a Continuation*

Blocked by the Wind during a Mountain Trip

The flying birds had crossed the layered peaks,
And everywhere a heavy mist was forming.
A whirling wind howled through the aged trees,
The lonely moon then paled a freezing sky.

Tones from a bell are floating through the clouds,
Sounds of a spring fall down next to my pillow.
Despite this quietude I cannot sleep,
And sit erect, as if in meditation.

Rising Early during a Mountain Trip

I'm walking through the mist atop the mountain
And hear the roosters crow on distant peaks.
This hidden realm is rich in country pleasures,
Of ancient temples we find hidden traces.
Worldly concerns follow the floating stream,
Deepest emotions love the aged pine.
The many magic realms of the immortals
Are hidden by white clouds, but only half.

On Ghosts

Is there reality to rites that save the souls from hell?
Up to the Qin and Han the customs were quite different.[20]
You want to know the whirling principle of life and death?
Going, retracting, coming, stretching: just one fleeting moment.

Lamenting My Husband's Father's Younger Brother

At that time my second son had passed away, and that's how I came to write this.

How could you, lonely and alone, become a roaming soul?
I cannot stop my bloody tears from splattering my gown.
Don't worry you will have no company there down below:
Take pity on your little nephew who will travel with you.

For Her Royal Highness the Mother of Prince Rui

In dark-green pine and light-green cypress I observe your bearing,
In floating stream and drifting cloud I can discern your nature.
Your shape resembles a disciple of the Buddhist school,
And you combine the talents of the students here at court.
Your high enfeoffment is not due to status long transmitted,
Your reputation in this age was earned by your fine verse.
How I admire your gracious love passed down through generations:
Around the steps the jasper grasses doubly spread their luster.

Emotions while Passing by the Abandoned Temple of the Pure Land Hermitage

In which year was this ancient ashram founded?
Today it has become a pile of rubble.
The broken walls are overgrown by weeds,
A lonely tower stands against the sunset.
The hall is cold—no incense here is burned,
And swallows flit between the empty beams.
The evening bell is sounded off and on,
But the old monk looks desolate and cold.
We find a hidden path by clearing shrubs,
And read the fallen stele cleaned of moss.
So, shaken by the thought of rise and fall,
I sigh about the rush of death and birth.
My stupid heart despises dreams of dust,
My waning years trust in the Brahman King.[21]
When I stop here and look around the place,
I cannot help myself from staying briefly.

Sitting Outside on a Summer Night

Alone, I'm sitting in the courtyard as the night grows late,
My shirt's light gauze fears an incursion of the evening wind.
The little maid does not yet know the joy of quietude,
And pointing at a blooming branch, she warns the moon is sinking.

From *Lamenting My Daughter (My Fourth Daughter)*

1.

Wasted all work of study and instruction by the window;
Memorization of the Classics turned out all for naught.
Talent and beauty—had I known they can't stay long united,
I had not overburdened your frail body to begin with.

2.

Your tender body struggled on while your disease was showing,
But still you hoped to come and visit your parental home.
How sad and lonely you must be down at the Yellow Springs,
As out of deep attachment to your mother tears still fall.

Lamenting Her Royal Highness the Mother of Prince Rui, with Preface

I was not acquainted with Her Royal Highness in earlier years, but after she saw the printed version of my *Collected Chantings of Cold Study* in the spring of the year *bingyin* [1806], she was so kind as to receive me, and thereupon we became close friends. For these last few years her feelings of friendship only continued to increase in depth. One day she stroked me and said: "The two of us have become such good friends! My only regret is that we have met so late. If at some later date our souls perhaps still have consciousness, I hope that you and I will be friends for life after life, existence after existence." How could there ever be an end to my gratitude for her appreciation of me! As I think of her today I cannot help my tears from gushing down.

In inner rooms I lost my knowing friend—
I weep for you and tears now soak my clothes.
My single book received your admiration,
Arousing ever growing gratitude in me.
  Not yet fulfilled—your wishes in this life;
Hard to foretell—a meeting in the next.
The autumn wind increased disease and illness,
So the clear moon brings now distress and grief.
  The ash is cold of papers in the burner,
Of zither on the wall the sound now rare.
Do not look on the sadness of the Springs—
In vain my dream will try to find you there.

From *Mourning Guizhen Daoren While She Is Still Alive,* with Preface[22]

My friend Guizhen Daoren is a gentlewoman of the inner quarters. Her nature is pure and strong and she is conversant with the Classics and Histories, but she excels even more in poetry. We have been friends now for a number of years: we sing in harmony like gold and orchid and are indistinguishable from each other like milk mixed with water.

One day she said to me: "Last night in a dream I came up with the following lines of verse: 'When spring arrived it carted off the blooming peach tree river, / It flowed into a dark ravine and then was lost to sight.' There is something very ghostly about these lines. Could it be that my remaining years will not be many? Our relationship, I think, has been out of the ordinary, and when I will have passed away, you are bound to write beautiful poems to lament me. But lost below the Double Springs I will not hear them. So why do you not gift me a few stanzas now we are resting here, so I will be able to hear the sound of your fine compositions in the moment of our eternal separation. It will be our parting song as I leave for the underworld and it will become a fine tale for the whole dynasty."

When I heard this, I was overcome by sorrow, and suddenly was beset by feelings of loneliness. Cherishing the present and thinking back on the past, I forced myself to complete a few rhymes to give expression to the sadness of some future day. "This enterprise of yours in grand and imposing. It is truly without precedent in the past and without parallel in the present. It is a new creation, an exceptional venture, and opens up an original aspect on the altar of poetry for all eternity. If ever the changing clouds change their deceptive shapes, of course I will write something. These pale imitations can only serve to dispel your tears and induce some laughter."

1.

A sudden midnight dream evoked the thought of separation;
Facing chrysanthemums in western winds a broken heart.
But the full moon does not yet know that she already left,
And still brings its white light to shine on broken parting fences.[23]

3.

I'm grateful for your diligence in teaching my small grandchild,
From dawn till dusk at the cold window always a companion!
This sentiment should only be engraved here on my heart—
Your virtue cannot be repaid except as dog or pig.[24]

5.

Easily moved in waning years I fear to meet with spring
When willow hues and flower splendor dazzle people's eyes.
But the emotion that I find most difficult to deal with
Is mourning Guizhen in the shadows of the setting sun.

8.

Alas, you did not meet the proper time when you were born!
Frustrated and depressed, you could not manifest your grit.
But these few poems I present to mourn you here today
Are equally the writings of the brokenhearted person.

11.

Meeting and parting in this life resembles floating clouds:
The time it takes to snap one's fingers and they are dispersed!
Now lost below the Double Springs you do not show yourself—
In vain I let my teary eyes gaze on your lonely grave.

12.

The only one I ever loved was you and no one else,
Filled with emotion I can't stop my tears from gushing down.
Please never say these feelings end together with this life—
They will not be exhausted after myriads of years.

The Fisherman

Shaded by willows, where he pleases, he just drops his line;
Why should he have to tie his boat up at some ford or quay?
Whenever he has caught a bass, he'll barter it for wine—
The squeaking sounds of moving oars in autumn on the river.

The Woodcutter[25]

He cuts osmanthus on the mountain without care for money,
A shoulder-load of *autumn colors near the stream and clouds.*
A madman's song he sings sometimes when he returns at night,
When from a grotto *evening clouds* arise and fill the sky.

6

A Tomboy in a Silly Dress

Mengyue

THE BIOGRAPHICAL NOTICE ON MENGYUE (DREAM MOON) IN Miaolianbao's sequel to *Correct Beginnings* reads:

> Mengyue's adopted pseudonym was the Four Counts Mistress [Siyan zhuren].[1] She was a Manchu, a granddaughter of the governor-general Korjishan [Ka-er-ji-shan; ca. 1670–1757; who received the posthumous title Zhuangke], a daughter of the governor-general Ding-chang [ca. 1700–1768], and the mother of the provincial graduate Mian-cheng, who [like her husband] was a member of the imperial family. She was decorated for her widowly chastity, and her writings were collected as *Selected Poems of the Bamboo Lodge* [Zhuwu shichao].[2]

Mengyue's grandfather and father were indeed major officials during the reign of the Qianlong emperor. The members of the family had served the Aisin Gioro house since the early seventeenth century. Korjishan's career was interrupted when he was dismissed by the Yongzheng emperor in 1735, but he was recalled by the new Qianlong emperor in 1736 and would steadily rise in office. From 1746 until his death in 1757 he served as governor-general of Fujian and Zhejiang. His son Ding-chang served as governor of Fujian from 1761 to 1766, after which he was appointed as governor-general of Hubei and Hunan.[3]

As a young girl, Mengyue accompanied her father during his period of office in Fujian. She and the other women of the household would accompany him when he made offerings to his father in the shrine the inhabitants of Fuzhou had erected in his honor outside the town:

> When my late grandfather was governor-general of Zhejiang and Fujian, the people erected a shrine for him on Drum Mountain in Fujian. In the *xinsi* year [1761] of the Qianlong reign my late father also became governor of Fujian. I accompanied him to his posting. Each year in the Third Month he would visit

> the shrine on the occasion of [my late grandfather's] birthday. That's why the members of his family, including women and children, had the opportunity to travel there and enjoy the sights.[4]

She also accompanied him when he moved to Hubei, where the ancient state of Chu was once located.

But while Mengyue's biographical notice mentions her father and grandfather, it does not mention her husband. From poems in her collection it becomes clear, however, that Mengyue's father-in-law was Hong-shang (d. 1781), a grandson of the Kangxi emperor as the thirteenth son of his eldest son Yin-ti (1672–1734). In the struggle over the succession of the Kangxi emperor, Yin-ti supported the emperor's eighth son, Yin-si. After he had suggested having the imprisoned crown-prince Yin-reng discreetly murdered and was accused of employing a Tibetan nun to cast a spell on Yin-reng, he was in 1708 deprived of his titles and imprisoned in his own mansion until his death.[5] Following the accession of the Qianlong emperor, Hong-shang had a long career in the banner administration, serving from 1770 to 1773 as Tatar general (commander of the Manchu garrison) in Fuzhou, and from 1779 till 1781 in the same function in Suiyuan.[6] Mengyue and her husband (whom she married in 1771 "by imperial decree") accompanied Hong-shang to his posts all over the country. Her husband, however, died after a marriage of eight years and before he obtained any official post, leaving her to raise two sons. One of them eventually passed the provincial examinations, but neither of them seems to have ever held office. Even though her circumstances later in life were very much reduced when compared to the days of her youth, that does not mean she lived in poverty. Her cousin Oyombu (1748–1811) steadily progressed through the ranks and eventually served as governor of Guizhou, while her elder brother Tai-fei-yin (d. 1803) also held a string of high positions.

Mengyue's collected poems have only been preserved as a manuscript. She describes the origin of this collection in some detail in her preface:

Preface to the Selected Poems of the Bamboo Loft of the Four Counts Mistress

> I was the youngest of my brothers and sisters, and the whole family doted on me, calling me the "Little Prince." Together with my brothers I [devoted myself to] brush and inkstone and so I could please my parents with my versifying. This is how I learned to write poetry. But following my marriage, I had no more leisure for this. Unfortunately, I lost my husband at an early age, and in the spare time left by serving (my parents-in-law) and teaching (my sons), I could not suppress my emotions: time and again I would grasp a theme and find a

rhyme. Even though the ancients said that words are the ornament of the body, what is the use of ornament when the body will remain hidden? I am a widow who is waiting for her death, so what use would I have for poetry? So as soon as I had finished chanting a poem, I would burn it.

But in their leisure hours my brothers would come and visit me. We would write linked verse on moonlit nights, then we would chant in competition on blooming days, and it was impossible for me to entrust my poems to the flames as soon as they had been finished. On top of that, my nieces would submit their compositions to me for correction, and when I would by chance remember one of my own works at some stage of my life, I would recite it to them, just to relieve my depression. Who could know that those who had come to me and listened would record that poem once they had left me!

Alas! My versifying has nothing to do with the poetry of the ancients. It is only the wild crane hidden in the mountains crying out all alone below an empty sky, the shivering cicada on an old tree chirping to amuse itself. So how can these poems been shown to outsiders? But my nieces disagreed, and put together this collection on my behalf, and therefore called it *Selected Poems of Bamboo Lodge.*

Written by Bamboo Lodge on the day before the full moon of the second winter month of the *mouchen* year [1808] of the Jiaqing reign

More details concerning the collection are provided in *Editorial Principles:*

This selection has been put together on my behalf by my nieces who heard me recite and explain these poems while they were waiting on me. Within a few years they gathered more than two hundred poems, but this is not a complete collection.

The sequence on occasion corresponds to the chronological sequence, and on occasion does not correspond to the chronological sequence (of composition). This is because they recorded these poems as they heard them. Once the collection had been completed I didn't have the energy to rearrange the sequence carefully.

It happens that a title says "five poems" or "four poems" but that there are only one or two poems. This is also because when we were talking I could not immediately remember the whole set, or because I had completely forgotten one or two stanzas, so these have not been included.

Only the first few poems in this collection are based on my written drafts, so in that case there is no mistake in the sequence.

> The poem entitled "Rising Late on a Spring Day" was written when I was still a virgin. For the other poems I do not remember [the dates of composition] anymore, so it is impossible to collect them [in chronological order]. But this is the reason why I put that poem at the beginning.
>
> The drafts of some of the poems in this collection may be preserved at the home of my elder brother Tong-yuan [Tai-fei-yin], at the home of my elder brother Xu-gu [Oyombu], or at the home of my elder brother Jing-ting. It is quite possible, of course, that there exist discrepancies between the authentic manuscripts of the date of composition and the versions as I recited them on occasion. So that is why I explain the matter here. Those who may have opportunity to see both versions should not be bewildered by the situation.
>
> The "Preface" by the Old Man of the Measured Hermitage[7] and my own "Preface" and "Editorial Principles"—these have only been written down at the very beginning after the selection had been compiled. My nieces had repeatedly requested me to do so, and I realized that it would be impossible to make this collection disappear even though I might wish it so.

The preface by the Old Man of the Measured Hermitage (Fashishan) that is mentioned in the final entry of the *General Principles* is not included with the National Library manuscript of *Selected Poems of the Bamboo Lodge* but found in Fashishan's prose collection.[8] But as is commonly the case of prefaces by highly respected men of letters to collections of women's poetry, his preface to Mengyue's collection is mostly concerned with defending women's poetry and not very informative about the author or her work.

Mengyue stands out for the liveliness of her poems, especially those in which she recalls the days of her youth and happy days of her marriage. A set of ten quatrains titled "Emotions on Remembering the Past" suggest that she grew up as a pampered tomboy, who was raised in the same way as her elder brothers, and who enjoyed the outdoor sports of riding, hunting, shooting, and fencing. Only when she turned fifteen was she dressed "just like some silly girl."

MENGYUE

Rising Late on a Spring Day

Last night we had a birthday party, late I went to bed—
When I woke up, the daybreak light shone on the painted railing.
Once I have put my hairpins in, I quickly eye the mirror:
All prim and proper now, I wish my parents a good morning.

Emotions on Remembering the Past, Ten Poems

1.
I still remember clearly how my parents, once while chatting,
Were holding me and put me on their lap and stroked my cheeks:
"The dream was true: the Buddha gifted us a bodhi-seed,
When we awoke, we smelled a fragrance as this child was born."

2.
They also said that as a child I played not like the others:
I would recite the Buddha's name, and chant *Amituofo*.
I plucked a twig of willow and then placed it in a vase:
With folded hands behind a screen I was the Bodhisattva![9]

3.
I learned to read when I was six, and later went to school;
My forehead covered by my locks, I wore no female dress.
I learned to paint, I learned the zither, and I learned to chant,
And visitors who called on us addressed me as "Young man!"

4.
A saddle of brocade—at twelve I learned to ride a pony;
The arrow-tips like freezing stars, a little bow of horn.
When I went hunting in the fields, all people loved to watch;
In their opinion I looked like the Bright and Shining Prince.[10]

5.
My hair was done when I reached fifteen—shimmering long clouds!
My rich chignon was pearls and baubles, and my skirt brocade.
I was in tears and asked my father: "This is all too stupid!
Why do I have to dress today just like some silly girl?"

6.

We learned to do our needlework seated around my mother:
A phoenix-chick the model for my seven-treasure basket.
The stitching done and a bright moon—then I would practice fencing,
And when I had a chance, I'd sneak away and pull the bow.

7.

I was selected on the twenty-first day of the Fourth Month of the thirty-sixth year [1771] of the Qianlong reign

With moth-eyebrows I first believed the Northern Star divine;[11]
His edict came—we welcomed it, and thanked Him for His grace.
The match was ordered by decree as we were joined by heaven:
The daughter of a loyal lord was married to a prince.

8.

Chrysanthemums in clumps of gold, a moon so round and full:
A noble house sends off a bride—the capital's abuzz.
The drums and fifes urge one to leave, the sky's about to break:
Alas, the pampered little chick still cannot leave her mommy!

9.

The mirror image disappeared: my husband now was gone;
My grief surpassed the wailing ape and moved the blue on high!
Oh, how I longed to go with you and share the hollow grave,
But shackled by our infant son I steeled my heart and guts.

10.

For full eight years I served my husband, till our karma's end;
Now locked here in my quiet cell I practice meditation.
I realize it's not a stone: my heart cannot be turned,
And feelings of deep loneliness have finally turned sweet.

Instructing My Son

Obey your lesson and you won't be scolded;
Please shirk no effort ever in your studies.
Each day renewed: the highest good will shine—
How could I bear to flog my darling boy?

Rising after an Illness, an Impromptu Poem

A poet's bones since ancient times have never sported fat;
On top of that, I'm often ill: my clothes are far too wide.
On this cold day, I try my silken blouses on to see:
My waist, compared to this year's spring, has lost another span!

Emotions upon Accidentally Passing by Our Former Mansion

Heron and gull have flown away, so brook and sand are cold:
Remembering those former days, I'm moved to heavy sighs.
What saddens my heart most, however, is a pair of swallows,
Which, twittering, still talk about that splendor and that glory.

An Impromptu Poem

I'm tired and put my needlework away to get some book,
As in its vase the sprig of plum has almost lost its fragrance.
I'm thirsty and I want some tea, but as my maid is young,
I fetch myself despite the cold some coals to light the brazier.

Contemporary Fashions

The eyebrows that are true they shave, and false ones they paint on,
While on their lips they place with art a round and ruby cherry.
They have no clue what virtue and obedience might mean,
As giant sleeves and drooping hairdo now are called "Meng Guang"![12]

People Often Call Me a Pedant (An Improvised Quatrain)[13]

I'm ridiculed by foolish people as a foolish pedant
Who all day long just bites her brush as long as light will last.
In their opinion inner chambers just house made-up dolls—
Nüwa, a woman, was the one who once repaired the heavens![14]

In My Youth, When My Late Father Served as Governor-General of the Provinces of Chu, I Once Accompanied Him on a Visit to the Yellow Crane Tower and Enjoyed the View. At That Time the Plum Rains Soaked the River and White Clouds Covered the Pavilion, and When I Looked Out to Parrot Island, It Was Just as in a Painting. But Alas, at That Time I Was Still Only a Young Child, and even though I Could See This with My Eyes, My Mouth Could Not Record It in Words, and I Did Not Realize That Such Fine Sights Are Difficult to Meet with Again, and That Such a Fine Season Is Hard to Reencounter. How Can I Suppress the Emotion of Remembering the Past like the Present? Sad, Isn't It?[15]

Thanks to my father I could travel in my early years—
Ten centuries before Cui Hao the crane had taken off.
Moved by the present and the past a person's feelings change,
Twenty-eight years have now passed by which I did not deserve.

People Say That It Is Bound to Rain on the Night of Double Seven, Because the Rain Is the Tears the Stars Shed at Parting. Last Year It Did Indeed Rain on the Night of Double Seven, but This Year It Did Not Rain at All, So I Wrote the Following Quatrain on the Spur of the Moment

The magpies bridge the Silver Stream and let them cross tonight;
The rain that drizzles down is said to be their pearly tears.
It is beyond my understanding why this pair of stars
Sheds oh so many tears one year, and in another, none.

A Letter to the Grave

My husband, please allow your wife to ask
How you are doing since our separation?
Please tell me, do the underworld illusions
Resemble those here in the world of dust?
  You have departed for your spirit tablet,
So how can I still dare implore your pity?
I follow in my actions your last words,
But cannot hope to do my duties fully.
  Moved by your virtue I spit blood for pain,
And shoulder labor to repay your favors:
Two boys without a father are your heirs;
Your aged mother has been laid to rest.
  Through study of the way of meditation
I spend my waning years in cultivation.
I write this letter with a broken heart—
Repeatedly my tears gush forth like fountains!

When I First Received a Letter from My Fifth Brother Xu-gu upon Arriving at His Posting in Xining, I Was Moved and Wrote the Following Poem[16]

Before the envelope is cut, the carrier is questioned:
The air is bad, the landscape wild, the customs are perverse!
It's hard, we know, to get accustomed to such new conditions,
And yet you write that all is well to please your distant kin.

A Description of Myself in My Poor Dwelling on a Spring Day

Don't laugh at destitute Yan Hui[17] or at his simple dwelling:
Once spring has come, it turns into a villa for the rich.
Fine flowers, just like maids, line up as ranks of servants,
And slim bamboos resemble guests by bowing to each other.
  Elm coins are strewn upon the ground as if I were a nabob;
The spear-like sprouts up to the eaves shame senior officials,[18]
And Heaven tells the orioles to play their festive music—
I am a carefree subject of the times of Lord Getian![19]

Written by Lamplight upon Returning from My Brother Tong-yuan's Place on the Second Day of the Third Month of the Xinyou *Year [1801] of the Jiaqing Reign*

Heaven and earth resemble one huge clam,
The sun and moon are like two shining pearls.
The world we live in is an "oyster-tower,"[20]
And time flies by just like a passing colt.
    Have you not seen
  How fame and profit are like hook and bait?
    Have you not seen
How laws and statues are one giant oven?
Down from the Son of Heaven to the people,
None can escape the verdict of historians!
  My study follows Master Zhuang of Meng:
Roaming outside creation is my joy.[21]
  I carry in my arms a string-less zither;
My fingers stroke a beard that has no hair.
Why meddle in the fight of right and wrong?
Feel free to call beasts either cows or horses!
  But there is one intention that is strong,
To straightway race and hurry to the West,[22]
Until I see, beyond the endless transformations, Shakyamuni—
Atop a pole of hundred feet my liberated me!

While Accompanying My Late Father-in-Law on His Journey to His Position as General of Suiyuan, We Passed by the Grave of the Brilliant Consort [Wang Zhaojun] and I Wrote the Following Poem to Mourn Her[23]

The horse's manes are frozen stiff, teeth chattering for cold;
The howling wind whirls up the sand and blows it in one's face.
The Second Month in southern mansions: flowers like brocade;

The Third Month in these northern lands: there's still no blade of grass.
  The generals failed badly to defend the state and nation,
But a mere woman knew her duty and bought China peace.
We halt here at the Verdant Mound and show her our respect:
A thousand years a Brilliant Consort—and eternal sighs!

Planting Bamboos

You don't need many when you plant bamboos:
Too many make the owner look so vulgar!
Just two or three that sweep the clouds are plenty,
More than enough to bring the clear breeze home.

On the Second Day after Clear and Bright My Elder Brother Jing-ting Came By. When He Saw How Opulently the Flowers Were Blooming, He Teased Me by Coining the Phrase "Rich Flowers of a Poor Owner." I Thereupon Wrote the Following Quatrain in Jest.

The flowers in my garden laugh at me for being poor,
But I laugh at those garden flowers that dare laugh at me.
The flowers laugh at me for being poor as poor can be,
But when I sing and chant my song, I'm richer than this spring.

Idle Chanting: An Autobiography

At fifteen I read poetry and prose,
At twenty I could still not versify;
At thirty I worked hard to teach my son,
At forty I can put my mind at rest.
  My son now has a wife and family,
So I can lay aside my needlework.
I have a grandson playing at my feet—
No need for any brush to write of sorrow!
  And even though I'm living in the city,
It is as quiet here as in the hills:
Bamboos in thousands kindly shade the house;
A single headrest is my solitary peak.
  When it has rained, I separate the mums;
In moonlit nights, I sound the simple zither.[24]
Closing the gate I keep out vulgar things,
So nowhere can be found one speck of dust!

Decorated by Imperial Decree for My Chastity I Am Moved and Write the Following

Our match was settled by a phoenix edict,
I'm decorated by His Dragon writ:
Such was the grace of these two emperors:
In the thirty-sixth year of the Qianlong reign [1771] my marriage partner was assigned to me, and in the eleventh year of the Jiaqing reign [1806] I was decorated.
Throughout the dynasty my fame will last!
My son passed the exams this autumn session,
And this old well, like ice, is clear and lucid.
But what afflicts the heart with pain is that
The one who passed away still has no title.[25]

Resting My Shoulders

For thirty years my simple heart has suffered all there is,
But now at last I am allowed to rest my weary shoulders.
Leaning against a pine I strum a zither without strings;
Walking in moonlit nights I hear a spring that rinses rocks.
Amidst a thousand acres of bamboos I built a little cottage,
And by the bank of one wide stream I moored my fishing skiff.
This tattered body should retire, it really has no use—
There are wise men who will take care of family and country.

Suffering from the Heat

A scorching sky and clouds on fire, an earth that gives off smoke—
All plants and trees are dry as dust, about to burst in flames.
Where do I find a chunk of ice to carve a fine pavilion
In which I temporarily can live like an immortal?

I Have Always Been Reading Buddhist Books and I Have a Summary Understanding of the Principles of Meditation, but I've Always Studiously Avoided Monks and Never Set Foot Inside Monasteries. Now, the Discussion of Pointing and Trance and the Explanation of True Emptiness Is Not the Business of Scholars and Gentlemen, and the Adoration of the Buddha and Veneration of Relics Is Not Proper for Sincere Officials. No Need to Say That It Is Not Tolerated by the Sagely Teaching and Strictly Prohibited by the Royal Administration! Everyone Like Me Should Carefully Consider This. But When Your Fine Nature Remains Deeply Hidden, Your Idle Feelings Have a Medicine, and When You

Quietly Stay on Your Orchid Chamber, and Keep to the Norms in Entrusting Yourself, Who Will Chide You for a Few Pages of Sutras, and the One Drop of the Willow Wand Will Have a Basis.[26] *In This Way You Can Read Your Buddhist Books at All Times, and You Definitely Will Grasp the Principles of Meditation. That's Why I Have Recorded My Insight in the Following Simple Lines.*

I love the Buddha but don't visit ashrams;
I meditate but I avoid those monks.
No need to still ask questions once your mind
Has fully understood the blooming plum.[27]

Hearing the Words of the Kitchen Maid to a Little Girl Servant

I overheard the kitchen maid as she went on complaining:
"No one on earth as simple as the lady of this house!
At dawn she rises and flips sutras at the northern inkstone,
Resting at noon she grabs a brush before the southern window.
While evening sun brings cooler hours, the zither does not sound,
And when the candle's light gives out, she's snoring in her dreams.
So all day long she has no worry and she has no trouble,
And never speaks a bitter word and never speaks a sweet."

From *Remembering My Trips to Fujian Long Ago, Ten Poems*

4. *Eating Lychees*

In the Sixth Month in Fuzhou lychees turn cinnabar red,
And when we plucked them, we would first present them to our parents:
The pearls of fire, drenched in a well, as cold as silver dragons;
We freezing maids of jade, lifting the plate in colored sleeves.
When you would peel them you would worry the red snow would leak;
You'd hold them and feel sorry for the damaged crimson cover.
A green gown of the highest rank: a fragrance sweet and rich;
A winsome girl of eighteen years would taste a little sour.

5. A Second Trip to Fuzhou

This event took place in the *kuisi* year [1773] of the Qianlong reign, when my late father-in-law became general in Fujian. That's why I could go there once again as a member of his household.

Together with my husband's father we arrive in Fuzhou:
On painted prows the banners flutter, dragon sails of silk!
Willows and flowers welcome us, their colors fresh and happy,
While hills and rivers, my old friends, are filled with warmest feelings.
My husband is a precious prince, enjoying highest status;
As members of the royal house, his family is noble.
But at the shrine[28] the people point to me and tell each other:
"She is a daughter of Lanbin, a grandchild of Danyuan!"
Lanbin was my father's style name, and Danyuan my grandfather's.

6. I Remember How We Ran into a Storm When Crossing the Yangzi When I Was Young

The boat on which I was traveling at the time was carried off by the storm, and when we had made it back [to the shore], the cables broke. A number of times we passed by Golden Mountain[29] and came back, and we were almost swept out to sea. It was truly a precarious situation! We then collected water from the river and brewed Mengshan tea. Body and mind were at peace, because I deeply realized that life and death are predestined. That is why I am capable of not fearing power.

The flags and pennants massed like woods, the colored cabin open,
But as the oars were screeching, snow-capped billows rose in heaps:
My hairpin-phoenix was adorned with every kind of jewel,
And a black dragon now made ready to reclaim his pearl!
We did not know that these huge waves were welcoming our boat,
So cursed the god-sent storm for speeding us out to the Isles.[30]
If only we that year had sailed away across the ocean,
We would have reached the realm of the immortals long ago!

7

Unbridled Energy

Yingchuan

IN HER *CORRECT BEGINNINGS*, YUN ZHU PROVIDES A SUMMARY of Yingchuan's life:

> Yingchuan's style name was Ruting. She was a Manchu of the Ningguta clan. She was a daughter of the Academician Reader-in-Waiting Ba-ke-tang-a and the wife of Minister Tie-bao. She was enfeoffed as a Lady of the First Rank, and authored *Ruting's Poetry Drafts* [Ruting shicao].
>
> Tie-bao's style name was Yeting. He passed the metropolitan examinations in the *renchen* year [1772] of the Qianlong period. He was famed for his talent.
>
> Ruting loved to read the Classics and Histories; she was competent in large cursive script, and skilled in depicting orchids and bamboos. She also excelled in riding and archery. She understood the grand scheme of things. Yeting occupied many positions at court and in the provinces and he was often assisted by her. Once, when visiting Jizhou, she climbed the Li Taibai Tower and composed poems while leaning on the balustrade. Her feelings were unrestrained, far beyond those of the common female poet.[1]

What Yun Zhu fails to mention, however, is that Tie-bao was not only Yingchuan's husband but also the man who taught her to read and write. Tie-bao was descended from a long line of military men. He was the first in his family to establish a reputation based on his writing and scholarship. After he passed the metropolitan examination, he was soon appointed to the Hanlin Secretariat. One of his most important compilations was *Elegant Chants* (1804). Starting from 1799, Tie-bao also served in a number of high provincial posts, including stints as governor of Shandong and as governor-general of Jiangsu, Anhui, and Jiangxi; Yingchuan accompanied him to these postings. Later he was banished to Urumchi and served in Kashgar, but from

1811 to 1814 he served once again in Beijing. Banished to Manchuria, he stayed there until 1818, and on his return to the capital he retired in 1821.[2]

During the last years of his life he compiled a detailed year by year chronology of his own life, in which he described his marriage in the following words:

> In the thirty-fifth year of the Qianlong reign period, a *gengyin* year [1770], when I was nineteen years of age, I took part in the special provincial examination for Shuntian [Beijing], and obtained the provincial degree as number twenty-one on the list. . . . Following the examination I married my wife, the second daughter of the Grand Secretariat Academician Reader-in-Waiting Ningguta Ba-ke-tang-a.
>
> My wife's style name was Ruting. She also used the style of Zhuxian. She only learned to read after our marriage. She studied the Four Books and the poems of the Tang and the Song dynasties. The quatrains she wrote from time to time clearly had their own force. She loved the large "grass" script. *Seventeen Models* [Shiqi tie] and *Master Su's Autobiography* [Sushi zixu tie] never left her side.[3] In the rush of excitement she would wield her brush with abandon, and strongly displayed a natural proclivity. By nature she was magnanimous and broad-minded. She was unaffected by all the things women enjoy and abhor. Whenever she expressed an opinion, it never resembled the chatter of the inner chambers. Her disposition was peaceful and she treated others amicably. I therefore benefited greatly from her assistance for several tens of years, as if she was a fellow student![4]

Some of the comments of Tie-bao have to be understood against the background of a society in which a man of Tie-bao's status would be expected to have several concubines, especially if his main wife did not bear a son. From Tie-bao's account of his own life we learn that his eldest son was born to a concubine.

> In the sixth year of the Jiaqing reign period, a *xinyou* year [1801], when I was fifty years of age . . .
>
> In the Fourth Month my concubine Lady Ma [Ma Ruren] died on board our boat at the Cheng Locks on the [Yellow] River. She was thirty-five years old at the time. She was the birth-mother of my eldest son, Rui-yuan. Her character was graceful and dignified and she rarely engaged in chatter and jest. She had waited on me from the age of fourteen. She assisted in running the household, and my wife Lady Ruting valued her highly—she addressed her as "aunt" and didn't call her by name. She gave birth to one boy and two girls.[5]

Tie-bao also provided a more intimate portrait of his married life with Yinchuan in a poem he wrote when she turned sixty in Beijing while he was returning to the capital from Kashgar:

A Poem Sent to My Wife on Reaching the Age of Sixty

At seventeen you left your home as bride
For me, your groom, who barely was nineteen.
Startled awake at midnight by a rooster—
Scissors and ruler never left your hands.[6]
From me you learned to write quatrains and verses;
In inner chambers you were like a friend.
We tried to please my parents in the hall,
And when they smiled, it was because of you.
At twenty I returned to Beijing city;
You ran the household, managed well and kitchen.
As secretary I received an income
Of modest means: you ate a lot of leeks.
In later years, providing education,
You were surrounded by our sons and daughters.
Domestic duties always have been many—
All those details of marriages and weddings!
So months and years have passed as in a rush;
We're startled by our partner's ugly age.
Once, long ago, you were a teenage girl,
But now you're married to a white-haired graybeard.
I am already well into my sixties,
And presently you also will turn sixty.
Facing each other with thin hair like silk,
Don't ask me for a seal big as a bushel.[7]
Last year I got permission to return,
But my replacement took more than twelve months.
Late in the year my luggage is all packed:
We will be reunited by late spring.
You have lost weight but still are hale and healthy;
The one who's ravaged by age is me.
Thanks to that free and lofty mind of yours,
You are much stronger than this hollow willow.
When I am back, we'll celebrate your birthday;
With lifted tray, you'll vaunt our lasting bond.

In front of sons and daughters we'll rejoice,
Get tipsy on the wine of the immortals![8]

When the couple's eldest son, Rui-yuan, had his father's works printed following his death, he also included the writings of his mother. "She left many drafts but never compiled them into a collection," so he arranged the 352 poems in two scrolls, as much as possible in chronological order.[9] It appears that most of these preserved poems date from the last two decades of Yingchuan's life, as the earliest dated poem in her collection is from 1792 and the last dated poem from 1810. The collection, entitled *Ruting's Poetry Drafts* (Ruting shigao), was printed in 1828, preceded by three lengthy prefaces penned by eminent students of Tie-bao and major intellectuals in their own right. As usual, such prefaces are strong on praise and weak on detail, while her son (actually the son of Ms. Ma) declined to sketch a more detailed picture of his mother's life because his late father had already written about her in some detail in his annalistic autobiography.[10]

YINGCHUAN

My Husband and His Younger Brother Langfeng Followed the Emperor and Took Part in the Autumn Hunt[11]

You journeyed both to northern plains: the Emperor's encampment;
You wheel your horse and draw your bow as thunderclaps resound.
You hunt down remnant animals and scare the fiercest tiger—
Who recognizes in those braves that pair of bookish pedants?

From *Trying Out Our Horses outside the City*

2.

On Clear and Bright[12] we ride on horseback through the city gate
At break of dawn, as spring winds blow, to Slender Willow Camp.
If you inquire about green hills, those hills are farther still,
And our proud steeds proceed through Blossoming Apricot Village.

Improvised When the Old Pavilion at Langfeng's Place Was Renovated

A new pavilion now confronts a student old and used—
The shadows of bamboos a maze, the moon right now so bright!
Remember how when you had not yet taken the exams
You studied there in freezing cold at night, always till midnight?

The Expression of Congratulations on the Completion of the Ritual [of Abdication and Accession] during the Early Morning Audience of the Initial Fifth Day of the First Month of the Opening Year [1796] of the Jiaqing Reign Period; Reverentially Recorded[13]

1.

The stars now sparse still sparkle on the jade steps all around
While silver candles brightly burn so we may know His face.
When night is done the rooster-men announce the hour of dawn
And from high heaven comes the order to align in rows.

2.

The curtain rises: golden hooks! The Phoenix Cart returns;
Embroidered banners, parasols proceed as clouds disperse.
In all twelve decorated halls the spring breeze wafts so warmly;
Amidst the sounds of pendant jewels comes immortal music!

3.

In pheasant gown I now first try to bow in Chaoyang Palace;
A fragrant mist, a heavy haze, drifts through the palace halls.
When we have paid obeisance a golden bell announces
His words: we hear we are awarded a sweet meal of gruel.

4.

Auspicious snow falls heavily in this praiseworthy hour;
Our sleeves invite the burner's smoke to warm these treasured seats.
When I look back on halls of quartz, the golden gates are far:
In highest heaven He now walks where even dust is fragrant.

For Lady Lengzhai[14]

A widow's life for thirty years—you know its tribulations!
How I admire your lofty virtue and your perseverance.
The ice and frost are even colder than the Third Month moon;
The light of pearl and jade emerges from your five-word verse.
You strum the zither all alone and play the ancient tune;
Who will inherit your tradition and provide new lyrics?
Do not complain when all falls silent that you have no friend,
As that will only add more sorrow to your thinning locks.

From *On Ascending the Li Taibai Tower*[15]

1.

I want to climb the tower and to mourn the ancient poet—
Alas, the scenery has been erased by all these years.
The broken steles and halved columns give no answer
But in the wind one still can feel his mood when he was drunk.

2.

Beyond the tower clouds and hills—a myriad autumn trees;
The vast and boundless lakes and seas—a spirit hard to tame!
What I love most on these clear days: climb to the top
And see a single wind-filled sail that floats to the horizon.

From *My Own Inscription on My Small Portrait in the Picture of Looking Out over the Ocean at Mountain-Sea Pass*[16]

1.

The snow-capped waves stretch to the sky as far as one can see,
And all dimensions in the end return to the vast ocean.
Then, barely visible beyond the setting sun, one sail
Races a myriad of miles before a mighty storm!

3.

A single tower in the shadow of the setting sun:
The waves that beat against the shore stir longings for one's home.
And when I turn toward heaven's edge and open wide my eyes,
A whirlwind carries me aloft—my body's lost all weight!

The Ruined Monastery

How desolate this ruined temple visited by none—
The place is filled with piles of straw both old and new.
Because the Buddha lacked divinity, the monks have left
And ashes in the incense burner have gone cold in vain.

Written in Joy upon Obtaining a Son in the Second Month of the Year Jiazi *[1804]*

This racing letter was dashed off at nighttime;
A goose will take it to those distant skies:
After ten years I had unlearned the custom—
Again we will spend baby-washing money!

While Traveling by Boat in Autumn, in the Eighth Month of the Year Jisi *[1809], We Encountered a Heavy Hail Storm*

1.

The clouds turned black and then the thunder roared:
The cabin roof was smashed by ice and hail!
It pierced one's bones, that chilly river wind—
It didn't care how thin I had become.

2.

After the hail, at night, my mind at peace,
I realized how weird that mad monk was:
If one is without any Chan-like insight,
A running mouth does not serve any purpose.
That day I had seen a mad monk. His appearance was very strange but his words made no sense at all.

On Board a Boat, an Impromptu Poem

The food smells great here in this little boat:
The fisherwoman makes a tasty soup
And the exhausted cormorants just sit
And vainly watch their owners eat their fill.

8

Releasing Butterflies

Wanyan Jinchi

WANYAN JINCHI (CA. 1770–CA. 1840) WAS THE WIFE OF YING-zhi, a member of the Imperial Guard. Her son Wen-xi reached the rank of prefect. He apparently inherited his mother's gift for poetry, and once he was grown up, she would often exchange poems with him (her husband never makes an appearance in her poems). Wanyan Jinchi's youngest daughter was married to Dorje Wangchuk, a minor Mongol prince of the Borjigit clan, who at the time of the wedding was a low-ranking official in Kulun (modern day Ulan Bator). The Manchu government pursued an active policy of intermarriage between Manchu nobles and Mongol counterparts. Just as marriages between upper-class Manchus were arranged by the government, such matches between Manchu brides and Mongol grooms were also determined by the administration.

When Dorje Wanchuk was summoned to Beijing in 1828, he brought his family with him and moved in with his mother-in-law. The preserved poems of Wanyan Jinchi cover the period from just before her daughter's departure to Mongolia to her imminent return to Beijing. Her collection contains both the set of four regulated poems she wrote on seeing her daughter off, and the poem she wrote when she learned she would come back; in between, in "Releasing Butterflies," she ponders the duty of a mother to release her children once they are adults. Dorje Wanchuk was never reassigned to Kulun, and his little daughter Naxun Lanbao was largely raised by her grandmother.

Naxun Lanbao provided an intimate and loving portrait of her grandmother in the preface she wrote for Wanyan Jinchi's *Poetry Collection of the Pavilion of Green Rue* (Lüyunxuan shiji), which Naxun Lanbao published shortly before her own death. That preface not only is our main source for information on Wanyan Jinchi, but also served to announce Naxun Lanbao's anthology project devoted to Manchu women poets, as discussed in this volume's introduction.

Preface

There is no lack of gentlemen and dignitaries renowned for their poetry among those who are registered in our banners. But when I start counting, there reigns an absolute silence in the inner chambers, except for Lady Cai and Lady Gao.[1]

I was born very late and I have been unable to link up with the fragrant guidelines of earlier generations, but I have observed that when daughters of family and relatives enter school and recite books, they often are equal to boys—but they distinguish themselves by the virtuous beauty of their customs. However, when these daughters reach marriageable age their parents as a rule do not allow them to practice poetry, and if these daughters occasionally do write poems, their parents warn them not to show them to outsiders, and for that reason few of their poems are transmitted.

For generations, my family lived north of the Passes [in Mongolia], so my aunts and cousins never received any literary education. I was an exception because I came to the capital when my father was appointed to the Imperial Guard, and grew up in the house of my maternal grandparents, where my maternal grandmother, Lady Wanyan, taught me my letters. At that time, the family of my maternal grandparents was noble and flourishing, and whenever the female relatives would meet, they would never deign to speak of domestic matters such as rice and salt, but they would always compete in poetry, and basically they all would have to admit defeat to my grandmother. They might excel in matters of style and prosody, but my grandmother would just give expression to her natural inspiration [*xingling*], without ever being obstructed. Whenever the moon was bright and the breeze pleasant, she would call for a brush and chant her poems, which she then would paste on the walls. Only I knew this, and her relatives knew this, but not others.

In those days, Yuan Jianzhai established his altar for chanting south of the River,[2] and Tie Yeting was in charge of examination administration in the imperial capital.[3] When my grandmother learned that there were women who submitted their poems to these gentlemen in order to become their disciples, she joined the others in condemning and ridiculing them. That was because the atmosphere was like that, and it was not only my grandmother who acted that way.

I have the ambition to compile an *Anthology of Poetry by Manchu Women* [Manzhou guige shichao]. Even though I already have a rich collection, I still fear that there may be overlooked pearls, and that is why I am still waiting and postponing. On the other hand, I am aware of my grandmother's efforts in feeding and raising me, and her grace in instructing and teaching me, and I also

> continue to be afraid that her work eventually may be lost. Therefore, I have first collated her poems and entrusted them to the printer. The poems composed by my grandmother were numerous, but once I was married I could not constantly serve at her side, and when she passed away, the servants lacked in care, so half of these poems were dispersed. Those that I now recovered from an old trunk carried the title *Poems of the Pavilion of Green Rue, Third Book,* so many of her poems must have been lost.
>
> My grandmother was skilled in embroidery, and in her days was praised as the Goddess of the Needle. She was very nearsighted, and when she wrote her characters, the brush often would soil her eyelashes. By nature she was peaceful and easygoing. All her life she never spoke a harsh word or showed an angry face. In general, she was much like her poetry.
>
> My grandmother's personal name was Jinchi, and her style name was Yunxiang. She was a Manchu of the Wanyan clan. She married into the Feimo family, and her husband Ying-zhi served as a member of the guard. Her son Wen-xi reached the rank of prefect, and her grandson Bin-yue served as prefect of Gongchang in Gansu.
>
> Respectfully composed by her granddaughter Naxun Lanbao on the day of the full moon in the Third Month, in spring, in the twelfth year [1873] of the Tongzhi reign period

If we assume that the collection is chronologically arranged, we must conclude that the collection mostly consists of the writings of a middle-aged Wanyan Jinchi, and that we have no poems from the convivial poetry parties that Naxun Lanbao describes as childhood memories, because one of the last poems in the collection portrays Wanyan Jinchi's joy over her daughter's imminent return from Mongolia.[4]

WANYAN JINCHI

Idly Chanting on an Autumn Day

A little courtyard with its chilly mosses—
The double gate stays locked during the day.
While incense burns, I copy ancient models;
As I pour wine, I think of autumn hills.
  No draft disturbs the brazier's rising smoke;

The shadows idle of the empty garden's trees.
I watch the falling leaves outside the window,
Blown hither and blown thither by the breeze.

Autumn Night

The guests have gone, the gate is safely locked;
The empty steps bathe in a chilly moonlight.
The dew is light, the insects keep on chirping;
The wind falls still, the call of geese persists.
  I cannot sleep, and often move my headrest;
I idly chant, too lazy to burn incense,
And somewhere faraway I hear the notes,
Rising and falling still at midnight, of a flute.

Sending Off My Daughter

1.

You followed me as if you were my shadow:
We've been together now for eighteen years.
But rise and fall depend for sure on fate,
And partings are determined by one's karma.
  When calling on his parents, walk behind your husband;
Yield to his elder brother's wife when serving them.
It is not difficult to make congee—
Let's hope his younger sister will be nice.[5]

2.

Who is the dearest and who is the closest—
What need is there to talk of true or feigned?
My daughter who last year wore swaddling clothes,
Now is a bride who marries far from home.
  Your purse is slim—accept your brother's gifts;
Your luggage light—your mother is but poor.
If I can know you will show self-respect,
That's better than an endless stream of letters.

3.

Once you have left, you will be someone's wife,
You cannot be a spoiled brat like before.
Behave yourself with constant vigilance,

Never be partial in your management.
  The principles have nothing hard to learn;
A reputation is not lightly gained.
You may be able to come back some day,
But I'm already past my "middle years."

4.

You are my youngest—yes, I love you best,
Your natural and utter innocence:
You only know to spoil the maids and servants,
And have no clue about who's near or distant.
  You gain your brother's praise by asking words,
When picking flowers fear your mother's anger.
How can I not be wounded in my heart
Now you today depart for this far journey?

Looking Out over the Fields

Now close to dusk the suburbs are just great:
The cloudy hills are everywhere serene.
An ashen mist congeals on far-off trees,
The remnant sun still clings to upper rooms.
  Leading her calf, a cow walks slowly by;
Teaching their chicks, the swallows softly chatter.
Right at this time the rain has stopped at last:
The river through the fields runs wild and fast.

An Ancient Monastery

How bleak and desolate the scene around us!
We face each other and are filled with gloom.
The walls collapsed, but still we see the traces;
The pines are old—no one can know their age.
  Only the wind will sweep the fallen flowers,
The swallows freely flit through empty halls.
And where the far-off hills form slanting lines
We vaguely see a rising deep-blue mist.

Visiting a Mountain Monastery

At daybreak coming to the mountain temple:
Its hall encircled by a cool clear breeze.

A hazy mist enshrouds a far pagoda;
The early sun shines on long corridors.
Bamboos cover a thousand layers of green,
Flowers divide into some realms of fragrance.
The waves of pine trees sound like surging billows:
You think yourself besides the deep-blue sea!

An Impromptu Composition on a Winter Night

The courtyard's still, the gate is doubly locked;
The hour is late, the night air now feels chilly.
The moon is new, the flower's shadow thin;
As autumn ages, trees just always murmur.
My slender body hates the higher headrest,
My lazy bones just love my oldest skirt.
No smoke emerges from the golden brazier:
I poke the fire to find the remnant fragrance.

Sitting Idly

I'm sitting in my little study, by the southern window,
And idly hear the pine breeze passing through the winding walkways.
I love the snow and tell the boy to wait to sweep the paths,
And warn the maid to add no incense as I treasure flowers.
Though poor, I still love having guests—I buy the wine on credit;
I call no doctor when I'm sick—I'll write my own prescriptions.
How wonderful is this clear evening in this hidden courtyard:
The one tree full of freezing crows disturbs the setting sun.

Impromptu Composition on a Spring Day

The single shower of last night turned courtyard branches green,
The water level in the pond has risen by some inches.
Swallows and sparrows fight on shady paths for thawing loam,
In the warm breeze of corridors the cockatoos now prattle.
But ever since my daughter left I rarely pick flowers;
A line of verse I often find now we have entered spring.
I'm fortunate that Heaven grants me peace in poverty—
Where would I be if Heaven did not let me have my son?

Releasing Butterflies

This raising butterflies resembles raising daughters:
Once you have raised them, you can't keep them any longer.
A person's heart may still be filled with love,
But butterflies already long for distant parts.
  You want to set them free, but cannot give them up;
If you don't set them free, they may not find a partner.
So I'll allow you now to find your way—
I'll hang the pearly curtain on its hook.
  When first they fly, they still stay close to home,
When next they fly, they cross the garden wall.
I'm not concerned about the butterflies' thin dress,
I am concerned about the winds and rains of fall.
  If you succeed in finding a fit partner,
Please come together, entering my room.
The dreams tonight here in my flower cell
Will be more somber than green window-gauze.

Following the Original Rhymes of My Eldest Son's "The Moon Outside the Window"

The chill outside the gauze comes to my cushion—
Who called the moon "bereft of any feeling"?
No wine is needed for this clear enjoyment:
I watch enraptured and ignore the hour.
  A jumbled mess: the flowers see their shadows;
Shedding its leaves: bamboo now hears its sound.
Facing each other I forget how tired I was before,
And hate the night for fast approaching dawn.

On an Autumn Night, While Ill, I Was Thinking of My Eldest Son, Who at the Time Was in Luanyang[6]

The moonlight penetrates the gauze of curtains,
Cicadas chirp close to the winding railings.
My weary eyes just love the nighttime dark;
My meager body quickly knows the cold.
  The frost, I fear, falls heavy in the mountains,
Your horseback gown, I worry, is unpadded.
I lie in bed, facing a single lamp,
And hear five watches to the very end.

Laboring on a Poem before a Rainy Window during an Autumn Night

By wind and rain below an autumn window—
With nothing else to do I face a candle.
When I drink tea, I see my hairpins' shadows,
When I rub ink, I hear my bangles clatter.
  I wish to write a poem like a painting,
So I must make each line exhaust the feelings.
But as my talents and my force diminish,
Competing with the ancients is beyond me.

Thanking Third Younger Sister Shilan for Sending Me a Gift

1.

I see this gift—I seem to see your face,
I open it, and seem to hear your voice.
This letter may be just ten words or so,
But without limit are my friend's emotions.
  How deep are these emotions of my friend?
She sends a pelt and also sends some money.
It is not hard to find a pelt and money,
It's hard to find devotion such as yours.

2.

Now let me wrap my recent situation
And send it to Shilan so she may know.
My face looks older now than long ago,
More gray than earlier shows in my hair.
  Till seventy few people live since yore,
And I am now already in my forties.
When comes the year that we will meet again,
And hand in hand confess our mutual love?

Completed in Joy as My Second Daughter Will Come from Kulun to the Capital

As in a flash these few years passed once you had gone away,
But now I hear that you'll be back I'm almost mad with joy!
I order servants to prepare the bench to watch the moonlight,
And tell my son to get some extra cash for buying flowers.
  For wine we'll open a new vat now smelling at its best,
The vegetables from the garden will be springtime fresh.
Which human power could accomplish this reunion?
It's Heaven's love that far surpasses private love of ours!

9

Seeking Refuge in Truth

Guizhen Daoren

OUR MAIN SOURCE OF INFORMATION ON THE LIFE OF THE PERson of the Way Who Takes Refuge in the Truth (Guizhen Daoren; 1770–after 1850) is the preface to her *Poems of the Hall of Ice and Snow* (Bingxuetang shi) by her female disciple Yuhua, dated 1840. This collection also carries a postface, dated 1834, by a prince of the second rank Cheng-shuo.[1] The postface is a very general laudatory description of her poetry, but it is the preface that provides a detailed description of the circumstances of Guizhen Daoren's life.

The Person of the Way Who Takes Refuge in the Truth was my mother's teacher. The Person of the Way lived very close to my maternal grandmother. As I lost my parents at a tender age, I was raised by my maternal grandmother, and that is why I could ascend her hall and receive her teaching.

The Person of the Way was surnamed Chen, and was a daughter of Master Rue-Window (Yunchuang Xiansheng) of the Plain Yellow Banner of the Imperial Treasury.[2] From her earliest years she was exceptionally intelligent. Once, when she was three, her father was reading a book and she was playing by his side. She pointed to the character "gate" [*men*] and said, "That is 'gate.'" Her father marveled at this and said, "This girl will definitely know her letters once she grows up." When she grew up, she tirelessly loved to study, but her family was poor and had no servants, while her mother was often ill. She did all the heavy household chores, and tasted every kind of suffering, but as soon as she found any leisure, she would compose poems, which she always submitted to her father for correction. Master Rue-Window said anxiously, "Don't do such things that shorten your life!"[3] But she did not listen.

At the age of twenty-five she married the grand secretariat secretary Hesheli Ba-ni-hun (whose style was Jing'an), a Manchu of the Bordered Blue Banner.[4] She gave birth to one girl and one boy. After only five years Jing'an's elder brother, who was brigade vice commander in Fuzhou, died.[5] It so happened that her husband's mother also was staying at his posting. Jing'an asked for leave to go to Fuzhou in order to bring back his mother and his elder brother's coffin. Halfway on his journey back he fell ill and passed away in a hostel in Pingding District. As soon as the Person of the Way heard this news, she wanted to follow her husband in death, but she desisted after everybody told her not to do so because her mother-in-law was advanced in years and her son still young. A year later in spring her son and daughter both died in a widespread epidemic. When her mother-in-law returned to her natal family, the Person of the Way was left all alone, without anyone to rely on. Moreover, there was no lack of persons who were jealous of her because she always had been famous for her talent.

She then asked her father and mother, elder brother and younger brother to come and live with her, but very soon her parents and her younger brother had all died, so she had only her elder brother and his wife to rely on. She kept herself occupied each day by teaching her female cousins. When the neighbors had young children and from time to time a mother would ask her to instruct them, she would teach them devotedly as well.

At the same time there were the Mistress of Quiet Joy (Jingyi Zhuren)[6] and the Mistress of the Cold Study (Lengzhai Zhuren)[7] who visited her because they had heard about her, and who became her good friends. But whenever these ladies would give her presents, she would adamantly refuse to accept them, saying, "I have nothing with which to repay these [gifts]." This was the way in which her sincerity became clear to others.

Alas! I have heard it is Heaven's doing if one's body and bones are worn out and if one's mind and ambition are made to suffer, but that it is the doing of fellow human beings if one is slandered and badmouthed despite one's great virtue. It seemed that despite her nature as a woman she was provided with a stellar talent, and yet it also seemed that her talent was hindered and blocked on purpose, with the result that she was not capable of fully displaying it. And it was not only that her talent was not allowed to be displayed, also her body suffered pain and illness in endless succession without any recourse. In such an extreme case as that of the Person of the Way Who Takes Refuge in the Truth, is this Heaven's doing? Or is it the doing other human beings? But if this was the doing of Heaven, why did Heaven have to bring her into life? If this was the doing of fellow human beings, why did they have to go so far as to cause her death? Was it Heaven? Was it human beings? I really do not know. Her works were collected in her *Poems of the Hall of Snow and Ice*, in one scroll. Her poems often describe the actual situations she experienced.

> Written by her female disciple Yuhua in the middle decade of the Tenth Month of the *gengzi* year [1840]

Unfortunately, biographical information on the Person of the Way's "female disciple Yuhua" seems to be lacking.[8] Yuhua's preface is followed by two five-syllable regulated poems that are signed by Guizhen Daoren's son Ming-chang Qi-chu, who may have been a son she adopted to continue the ancestral sacrifices for her husband.

Naxun Lanbao's collection contains a long poem occasioned by the *Poems of the Hall of Snow and Ice*. It also contains a poem on the occasion of the eightieth birthday of the Person of the Way, in which Naxun Lanbao declares herself to be a disciple of the Person of the Way. Some critics state that Naxun Lanbao studied with the Person of the Way as a little child, just like Yuhua, but while this is not impossible, it is unclear to me how hard the evidence for such a statement is.

Poems of the Hall of Ice and Snow is a substantial collection, which runs to almost seventy double pages. One remarkable feature of this collection is that it contains a large number of long sets of poems. Many of these sets are a conspicuous display of virtuosity as each poem in the set utilizes a different rhyme category. This applies, for instance, to the thirty quatrains on the topic of "Autumn Angling on the Long River" (3a–6b) and the thirty regulated poems "On the Chrysanthemum" (56a–63a). Other large sets are the twenty quatrains devoted to "Roaming with the Immortals" (39a–41a) and the ten quatrains titled "In Response to Someone's 'Giving Expression to My Feelings,' Ten Poems" (53b–55a). To the extent that the following selection hardly includes any poems from these longer sets, it fails to be representative, but it is difficult in unrhymed translation to reproduce the virtuosity of using all these different rhyme categories.[9] Yet another category of poems that is underrepresented in the following selection are the occasional poems. The Person of the Way addressed many poems to her female patrons the Master of Quiet Joy and the Lady of the Cold Study from 1804 on. There are also some poems addressed to male patrons, but these are much smaller in number.

GUIZHEN DAOREN

On the Night of the First Prime My Father Entertained His Friends; Respectfully Composed at His Command

I was assigned the character *tai* [terrace].

With joy I see on this fine night a festive banquet spread;
How truly pleasant is this splendid age, this rising peace!
The Jade Clepsydra may urge one to leave on horseback, rambling;[10]
The Golden Cudgel welcomes those who come with song and dance.[11]
  The Silver Toad allows her light to float on flower markets,[12]
The giant candles' shaky glow in wine cups is reflected.
Here at this stellar gathering tonight in this high hall
The Virtue Stars are congregating at the Triple Terrace.[13]

Writing Down My Deepest Feelings

I pull my sword and sing out loud—frustration without end!
Braving the wind time and again I loath this empty floating.
Ambitious to inscribe the bridge—but it cannot be done;[14]
Unsuited to throw out the brush—how could that be accomplished?[15]
  Going through life not capable of walking the Great Way;
In all my acts only expected to stress gentle warmth:
I hate how I am sitting in a well and watching heaven—
How can I find a raft and sail up to the stars above?[16]

A Reaction to Certain People

Don't laugh at me because I am addicted to these books!
Who knows the many hidden meanings to be found therein?
All my activity all day has only this one aim:
It is just meant to polish bright the mirror of my mind.

My Sick Rooster

I have a rooster that is very tame. When I married, I took it with me and kept it in a separate courtyard. Suddenly one day it fell ill, but when it sees me, it limps over to be close by. Moved by the spectacle I wrote a quatrain.

I still remember how in years gone by I deeply loved you,
But nowadays you do not grow new feathers anymore.

How pitiable this meager frame with bones all sticking out—
Yet still you love your master and you want to cling to her.

When in the Last Month of the Fall of the Jiwei *Year [1799] the Passing-Away Letter Arrived in the Capital, We Learned That My Husband's Elder Brother Had Died at His Posting. In a Personal Letter, the Lady My Mother-in-Law Ordered My Husband, Jing'an, to Come and Escort the Coffin Back to the Capital. At That Time the Mountains and Rivers Were Dangerous and Difficult and the Border Regions Were Suffering from Extreme Cold, So I Was Greatly Worried (Two Poems)*

1.

The many feelings at departure as you left in haste—
Craning our necks toward Yan and Qin we find our sight is blocked.
Mountains and rivers, people say, are frozen and deserted,
And so my dreaming soul is always on the roads you travel.

2.

The border storms and northern snows are always on my mind:
I try to rid myself of worries but these worries never end.
Three thousand miles of traveling—are you still in good health?
By now, I reckon, you must have arrived in Fuzhou.

Lamenting My Husband in the Second Month of the Gengshen *Year [1800] (Two Poems)*

In the Twelfth Month of the *jiwei* [1799] year my husband departed from Fuzhou, at the order of the lady my mother-in-law, escorting his elder brother's coffin back to the capital. On the road he fell ill, and he passed away in a hostel in Pingding District on the twenty-sixth of the First Month of the *gengshen* year [1800]. The night before I dreamed that I ascended to Heaven and chanted a poem, containing the lines: "Heaven's wind is cold on the nine stretches of the journey back, / When looking down to the realm of men the Jade Capital is blocked." When I woke up, I could not understand the meaning. Only later did I learn that Pingding District is located nine days from the capital. Could it really be that his fate was contained in these lines? Or was there another connection between the living and the dead? How wounding this all is!

1.

To be together till old age—I thought such was the norm;
How could I know that I this day would have to call you "gone"?

The breeze so clear, the moon so bright—leaving in vain this grief;
A hidden jade, a hidden pearl—a heart for no cause broken.
The legends tell of herbs that lengthen life on the Three Isles,
But no one finds in the Ten Lands such soul-restoring incense.[17]
I shared five years with you and these resemble now a dream,
And in my memory your face and voice become a hazy blur.

2.

As I've poured out the fragrant wine, my gown is soaked by tears—
Oh, if your soul would have awareness, it should come back home!
The living and the dead are separated far, for ever;
And all my hopes and strivings are frustrated now for good.
The world is like the road to Shu,[18] and I am left alone;
My body's like a floating stick—on whom can I rely?
But you today are sound asleep for an eternal night
And do not care for right and wrong here in the realm of men.

Written at the End of a Scroll of Planchette Poems[19]

The world of shade we cannot know—no need to speculate;
How could one ever really think that death surpasses life?
But if indeed the realm of darkness is as here described,
I'd rather be a ghostly poet than a human being.

Lamenting My Dog

You, Brown Ears, had retired from night-guard duty,
And only rarely did we hear you bark.
I cannot keep myself from cold and hunger;
Frozen and starved you are the first to go.
I have no means to have you nicely buried,
But you will not refuse to take a letter.
If you will meet your master down below,
Please tell him that the tears still soak my gown.

Self-Consolation

The world of dust and I have never been in harmony,
On top of that I've lodged my body in a swampy moor.
The world of men has medicine, but not to cure the vulgar;
And the Creator does not care—He only envies talent.
Riches and status, fame and merit cannot be predicted;

Equally pitiable are kings and insects, ants and princes.
When comes the day I will depart and join the realm of shade
To rest amidst the tares and grasses, sleeping undisturbed?

To a Feathered Gentleman[20]

You have achieved the gold elixir and your Way is perfect;
Returning to the world of men, you want to help us mortals.
Inside your flask the sun and moon, so spring is always present;
A hazy mist beyond our world—your energy is pure.
My shallow karma hinders me from spying secret teachings;
How can I praise your lofty manner with my little talent?
I'd like to follow you and leave behind the realm of dust—
When will I fly on crane or phoenix to the world of jade?

Returning from a Visit to the Lady My Mother-in-Law, I Learned That the Master of Quiet Joy Had Sent Me a Copy of Her Newly Printed Poetry Collection and Also Had Gifted Me with a Potted Plum; by Lamplight I Improvised the Following Lines

Because I visited my husband's mother,
I learned once back that I received some mail:
The printed version of your white-snow verse,
Together with a plum that blooms in winter.
I love the flowers for their frozen splendor,
Admire the lofty talent in your writings.
To my great fortune I am joined tonight
Here in my little study by the moon.

Reading the Poems of the Lady of Cold Study on a Rainy Night

The single lamp gives but a little light,
At midnight now the time is crawling by.
The rain today is thus the perfect moment
To read and savor poems of Cold Study.
Holding the book, I love your lofty thoughts,
Imagine in the wind your jade-pure form.
We're living only a few feet apart—
How come we never came to know each other?

Inscription on a Painting

A fishing skiff crossing an autumn river,
A hermit gazing at the distant mountains.
A little cottage far from worldly dust:
A heart as idle as the floating clouds.

Memories, Two Improvised Poems

1.

It is now sixteen years, my lord, since you have passed away:
A single person, all alone, I've had my share of pain.
If you but called me from the Yellow Springs[21] or Highest Heavens,
I would not have to be a grieving woman in the world of men.

2.

That fabled land of ghosts most likely is, I fear, an empty lie,
Because how could one otherwise never receive some letters?
But if your soul still has awareness and remembers me,
You must be equally heartbroken at the Yellow Springs.

Lamenting Lady Quiet Joy

1.

I first met you, I still remember, in the spring of *jiazi*:[22]
You grasped my hands, filled with affection, and became a friend.
Who could have known that sea and land would change all of a sudden?
How I regret that I that year had come to know this person!

2.

On moonlit nights and fragrant days we chanted our emotions;
Dividing themes and setting rhymes, admiring your pure talent.
Your gentle tapping at my door from now on is all gone
And never will you send me your new poems anymore.

From *In Response to Someone's "Giving Expression to My Feelings, Ten Poems"*

1.

Words that are right will never suit the heart of anyone—
Since ancient times it has been thus, not only just today.
Great wisdom is in short supply, stupidity comes cheap:
Why did Qu Yuan then have to soak his shirtfront with his tears?[23]

2.

It's clever words and dazzling colors that will please the crowd,
The noble prince, however, never practices such wiles.
So even if Confucius would from his grave emerge,
The man would never gain the reputation of a sage.

3.

Not sticking to the golden mean, they all love heresy:
The common crowd is mean and fickle, filling one with fear.
A ruler like a Yao or Shun, a teacher like the Master[24]
Would find it hard to change the evil customs of this age.

7.

One's blessings are by talent broken—but I have no talent!
My guess is that the Lord of Heaven broke them by mistake.
The Way of Heaven can't be fathomed, fate is arbitrary:
Whether you fall on moss or shit, do not rejoice or grieve.

10

Traveling throughout the Empire

Baibao Youlan

BAIBAO YOULAN (CA. 1800–1861) WAS A DAUGHTER-IN-LAW OF Gui-liang (1785–1862). Gui-liang's father, Yu-de (d. 1809), had reached the rank of governor-general of Fujian and Zhejiang. Gui-liang had, as a tribute student, bought an official rank in one of the ministries. His first substantial post, however, was his appointment as prefect in Sichuan in 1819. He continued to serve in this province until 1830, by which time he had reached the rank of provincial administration commissioner. In the same function he would subsequently serve in Guangdong and Jiangxi. From 1834 to 1839 he served as governor of Henan, then was appointed as governor-general of Hubei and Hunan. Next he was transferred to the same position in Yunnan and Guizhou. Stationed in Kunming, he continued in that function until 1845, when he was recalled to Beijing. He would go on to serve in a variety of powerful positions in the capital and in the provinces till his dying day.[1] While we know little about Gui-liang as a writer, his elder brother Bin-liang (1784–1847), who also had a distinguished career (he died as imperial resident in Lhasa), enjoyed quite a reputation as a poet.[2]

When her husband, Yan-zuo, died one (or ten) year(s) into their marriage, Baibao Youlan was pregnant. She gave birth to a baby boy, and, as members of Gui-liang's household, mother and son (Lin-zhi, d. 1861) followed him to his various postings throughout China, up to his return to Beijing in 1845. As she had already accompanied Gui-liang to Sichuan, she probably joined the household before 1819. Her poems describe the scenes she encountered on her continuous journeys throughout China, and often testify to her homesickness. Gui-liang's family must have been very large (in 1848 his tenth daughter, born in 1834, was married to Yi-xin [Prince Gong; 1833–1898], the sixth son of the Daoguang emperor), and at least on one occasion Baibao Youlan hints at tensions within the family. After 1845 she lived in Beijing with her now grown-up son. When in 1856 Lin-zhi had been appointed as prefect of Jinhua, she followed him to his posting in the Jiangnan area, which at that moment was ravaged by the Taiping Tianguo rebellion. She and her son both died in the final days of 1861, when the city of Hangzhou was taken by the rebels. When the rebels had first taken the city in 1860 they failed to capture the compound that housed the Manchu garrison, but when they returned they succeeded and massacred the troops and their dependents—ten thousand people are said to have died.[3]

Baibao Youlan's *Collected Poems of Cold Reds Studio* (Lenghongxuan shiji) is exceptional in that is was printed three times in the second half of the nineteenth century. The first edition was first printed in 1857. It consists of a main collection, which includes poems written up to 1845 (*Lenghongxuan shiji*); a sequel, with poems from the years 1854 to 1856 (*Lenghongxuan xuji*); and a modest collection of song-lyrics (*Lenghongxuan ci*). This edition includes a preface by the author dated as early as 1837, which is an ambitious attempt to place her work in the tradition of Chinese poetry, whether by men or women:

> Poems are texts that have rhyme. They originate in tracing one's feelings, and are done once one has expressed one's intentions. As they are able to express in detail whatever the heart aspires to and each scene one has experienced, one may extend the words and sing them. So they can provide a stimulus, allow observation, unite a group, and vent resentment.[4] Since ancient times, their origin goes a long way back!
>
> From the Han and the Wei dynasties down to the Ming dynasty every generation has had its authors, and every kind of beauty is fully provided. In the inner apartments, Concubine Ban[5] and her "Round Fan" and Su Hui[6] and her palindrome were called the Xiangrus[7] among women and they provided scholars inside the palace. Those whose writings left a fragrance and were praised for their song on willow floss[8] were more than can be easily counted. If I look up to that past splendor, how grand it is!
>
> From my earliest youth I have been obsessed with brush and inkstone, and from birth I've loved poems and lyrics. Whenever I would encounter a fine stanza, I would promptly chant and hum it, unable to put it aside. When at times I would imitate the masters and select rhymes, those who read my compositions would often express their approval, and so my addiction grew only more intense. Eventually it resulted in this collection.
>
> Thinking upon the Way of poetry, I have come to realize how hard it is! If one does not read many books, one cannot achieve broad elegance and wide understanding. If one does not travel broadly, one cannot escape from empty prejudice and nearsighted myopia. Without the elegance of careful diction,

"other mountains"[9] will be of little help; and without hours of carefree leisure, one's own achievements will only be minor. I have never devoted myself to a life a study, so how would I dare say to have read five cartloads of books to shreds?[10] But accompanying my father-in-law on his travels as an official, I have passed through a myriad of miles on the road. Like spring grasses on pond and reservoir I have brothers and sisters who share my passions, and at Double Nine with its wind and rain we are without the burden of collecting rent, so it is only fitting that since a long time I've engaged in cutting out greens and fashioning reds while beating the rhythm on a bowl and setting time by making marks on a candle.

I live far away from my parents' home and often fail to make the fixed visits. Quickly upon my marriage I lost my husband, and this life of obedience and chastity requires all my effort. Whenever I raise a song on the rocky road, I am filled with admiration for pine and bamboo.[11] As for longevity, I remember cedrela and daylily[12]—as I chant "Hovering Clouds"[13] my emotions are intense; as for infants I pity my child, hoping for the clear call of the Phoenix chick. In this way I distinguish sour and salty beyond taste, and by "extended words"[14] dissipate the massive lump in my bosom. It truly stands in for my wailing.

As to the waning moon and the morning breeze, carved carnelian and polished jade—if on occasion I write a short lyric, it is still an "extension of poetry."[15] I am guided by pure authenticity and do no seek beguiling charm. It may be compared to Yu [Xin]'s purity[16] versus Bao [Zhao]'s bravado;[17] Cao [Zhi]'s inner room[18] and Liu [Zhen]'s outer hall.[19] I do not just attempt to display beauty in flowery language, but to entrust the highest taste to simple antiquity. But my "roaming and hunting" has not been deep, and I am far from having achieved my ambition. Whenever I encounter a scene that moves my emotions, I freely wield the brush to express my intent. As for talent and thought I am ashamed of Bao Linghui's[20] extensive erudition—one hundred pieces on fragrant tea, but as for virtuous conduct I aspire to Ban Zhao's scholarship and habitus—one single song of the hidden orchid.

Written by the month of the chrysanthemum in the *dingchou* year [1837] of the Daoguang reign by the Changbai female scribe of the Sakeda lineage in the Cold Reds Studio of the governor's office at Kaifeng.

The other prefatory materials also include "a poem in large characters" (printed in the original calligraphy) by Bin-liang, which is one of the last works in his extensive collection and dates from 1846. It must be based on his perusal of the main collection in the 1837 version. This work is the first source to inform us of Baibao Youlan's act of *gegu* on behalf of her father-in-law, though it is not recorded when Baibao Youlan committed the gruesome act of self-sacrifice:

An Inscription for Poetry Drafts from the Studio for Befriending Orchids *by the Wife of My Third Nephew*

A volume full of ice and snow of flawless purity:
Invited to inscribe a poem, I am highly pleased.
If one's a woman, to have talent does not mean good fortune,
But if the grandson will work hard, he can revive the house.
A filial child, she sliced off flesh to use as medicine,
When my younger brother Yanshan [Gui-liang] was critically ill, my nephew's wife sliced flesh off her arm, mixed it with herbs and used it to prepare a broth to cure him; she also addressed prayers to the gods. In this way he recovered. Her unadulterated filial piety was such by nature—this is truly commendable!
Such bitter virtue pains the heart of one who sips the broth.[21]
So, once she'll have her son reach high position by his studies,
Her phoenix-rank and pheasant-rig will show the Emp'ror's grace.[22]

Concrete steps for the publication of the collection were apparently only undertaken when her son Lin-zhi had grown up and had become an official of some substance himself. The 1857 edition, prepared when he served as circuit intendant in Jinhua, carries three prefaces, by Yi-xin , Peng Yunzhang (1792–1862), and Tao Liang (1772–1857), all dated to 1855.[23] Yi-xin by that time carried the title Prince Gong and was one of the most powerful men at court; Peng Yunzhang was one of the highest officials; and Tao Liang enjoyed fame as an arbiter of taste. These three prefaces are followed by undated "dedicatory inscriptions" (*tici*) by Lianzhai sanshou, Foyunbao (b. 1832), and Li Jinchun. Foyunbao was one of the granddaughters of Wanyan Yun Zhu, and a poet in her own right. The collection also includes two postfaces, one of which is by her son Lin-zhi, and one by the poet and painter Lao Yuan'en (1802–1858), who had served as editor. Lin-zhi's postface reads:

The Poems of Cold Reds Studio have been written by Her Ladyship my mother. Her Ladyship was conversant with the *Odes* and *Documents* from an early age, and excelled at chanting and singing when she grew up. When she married her late husband, my late grandmother had already passed away so she could not serve her, and only my grandfather was still alive. She obediently served him with greatest diligence. Before ten years had passed, her late husband passed away, leaving behind me, his son Lin-zhi, as a posthumous child. Desolate and alone, she lived the lonely life of a widow, filled with sadness and grief, without any joy.

In the time left from caring for her son, the composition of poems was her only consolation. But all her words were gentle and bland, as she never indulged herself in sounds of deep sorrow and grievous lament, out of fear that my grandfather would be hurt in his heart upon reading her poems. At one moment in the past my grandfather fell ill and Her Ladyship sliced flesh from her arm as a medicine, upon which he was cured. When her servants saw her wound, they were all overcome by emotion.

My grandfather served for a long time in the provinces. For over ten years he traveled to Shu [Sichuan], to Yue [Guangdong], to Chu [Hubei], to Yu [Henan], to Min [Fujian], to Wu-Yue [Zhejiang], and to Dian-Qian [Yunnan], and Her Ladyship accompanied him to all these places. The mountains and rivers she passed during those years, the scenic sights she observed, and the emotions she experienced all became the subject of her poetry. That's why the number of her poems became ever larger and why the content of her poems became ever more original.

When my hair was tied up and I was taught my letters, Her Ladyship would personally supervise my lessons. If there was any leisure time, she would teach me poems. Each time she would instruct me: "In bitter suffering I have raised you and taught you, and I do not dare hope that you will achieve riches and glory. My ambitions would be satisfied if you would be able to pass the imperial examinations." But when I had become a young man and could write essays, I was failed every time I sat for the tests, and on each occasion Her Ladyship would heave a heavy sigh and be depressed for days on end. At present I have achieved office because of hereditary privilege and through the Emperor's Grace I have been appointed to a provincial post. My salary and care may be sufficient to console my mother's heart, but I still regret that I have never been able to pass a single examination. Whenever I think of this I am flustered and covered in cold sweat, blaming myself for my lack of perseverance.

This autumn she joined me at my official posting. When I took up my office in Jinhua I had quite some leisure and I repeatedly asked Her Ladyship to collect the poems she had written throughout her life. These amounted to a considerable number and I divided them into two scrolls. I reverentially collated them and copied them out in my own hand. Now the blocks have been

> carved, I respectfully write some words at the end of the book. It is not that I would dare glorify Her Ladyship in this manner. But now these poems are published, there will be readers who will measure the person by reading the poems. And so Her Ladyship's chastity despite bitter suffering and her practice of pure filiality will enjoy lasting fame through this collection.
>
> Respectfully written by her son Lin-zhi on the first day of the Last Month of the seventh year (*dingsi*) [1857] of the Xianfeng reign.

Following Baibao Youlan's death, her poems were reissued in 1873 by Naxun Lanbao. Naxun Lanbao reduced the number of poems included by roughly a third. And whereas the 1857 edition had consisted of a (main) collection (*Lenghongxuan shiji*) and a sequel (*Lenghongxuan xuji*), she reorganized the collection into two scrolls, but maintained the chronological arrangement. In Naxun Lanbao's edition of Baibao Youlan's poetry, the first scroll includes poems dating from the years 1819 to 1839, while the second scroll covers the years 1839 to 1845 and then the years 1854 to 1861; no poems from the intervening decade are included, even though this must have been the period when the two women were good friends. Naxun Lanbao reduced the collection of song-lyrics (*Lenghongxuan ci*) that is included in the 1857 edition of Baibao Youlan's poetry to a small appendix.[24] Most likely she considered this edition as one of the first installments of her projected *Anthology of Poetry by Manchu Women*. Naxun Lanbao's edition does not include the paratextual materials of the 1857 edition, and she prefixed the collection with the following preface of her own:

Preface

> Virtue, appearance, words, and work are the great basics for a woman, while loyalty, filial piety, chastity, and righteousness are the great norms of human life. As long as one obtains one of these, it is enough to shake and melt past and present, and to shine and blaze throughout the cosmos. How much more so if all of these are combined in one person! But in such cases your treatment by Heaven will be such that He afflicts you with labor and suffering; you will encounter hardship and trouble, stumble and fall till the day of your death, without any relief. But how could this be Heaven's deliberate intention? By making your experiences bitter, your reputation will be sweeter, and by treating you parsimoniously in the present, your posthumous reputation will be richer. But that Heaven fully perfects such a person with greatest care truly is not easily achieved apart from the concentrated nurturance of mountains and

rivers and the accumulated blessings of generations of ancestors. But if even stalwart heroes and men of determination are incapable of accepting Heaven's mandate without change of heart, and of not departing from a steadfastly chaste and unshakeable conduct, it is even more to be marveled at if such a person appears in the inner chambers!

My friend Lady Youlan was surnamed Sakeda. She was a daughter of the Manchu duke Xing, and her family was poor. When she was studying with her brothers, her sharp intelligence was extraordinary. At the age of ten she could compose poetry, and when she reached marriageable age, she was conversant with the Classics. She married Yan-zuo of the Gua'erjia [Guwalgiya] clan, which meant she became the wife of a son of Wenduan, the late chancellor Gui-liang. Wenduan's surely was a great family! But within ten years her husband died, and she raised his posthumously born son Lin-zhi, the [later] Duke Zhuangjie. Tasting ice and eating yeast, she never again smiled or laughed. There were also many disharmonies amongst the relatives. Raising and protecting her infant son she obediently served her parents-in-law. Compared to the wife in a poor family, her sufferings were more than ten times as many! In the meantime she followed Wenduan to his postings for a number of years. When Wenduan fell ill, the Lady scraped flesh from her arm to cure him, and Wenduan indeed recovered. When Wenduan was appointed to a posting in another province, he left the Lady at home [in Beijing]. All alone and without support she could not live with her husband's relatives anymore and had to hire a small house in a poor neighborhood. She had to do the physical work of hauling water and stamping rice all by herself and on occasion lacked clothing and food. This lasted for almost twenty years.[25]

In the year *bingchen* [1856] of the Xianfeng reign-period, Zhuangjie, then a director in one of the ministries, was appointed as prefect of Jinhua. At that time the Cantonese rebels had already spread widely to the south and the north of the Yangzi.[26] Many urged her to stay in the capital, but the Lady was of the opinion that as she taught her son to be loyal she should not try to avoid danger herself, and she resolutely went to his posting. In the winter of the year *xinyou* [1861], when Hangzhou was besieged for a second time,[27] Zhuangjie, then the Jin-Qu-Yan Circuit Intendant, was the acting governor, and was living with the Lady in the provincial capital. Each day the Lady urged Zhuangjie to lead his trained braves, and repeatedly he repulsed the bandits. But when the city was about to fall, the Lady offered Zhuangjie a cup of wine and ordered him to give battle in the streets and kill the bandits, and on no account to return or look back. She then herself kowtowed toward the north, and clutching the seal of the Provincial Administration Commissioner of the Provincial

Administration Commission for Zhejiang, she drowned herself in the pond in the garden behind the official mansion. Alas, the Lady may be said to have in this way achieved the full measure of human qualities! I had always known that the Lady would be capable of this!

I had been a lifelong literary friend of the Lady at the imperial capital. Whenever we would get together and talk, it would often last until deep into the night, and when enumerating the many deeds of chaste virtue since ancient times, we would heave a heavy sigh and shed tears as we promised to follow these examples. It must have been Heaven's will that eventually she was able to accomplish this! If one adds up all the bitter chastity of the Lady, she was renowned for her filial piety in her hometown for forty years, and in her final years she sacrificed herself for her country. Such loyalty and righteousness has been rare in recent times. As to her other accomplishments, whether it was the study of the Classics or the understanding of the Histories, the composition of poems or the composition of lyrics, the making of paintings or playing the zither; the game of go or needlework, there was nothing of which she was not capable and there was nothing in which she did not excel. This must mean that such a person has been given life by Heaven in order that she above all others should bring glory to us women in the banners! So I do not pity the Lady but deeply think it my greatest good fortune to have been the Lady's friend.

After the disturbance, the deeds of Zhuangjie were reported to the throne, and the Lady was honored according to the regulations. When her son's wife arrived from Shanghai with the fatherless children, I asked her for her collected poems. I combined these with those I had stored in my trunks, and after selecting and editing them, I preserved them at home. This year in spring I wrote this preface in preparation for printing. From the Lady's standpoint this may only be a minor matter, but in this way we will preserve the Lady, as in this manner those who in later ages will compile biographies of exemplary women will have something to base themselves upon. This is why the Lady may well deeply approve.

Respectfully composed by Naxun Lanbao, Female Scribe of a Foreign Fief, in the Third Month of the spring of the twelfth year [1873] of the Tongzhi reign-period

This edition of Baibao Youlan's poems by Naxunlanbao was reprinted in 1882 by Baibao Youlan's sole surviving younger brother, Chong-bao, who added a short postface of his own.

Baibao Youlan's poetry is very much a widow's poetry, so we once again encounter many poems in memory of the husband who passed away before he could realize his ambitions, alongside numerous poems in which the orphaned son is urged to study hard in order to continue the family tradition. Also when her son Lin-zhi had been appointed to an official position and quickly was promoted, she continued to provide him with moral advice on his duties as an administrator. This advice culminated of course in her prose advice to her son to fight till the last, a plea that was strengthened by her own suicide. The most original aspect of her collection is, however, Baibao Youlan's landscape poetry. Baibao Youlan traveled widely in southern China, and while traveling eagerly observed the mountains and rivers, and the people who lived there.[28]

BAIBAO YOULAN

Enjoying a Cool Breeze in the Pavilion on a Summer Day

Because I'm tired and take a noontime rest,
I silently sit in this small pavilion:
Here ancient trees reach, green, up to the sky,
And idle flowers brighten, red, the stream.
  Nobody can forget the sultry heat,
So Heaven gives us a refreshing breeze.
Once more we see the strange peaks rising,
As shafts of sunlight fall through holes in clouds.

A Dreamed Return Home

My dreaming soul accompanied migrating geese in flight
And in a moment I had crossed the thousand miles back home.
I met a friend and just while I described this other place,
A rooster crowed and I awoke as moonlight filled the door.

In the Garden, an Impromptu Poem

The winding balustrades protect the emerald-green pond—
Who understands the proper pleasures of a little garden?
A meal is spread once the incessant rains have cleared away,
And we are tipsy while the setting sun has not yet sunk.
  The maple leaves are turning red: as if they're flushed by wine,

Chrysanthemums are now in bloom: fit subject for a poem.
This scenery and this occasion—hard to wind it up,
But suddenly the shadows on the window move their place.

Heavy Snow

Snow-images are dancing in the sky,
As if the floss of willows has gone crazy.
The pine tree branches have increased in splendor;
The plum's desire just wants this spring to stay.
    I find a verse when opening the window,
And brew my tea to entertain a guest.[29]
Wrapped in a cloak and gazing with fixed eyes
I do not feel how cold the north wind blows.

The Pine Tree, Two Poems

1.

When other trees are bare and empty branches,
One marvels at the pine—despite the cold
It does not shed its needles like red leaves,
But uses the white clouds to fix them firmer.
    Its spreading canopy invites the crane,
Its coiling roots are set to change to dragons.
As long as northern winds continue blowing,
Its verdant shadows come in many layers.

2.

The time has come, no flowers now are left,
But its dark green will never change its color.
In ice and frost it still maintains its manner,
In wind and snow its rhymes sound even purer.
    Its character surpasses other trees,
And in adversity it shows its virtue.
Bamboo and plum are famous as its friends:
It keeps their pact in winter's coldest month.

Mooring for the Night at Yijun[30]

As far as one can see it's tied-up boats,
This orphaned city in the sunset glow.
Clouds, multihued, emerge from blue-green mountains,

Herons and gulls descend on level sands.
  On far-off reaches fires of fishermen,
In frosty groves crows gather for the night.
By white smoke in between red leaves one knows
The place of houses even from this distance.

When Our Boat Stopped at Badong I Saw the People Living on the Mountains[31]

Which family here built its snail-like cottage near the rocks?
Their gate faces the River's flow—no painting matches this![32]
A multitude of trees surrounds the little thatched hovel,
The farmer hoes his taro field, sun burning on his back.

Getting Up at Dawn in Wanxian [While Traveling on the River]

Once startled from my predawn dreams I cannot fall asleep,
So I get up and watch the sky that is about to break.
The river fog and mountain haze here cannot be distinguished,
But calling birds rip with their song the mist on many peaks.

At Night I Hear the Swelling Waters

I listen to the swelling waters, sounding just like rain,
Then suddenly I feel a freezing cold throughout the cabin.
So, hastily, I call the maid, who opens up the window—
Look! Frost descends on sky and river under a full moon.

Stopping for the Night While Traveling by Boat on the River in Chu[33]

The vista of the River's banks in Chu
Moves one who travels by its boundless vastness.
New geese have landed on the white-sand beaches,
Red trees are shining in the sunset glow.
  The ferry's near: returning people's chatter,
The village's far: the noise of barking dogs.
Dark haze now gathers on surrounding hills,
And with no wind, the stream and clouds are level.

Emotions, Improvised Verses

1.

The feelings of this world are thin as paper,
As people's passions all are ruled by gold.
Status and rank are mostly an illusion—

So I lodge my emotions in these ditties.
I teach our son ambition for the future,
I stick to fasting for my present mind.
His Xiang Ping, once I'll have arranged his marriage,
I'd love to join you in the world of shades.[34]

2.
We're setting sail: the final month of autumn;
I'm deeply moved: no tears of blood are left.
Passes and mountains weary strength of mind,
And wind and rain revive the spirit's sickness.
Emotions stir poetic inspiration,
Sad and alone I lack my trusted friends.
In which direction do I find my hometown?
The River's covered by the evening clouds.

3.
Whenever I meet with a postal courier,
I hasten to compose a letter home.
Before I lift the brush, my tears fall down,
I search my breast, cannot express my mind.
From dusty dreams awakened as of now,
No longer plagued by any great ambitions.
In vain I long for simple hometown foods—
Oh, when will I go back to my old house?

4.
In Western Shu it's only mountain tracks[35]
I've traveled up and down for many years.
The dust of roads again fills gown and sleeves—
A single shadow, back to pass and river.
Between the crowing cocks my dreams in inns,
And on Chu's streams poetic inspiration:
Long journeys easily weary the mind,
I envy now the local peasants' leisure.

On the Pearl River; Sent to Elder Sister Ruiliu[36]

1.

My sickly body is invaded by that "pair of urchins,"[37]
So the arrival of your letter has enormous value.
The people here are commonplace: I have no bosom friend,
Only your words are capable of comforting my heart.

2.

After I read your recent works, my tears gushed forth in streams:
Recalling me you often look at that once-given bracelet.
We may be separated by ten thousand miles of mountains,
But hearts of one inch square ensure spiritual communion.

3.

When I gaze out, the road to my old hometown stretches on,
The blood I weep has stained and spotted this white piece of silk.
If you would ask how I have been most lately, I would say:
My pearly tears are truly like the tidal bore of Hangzhou.

4.

In sorrow and in sickness I have spent the months of spring,
Ashamed at having no recipe for comforting this body.
I crane my neck at heaven's end, bereft of "flesh and blood,"
Each time because of autumn floods remembering "that person."

Mooring for the Night at Zhang River[38]

1.

One landscape scene of cloud-wrapped groves,
Its colors painted by the Lord of Heaven.
At dusk the crows amass in mist-clad trees,
While village dogs follow returning farmers.
  The remnant light beyond the level hills,
A final glow on distant river banks:
If one could only catch this in a picture,
That sketch would demonstrate unequalled skill.

2.

While leaning on the cabin window, watching
The many houses on both river banks—

Shimmering ripples shake the legs of sunlight,[39]
As darkness rises from the mountain roots.
A few bright spots of fires of fishermen
And traces three-rod high of raising floods.
Then suddenly the sail of reed is lowered:
The boat is moored right at the nearest village.

On the Fuchun, an Impromptu Poem[40]

The river, swollen in the spring, gleams green as oil,
On both its banks, the halcyon glow of mountains seems to float.
The wine is done on painted boats, the guests have all dispersed,
And in the dark-blue sky a hook-shaped moon is hanging sideways.

The Scenery at Huai'an

Some drops of rain, some gusts of wind, and wildly fluttering petals,
And then there is the flapping curtain of the village wine house.
A few old local farmers with no worry in the world
And shaded by green poplars talk of mulberry and hemp.

Bowing to the Kitchen God

I bow before the Eastern Kitchen's Arbiter of Fate
And pray he will transmit my wishes to the Lord of Heaven.[41]
There is no need to ask for much here in the inner chambers:
I hope my parents will stay healthy—let my son be smart.

When I Got Up This Morning and Looked in the Mirror, I Saw a Few Strands of White Hair at My Temples. So I Pondered That Years and Months Are Like a Stream and That Half My Life Had Already Passed, and Deeply Moved I Recorded My Emotions.

When comes an end to this long march to home and garden?
My deepest wish is after all these years not yet fulfilled.
I'm startled by the new white hairs appearing in the mirror,
As time flies by I am afraid I may betray my mission.

Because I Earlier Saw Some White Hairs I Was Deeply Moved and Wrote a Poem, but Later I Pondered the Line of an Earlier Poet, "For Men It's Truly Rare to Live to See Their Hair Turn White," and So I Improvised Yet Another Quatrain.

My little heart turns round and round, always beset by sorrow,
So it is only fitting that my temples should turn white.
Facing the mirror sunk in thought, but then again comforted
As I am flooded by the memories of thirty years.

Ridiculing Myself

This poetry is truly my addiction!
My greatest pleasure is to polish verses.
At leisure I just chant without a rest,
A book is always opened until midnight.
With ink of dew I punctuate the *Changes*,[42]
While incense burns I chant *Songs of the South*.[43]
It may be called "an otter's sacrifice,"[44]
But it's a joy of which I never tire.

From *In the Night of the Mid-Autumn Festival I Dreamed That I Arrived at Jasper Tower. The Jade Palaces Were Quite Different From Those in the World of Dust. Immortals Were Coming and Going, and All Seemed Old Friends. When I Recalled This after I Woke up, I Used Various Rhymes to Write in Jest Fifteen Quatrains on the Subject of Roaming through the Realm of the Immortals. (Twelve Poems)*

1.
By chance I entered in my dream the Pearly-Pistil Palace,
The music played was "Central Heaven," crimson candles glowed.
All filled with joy I sat there briefly next to Flying Jasper—
When I awoke, my gown still bore the traces of that fragrance.

5.
It's hard to know the right or wrong of dreams and their illusions:
All of a sudden I became a crane and soared with clouds!
Along the winding balustrades the screens are highly raised,
And for a while I serve on Penglai as the jade queen's maid.[45]

7.

I don't yet know: is present me the same as former me?
I'm filled with doubt as I first enter the immortals' city.
My female friends of former times are making fun of me,
Because I lost the pearl of memory of years gone by.

8.

I may be back in Langyuan but I do not know the way,[46]
It's difficult to recognize my old room's green-gauze window.
A serving girl shows an inscription in the western hallway
That I wrote out when I was banished to the red-dust world.

9.

The moonlight, white and clear like water, fills the jasper steps,
And fragrant dew without a sound soaks through embroidered boots.
When I return from "fighting flowers,"[47] chatting with companions,
I've won for my chignon a halcyon and phoenix hairpin.

Self-Description

1.

I quickly do my needlework, and then intone my texts,
Always concerned I might miss out on any idle moment.
How can I ever finish those ten thousand scrolls of writings?
I hope and pray that in my next life I may be a bookworm!

2.

A lightning flash, a spark from stone: no longer than an instant,
Why burden my so sickly body with these idle sorrows?
This floating life, I'm well aware, is only an illusion—
Ridiculous that fool from Qi who feared the sky might fall!

Emotions upon Finding in a Book a Poem by My Late Husband

Awakened from your dream of an immortal,
Your worries disappeared like floating clouds.
Your poem was still hiding in this volume,
While you had left and gone to Jasper Tower.[48]
  We made an oath to share our next existence,
It left me with a lifetime of vain sorrow.
Your orphan son has started on his studies—
But will he follow in his father's footsteps?

For Little Monk[49]

Your daddy's eyes are watching you from way beyond the grave,
Your mother's heart has toiled and slaved for more now than ten years.
Let me admonish you, my boy, with this advice: Don't slacken,
Who wants to study books must treasure each and every moment!

From *Improvised Verses While Traveling from Bian [Kaifeng] to Chu (Four Poems)*

1.

The burning sun, so fiery hot, fills travelers with fear,
This is a day on which to sing "The road is hard to go."
One envies now the village women living by the brook—
They share their breakfast in the shadow of green poplars.

2.

To Jing and Wu and Yue and Shu I flew on winds and rapids,
To Qin and Jin and Qi and Liang I rode in a jade saddle.
I've trekked, it seems, through nearly all of the Nine Lands,
When comes the day my horse will halt and rest in Chang'an city?[50]

On the Scenery Seen from Our Boat

A one-leaf boat, a wind-filled sail, so do not count the road—
One only sees in distant skies the geese migrating southward.
The reeds are white, the maples red—there is so much of autumn!
We travel on, it seems, inside a painting of Mount Heng.[51]

On the Way from Bian [Kaifeng] to Dian [Yunnan] I Dreamed at Shuangxikou [Couple Brook Junction] That I Returned Home

I fly across ten thousand peaks: an instant and I'm home!
The relatives come out to greet me and we laugh and talk.
But once awakened from that dream, then this looks like a dream:
Beyond the inn at Couple Brook the moon slants to the west.

The Scenery on Xiyang Ridge

At break of dawn we start on our long march:
I carefully observe the mountain shapes.
The clouds rise up from underneath our feet,
While we as humans travel through a painting.
  A rocky ledge connects to native bridges,

While mist and fog are spreading everywhere.
On either side the pines and firs rise tall,
As vines and creepers hang from steepest cliffs.
The curving brook just turns at every bend,
The strangest peaks rise right before your eyes.
The tricky pathway robs you of your courage,
The utmost pinnacles increase your fright.
I lift my head and see the heavens distant,
I gaze around and find these vistas pure.
How marvelous the beauty of these mountains—
When it is raining, and when skies are clear.

A Small Pine Tree

This pine tree by the roadside is still small—
How new is all its halcyon-like green!
There's bound to come a day it touches heaven
And shades the traveler with its dense shadow.

Visiting the Flying Clouds Cave and Venerating the Stone Guanyin (Passing through Huangping in Guizhou)

A sheet of silk, as white as silver, bounds the blue-green peak;
Serene and pure, the winding path makes for a pleasant walk.
The supernatural depiction shows a pulse divine,
Its free and easy majesty inspires one to devotion.
The hazy mist of mountain air drips down as sweetest dew,
The monastery is blocked from view by rising incense smoke.
And waves of pines, rhymes of bamboo, and roaring waterfalls
Transform into a Sanskrit hymn performed by the celestials.

Encountering Rain on the Road through Langdai Mountains

I'm back from dreams; the roosters have shut up,
The towering crags are doubly cold at dawn.
As misty hazes shroud bamboos and trees,
The cloudy vapors moisten gown and skirt.
The bells just keep on chattering in the wind,
And on the roadside cliffs the flowers smell.
We're running into pestilential rains,
So do not sing "I'm longing for my hometown"!

From *Old Eagle Cliff (Eight Poems)*

4.

A hazy halcyon-like green—it almost reaches heaven,
This single mountain rises high—linked to ten thousand others.
When I look back and see the road down in the world of dust,
A single breath of azure sky escapes to outer regions.

5.

Cliff and ravine serene and pure: one feels refreshed and free,
The landscape at this spot requires a poem for its fame.
Beyond the sky—who sees the traveler who flies and soars?
Just visit many famous mountains and you're an immortal!

On Middle Prime I Sent a Letter to My Late Husband, to Which I Appended Three Quatrains (This Poem and the Following Were Written in the Governor's Office in Yunnan)[52]

1.

The days and nights of these ten years have passed as in a flash,
How can I know how you are doing in the realm of shades?
Despite your talents you did not achieve your life's ambitions,
But did you rise, thanks to your writings, to the highest heavens?

2.

In vain I write my loneliness on little sheets of paper,
The memories of those shared years increase my somber mood.
I have one bundle paper money and a thousand tears,
And I want both of these delivered to the Yellow Springs.

3.

Repeatedly I scratch my head as I ask Heaven: Why?
I burn the letter that I wrote in hope it will be sent.
There's one thing I must tell you, as it may provide some comfort:
Your little boy now can recite the orphan's sagebrush song.[53]

From *For Little Monk*[54]

2.

An inch of gold could never yet buy one an inch of time:
Now memorize this proverb as it gives you good advice!
Please do not disappoint the many efforts of your mother—
The hopes for you of your late father will be even higher.

3.

You're fortunate in serving a fine teacher in your study,
You will become acquainted now with books and candlelight.
Glory and shame for all your life are not a minor matter:
Make sure you will have no remorse when it will be too late!

4.

It's urgent now to rid yourself of childish playfulness,
Your future and career depend on study of the Classics.
You have to grasp and understand your father's great regret—
You must continue the tradition by becoming an official!

On a Spring Day We Ascended the Heaven-Sea Pagoda and Gazed at Mountains Such As Gold Horse and Blue Cock

Because we loved the flowing brook that rippling went its way,
We followed flowers and we crossed, on foot, the little bridge.
By chance we climbed the high pagoda, peering at Gold Horse,
At leisure leaning on the railing we discussed Blue Cock.
We saw some fields of blooming herbs—the fragrance carried far,
We noticed too some willow trees—just barely clad in green.
The pleasant breeze felt oh so good, the spring light was alluring,
And then we heard new orioles that twittered in the hills.

An Impromptu Poem of Late Spring

The doves are cooing on the roof, the rain falls down like threads,
The flower business of the spring is now reduced to roses.
The day lasts long and I'm too lazy to pick up my needle,
I brew some tea and burn some incense, reading Du Fu's poems.

Dreams

A tangled mess—you doubt they're false, and then you doubt they're true,
The scenes you see are an illusion, yet may have some cause.
I've realized that human life is just like this in nature,
But by what means may one then know an earlier existence?

My Shadow

You keep me constant company by light of lamp or moon,
Inseparable! You do not leave me where I walk or sit.
In sticking closely to another, you are just like me,
But you are free of any thought, so I must yield to you.

While Ill, an Impromptu Poem

In bed while ill I fail to fall asleep,
And late at night the blanket gives no warmth.
The roaring winds howl even in my cushion,
And moonlight silently clings to the gate.
"A floating stick"—alas, such is my life,[55]
The mountain passes block my dreaming soul.
My true desire has long been contradicted,
With whom can I discuss my deepest longing?

From *About to Return, an Impromptu Poem* (Two Poems)

2.

I've finished packing all my luggage, yet I feel depressed,
My hometown lies ten thousand miles beyond the misty clouds.
The travel plans for going back now finally are settled,
My remnant life of bitter toil still fills my heart with grief.
The stains of tears here on my shirt are due to memories,
The hairs reflected in the mirror tell of my lost youth.
Admittedly, there is one thing that, yes, will be some fun:
I'll practice poetry again together with my siblings!

Visiting Flying Clouds Cave in Huangping Once Again

The days and nights of these ten years have passed as in a flash,
Again I burn my bit of incense to Vimalakirti.[56]
A dharma-rain that has no bounds is falling down from heaven,
Clouds of compassion without limit gather in the caves.
Awakened from the sea of nature, one is always free,
Rid of the devil of one's passions, one can move at ease.
Let common people never call the Lotus Throne too distant:
A full moon is reflected here at midnight in white waves.

Parting Poems for Lianyou, Written at the Banquet When Leaving for Jinhua[57]

1.

My heart is filled with parting thoughts, my mind feels paralyzed,
When this one cup of wine is downed, I'm off to heaven's edge.
We're of one mind, but when again will we be reunited?
As of today I'll look with sorrow at the sisters-flower.

2.

A single whip, and once again I leave the metropole,
When I look back at stream and bridge, it's bound to break my heart.
I take a handkerchief and wipe away those tears of parting—
The stains of these new tears mix with the stains of older tears.

On Our Way to the Temporary Posting at Wuzhou; also Shown to My Son Lin-zhi

While leaning at the cabin's window I recall past journeys,
A wind-filled sail—again I travel in a Wuling boat.[58]
In brocade dress you love to do the dance of Laizi's dress,[59]
Efficient government should come from moral government.
  Ten families the town, and still you'll be the people's parent,[60]
Two thousand bushels was a feudal lord in ancient times.[61]
You have—how great our nation's grace—received your father's rank,
Repay that favor with pure diligence and old ambition!

The Tianzhu Monastery[62]

1.

The morning mists encircle tall bamboos,
To roaring sounds of springs beneath the rocks.
The lake and hills surround this dharma realm,
Where Sanskrit hymns descend from highest heavens.
  The mountain haze is chilly on the cheeks,
The stupa's image in the sky is rounded.
I'm carried up—the road back home so far,
And look around—one white expanse of clouds.

2.

The first stage we have barely reached just now,
The storied peaks rise up above the trees.
Through tall bamboo the path to the Three Zhu,
Pure chimes resound at Hundred Flowers Altar.
  This marvelous domain shows a new face,
Clouds of compassion enter the Grand View.
In the light breeze the rhymes of pines stay silent,
In sunset light the mists of dusk amass.

Looking for Plums on West Lake[63]

1.

The lakeside hills are twenty-four and tie one's dreaming thoughts—
This time we come here, to my joy, right in the early spring.
And when our slender boat starts up the route of Western Brook,
A fragrant snow comes fluttering and falls into our wine cups.

2.

No drooping branches yet on the Six Bridges' misty willows—
It's now the moment when the snow has cleared on Orphan Island.[64]
I earnestly implore the eastern wind not to create a mess,
But let their fragrant form stay here and let us find new verses.

For My Son Lin-zhi

A single sail so lightly passes through deep river clouds,
Flowers and moonlight, springtime streams: together we chant verses.
Enjoying sights, our boat will stop at fords of fragrant grasses,
Searching for scenes, we then will walk though groves on river banks.
This parting sorrow—don't ask for my thoughts in idle moments,
We better find some striking lines here from this gorgeous landscape.
An unrestrained and easy manner frees one from the vulgar,
So let no worldly worries now disturb the first impulse.

11

A Proud Descendant of Chinggis Khan

Naxun Lanbao

NAXUN LANBAO (1824–1873) IS NOT THE ONLY KNOWN MONgol woman poet of the Qing dynasty, and she is also not the only one to have authored a collection, but she is the only one whose collection survives.[1] This has made her somewhat of a cultural icon in Inner Mongolia. Her work has been published in a modern annotated edition,[2] and has given rise to an ongoing series of articles in which she is praised to the skies.[3] Since the appearance of the first of these in 1982, critics have praised her strong sense of Mongol identity and her insistence on a unified China, her attacks on patriarchal values and her defense of women's talents, and her love for her husband and her care for her servants. Critics also praise her poetic skills as displayed in her poems on the changing seasons and on her outings to the Beijing suburbs. In some of these recent publications she has even been hailed as the "Mongolian Li Qingzhao," but, without wanting to denigrate her accomplishments, one has to say that such a comparison to China's greatest female poet is grossly overdone.[4] Naxun Lanbao left a small and finely crafted—but in many ways rather conventional—collection of ninety-one *shi* poems. Upon her death these were printed in 1874 by her second son, Shengyu (1850–1900), as *Preserved Poems of the Hall of Fragrant Rue* (Yunxiangguan yishi).[5]

Naxun Lanbao was born in Kulun, modern-day Ulan Bator. Her father's family, the Borjigit clan of Khalkha Mongols, traced its ancestry back to Chinggis Khan. Ever since the Khalkha Mongols had submitted to the Manchus in the late seventeenth century, the Borjigit princes were their staunchest allies, guarding the sensitive border with the Russian empire. Many of the Borjigit princes received women of the imperial Aisin Gioro clan as wives. Naxun Lanbao's father, Dorje Wanchuk, however, was only a younger son, and while his wife was Manchu, she was only a Feimo. In 1828 he was summoned to the capital to serve in the Imperial Guard, and when he arrived in Beijing, he and his wife and children lived with his parents-in-law.[6] Little Naxun Lanbao from that moment was primarily raised by her maternal grandmother, Wanyan Jinchi, as we learned from her preface to her grandmother's collection.

To the best of our knowledge, Naxun Lanbao never left Beijing again, except for short excursions to the Western Hills and Haidian (to the northwest of Beijing, on the road to Yuanmingyuan, the "old summer palace," which was destroyed in 1860 by French and English troops). Her husband, Heng-en (d. 1866), belonged to the imperial clan as a grandson of Yong-xi (d. 1821), the sixth Prince Su. When Heng-en, who was a younger son, was thirty, he was adopted as son and heir by an uncle, Yong-xi's fourth son, Jing-zheng (1785–1851), who eventually reached the rank of assistant grand secretary (1842–1845). In his own career, Heng-en rose to the rank of assistant vice president of the censorate (1864–1866). The couple's most successful son was Sheng-yu, who passed the provincial examination in 1870. Later, in 1877, he passed the metropolitan examinations, and served with distinction in the Hanlin Academy and the National Academy, from which he retired in 1888 to devote the remainder of his years to scholarship.[7]

When Sheng-yu published his mother's poems, he provided the collection with the following postface:

Postface to *Preserved Poems of the Hall of Fragrant Rue*

> My late mother entered the family school at the age of seven, could write poems at the age of twelve, grasped the Five Classics at the age of fifteen, and married my esteemed late father at the age of seventeen. She not only served her mother-in-law assiduously, but also lived in harmony with her sisters-in-law. In the spare time left by her domestic duties, she continued to practice "chanting and singing." The poems she wrote had been accumulated into one huge tome. But entering upon middle age, she loved to read useful books, and in her final years she busied herself with the Classics and Histories, and she only rarely would write poems. By the year of *bingyin* [1866], when my esteemed late father had passed away, she did not write any poems anymore as she was exhausted each day by arranging internal matters and warding off outside worries.
>
> On one occasion she said to my younger sister E and me: "I have had the good fortune of achieving a certain provisional understanding of poetry. But what I wrote in my younger years is mostly idle verbiage, not worthy of being ridiculed by later generations. So you should not have my poems printed after my death. If Heaven grants me the years and you have established yourselves

so I will no longer be burdened by domestic tasks, I may take up my earlier study of poetry once again. If I produce something by 'molding and melting,' it may perhaps be able to compete with works of ancient times." Alas, while these words were still ringing in my ears, my late mother abandoned the world of men in the autumn of last year.

I, her son, am muddle-headed and confused, and I do not know which of her poems merit transmission. By printing all her poems I would disobey the order of my late mother, and that would be a grave sin, but if I did not print her poems, the words of virtue of my late mother would have no means of transmission, and unavoidably end up getting lost, and that sin would even be graver. So I asked the elders of our neighborhood for advice, and they deemed upon inspection the poems of my late mother to be pure and manly, graceful and beautiful works, poems that well merited transmission despite her own dissatisfaction. That's why I have dared [to print her poems], basing myself on the manuscript she compiled herself in the year of *dingsi* [1857], to which I added what I collected. In total I obtained ninety-one poems, which I have arranged in two scrolls. This I have entrusted to the block-carvers.

Alas, my late mother did not want to be remembered because of her poems, and therefore many were scattered and lost, without any hope of retrieval. If I only limit myself to her poems, not one-tenth of the many hundreds have been preserved. And how much less has been preserved of her stellar virtue and noble words, which truly far transcend her poetical compositions! It is my sincere hope that later readers may deduce her habitual behavior from her poems, and not treat them only as verbal artifice. This is my only intention in printing the poems of my late mother.

Respectfully written by her unfilial son Sheng-yu in the Fifth Month of the thirteenth year [1874] of the Tongzhi reign period[8]

Preserved Poems of the Hall of Fragrant Rue is a relatively small collection, only containing ninety-one poems. In the original printing, the second scroll starts from "My Second Elder Brother Yingjun Was Appointed to Kulun, Which Is Our Old Hometown. On the Day I Saw Him Off, I Dashed Off This Poem." It seems safe to suppose that the first scroll reproduced the manuscript Naxun Lanbao had prepared in 1857, and that the second scroll consisted of the poems Sheng-yu had been able to collect from her friends and relatives, because this section mostly consists of social poems.

The more substantial poems are found in the first half of the collection. As is only to be expected, we find many poems marking the passing seasons of spring, summer, fall, and winter (and, as this is Beijing, the winter brings snow). We observe the author, an aristocratic lady, indulging in her hobbies of socializing, gardening, painting, and writing poems. At their best, these poems are distinguished by wit and self-irony. A number of poems describe excursions, to Haidian and the Western Hills. Modern critics like to point out the originality of the poems she addressed to an elderly servant, and hail it as proving Naxun Lanbao's sympathy for the lower classes. The two longest poems are inspired by poetry collections of other women writers. When Naxun Lanbao succeeded in buying a copy of *Orchid and Snow* (Lanxue ji) by the thirteenth-century woman poet Zhang Yuniang, she composed a long poem recounting the tragic story of the author (not included in this selection). Another long poem was inspired by her teacher Guizhen Daoren's *Poetry Collection of the Hall of Ice and Snow* (Bingxuetang shicao). In her poem, Naxun Lanbao recounts her teacher's long life of chaste widowhood, voices her (by that time quite trite but still very proper) views on the nature of poetry, and insists on women's right to write verse, in an obvious attack on the common saying "In women a lack of talent is a virtue."

Some other poems are parting poems, seeing off relatives who were leaving the comforts of Beijing for the rigors of a provincial posting. More parting poems are found in the second *scroll*.[9] The most remarkable parting poem is the one she wrote for one of her brothers, when he was posted to Kulun. This is the only poem in her collection in which she explicitly speaks about her Mongolian background. Critics from Inner Mongolia read this poem as a strong and straight assertion of Mongolian identity, calling at the same time for the unity of all minorities within a unified China, but the poem is more interesting than that. While Naxun Lanbao proudly recounts the family's heritage, she also admits that she herself has completely adapted to life in the capital and doesn't speak a word of Mongolian anymore. In a note to one of his own poems, Sheng-yu recounts that at one stage of his career a fellow official, quoting this poem in an indirect attack on him, asked for the destruction of the printing blocks of his mother's collection because she had "forgotten her roots."[10] Apparently the expression of Mongolian patriotism was not as explicit to Qing-dynasty readers as it is to contemporary academics.

We also find in this second scroll the poems Naxun Lanbao wrote when Baibao Youlan left for the Jiangnan area after her son had been posted there in the late 1850s, and the poems she sent in reply to those she received from her friend. The same scroll also includes the poems she sent in the 1860s to her friend Jiang Zhongshen (d. 1879) in Tianjin to thank her for her gifts. Jiang Zhongshen (also known as Heyou) was born in a Chinese banner family and married Wanyan Chong-hou (1826–1893), a grandson of Yun Zhu as the second son of Lin-qing, who resided in Tianjin from 1861 to 1870 as superintendent of trade.[11] Naxun Lanbao also was a good friend of Foyunbao (d. 1856), one of Yun Zhu's granddaughters.

While the filial son Sheng-yu stressed in his postface his mother's modesty regarding her poetry, we learn from Naxun Lanbao's preface to her grandmother's collection that in the final years of her life she had conceived of an ambitious project to compile a large-scale anthology of poetry by Manchu women, discussed in this volume's introduction. Modern critics, however, tend to base their discussion of Naxun Lanbao exclusively on her *Preserved Poems of the Hall of Fragrant Rue*, which they search for Mongolian characteristics.

NAXUN LANBAO

Impromptu

The heat has gone, new autumn has arrived,
The wind is cool, the air is clear and crisp.
When done embroidering I take my brush,
As flowers' shadows reach up to the window.

Early Summer

1.

The curtain hanging in the doorway lightly sweeps the ground,
As floss and fallen petals float around the roof and pillars.
The courtyard filled with shade of green, from red dust oh so far—
From time to time one hears a bird descending to the ground.

2.

On a small bench in the shade of pines I enjoy the cool of noon.
Floating gossamer is caught by the long strands of the willow.
When the sky clears up, all of a sudden the roses are blooming:
I smell their fragrance on the other side of the gauze window.

3.

Spider webs add to the gossamer, magpies fight over nests,
At the horizon, dense and towering trees join each other.
This is the idle life of watering plants and raising cranes—
Sitting down I write out my own copy of *The Many Flowers*.

How Hard the Road to Go!

Carved wheels that are square, and a horse with three legs—
Why don't you rest for a while in this small little cabin?
Heaven and earth are thorns and brambles wherever you go,
So what's the purpose of this restless wandering and striving?
    The frost of autumn descended last night on the winding slope,
But under mulberry and elm the spring breeze is always warm.

Late Fall. An Impromptu Poem

The weather is not yet cold but the wind is getting colder,
And the maple forest, dyed by frost, is slowly turning red.
After midnight longing for home is generated by cicadas,
The finest foliage of the year is found in wutong leaves.
    Bells of pigeons, lines of geese: a thousand miles of cloud,
Plots of herbs, a patch of cabbage: one square rod of land.
So we better enjoy ourselves by having a cup of wine—
Last night the chrysanthemums opened east of the fence.

Searching for Verses

Burning incense in the still room, I sit and search for verses,
As always, the reed curtain and paper pavilion suit me fine.
The lamp's glare on the folding screen really bothers my eyes,
And the fierce cold outside the window smartly hits my skin.
    Falling leaves beat the gate as the wind sighs harmoniously,
Tattered flowers fill the ground under a more graceful moon.
The clear night looks like water, so let's not miss this moment:
I never grow tired of taking out books and spreading them out.

A Voracious Wind

1.

All day long the wind is extremely voracious,
In the inner quarters we keep our doors closed.
The freezing trees compete for the sun's light,
But a weak wine displays traces of spring.
    Bamboo casts its shade on the hermit's curtain,
While plums are fragrant in his old wife's tubs.
They don't care for the cold outside their window,
All through the night the burner's fire stays warm.

2.

There's no end to the strands of idle sorrow
Which fill each corner of this desolate room.
The lamp on the wall casts a cold glare, and
The wind whistles through the paper window.
The thin blanket cannot warm all of my body,
And throughout the night no dream comes to me.
Bereft of sleep I count the drumbeats of the watch,
While the moon descends, east of the courtyard.

Autumn Night Chant

All of a sudden the scenery has turned to undiluted autumn,
And a tender cold sneaks into the tower by the waterside.
With half a window of cool moonlight, the flowers can fade,
In the clear breeze filling the courtyard, the bamboo darken.
Does one have to understand poetic scenes from books?
Don't try to acquire a cunning mind from the game of go.
You have to enjoy those moments in life you can enjoy—
Slowly but surely years and beauty leave, they will not stay.

Enjoying the Snow

When morning came the whole world was wearing a new dress,
The air was fragrant as all dust and grime were now suppressed.
When bamboo leaves touched, the silver sounded in harmony,
Where plum blossoms were covered, their jade gave off a scent.
Sweeping the pathways with a broom the children were happy,
Poking the fire, melting snow for tea, my sisters were busy.
Before we had finished a jug of wine, the bright moon rose—
How I loved that heaven and earth were equally cool!

A Visit to the Western Hills

1.

At break of dawn we mount a covered cart
To arrive at the foot of the hills after noon,
Not shirking the fatigue of the bumpy ride—
We've an appointment with the mountain god!
The winding road enters into misty clouds,
On looking back, the city walls have disappeared.
The steep stone stairs are overgrown with pines,

And one hears the bell of a distant monastery.
Its orphaned gray marks a peak far away, and
A myriad of greens compete for a single ravine.
As we go on, we step down from our litters,
And walk with giddy steps on the narrow path.
But our guides ask some convent cells for us,
As the red sun sinks on this endless expanse.

2.

I truly love the Secret Demon Cliff:
The strange rock loftily supports the heavens.
I also love the Grotto of the Precious Pearl:
One looks straight down to the level fields!
How great it is to ride the winds and travel!
For one moment one becomes an immortal.
Seeking out the hidden and secluded spots,
One wants to be the first to find the sights.
To my regret my legs and feet are small,
I have to call a maid to lend me her support.
Besides the road, the acorns rise in layers,
Between the rocks, a single flower blooms.
Lingering on, I completely forget to return:
Peak upon peak fixates the evening clouds.

Staying the Night at the Monastery of Great Enlightenment [Dajue Si]

The whole monastery is cool because of its ten acres of pines,
The view of the hills is blocked by the waterfall's single sheet.
The gray of peaks and summits closes in on us and clothes feel cold,
The red of burning candles meanders on the long mountain road.
From time to time we smell a light fragrance coming from the statue,
Occasionally we hear orphaned chimes emerging from a monk's cell.
We visitors sit opposite each other, without any sleep, only too eager
To ascend the mountain and venerate the Buddha first thing tomorrow.

Spring Night

I found a line of verse, which still requires pushing and pounding:[12]
"I love the moon but then again I hate the tangled shades of trees."
When I try to walk past the slanting part of the painted balustrade,
A pair of sleeping butterflies rises up from their flowering branch.

Spring Days, Three Poems

1.

Suddenly warmer, the weather tells the rain to stop its cold,
Without a worry, I now notice that the days grow longer.
Bees, loving the heavy dew, are loath to return to the hive,
Swallows, using the slight breeze, skim low across the wall.
Whenever I paint a picture, I splatter my gown with ink,
When I pluck a flower, at least my sleeves stay fragrant.
All spring long, carefully considered, I've nothing to do:
Let me busy myself by finding a theme and writing verse.

2.

The blue sky, cleared of clouds, is covered by a light haze:
The light warmth and the light cold of the Second Month.
Bamboo printed on the white wall becomes a painted sketch,
Note paper hidden in my sleeve makes it a poetry container.
By chance addicted to light drinking I forget my domestic duties,
Time and again I neglect my needlework because of my chanting.
This is the place where spring colors most demand our attention:
The apricot blossoms just have opened east of the little tower.

3.

The courtyard now the sky has cleared is filled with warm fragrance,
As the single string of a paper kite pulls in the radiance of spring.
This season is truly enjoyable—just look at the smiling flowers!
This time of year is full of passion—even grasses are fragrant.
The heavy dew of the apricot garden seduces the butterflies,
Mandarin ducks are sleeping on the warm sand under the willows.
Without a worry I only feel that this best suits my body, so after
Sweeping the green moss by myself, I sit down in the evening sun.

Wanting to Do a Painting

One slight trace of spring pierces the window's crimson gauze,
And the new pinks stimulate an overflow of painterly feelings.
Some lip-dotting red has been left from this morning's toilette,
I figure I can use that to add apricot flowers to the branches.

The Servant Woman Surnamed Li Has Been with Me for Six or Seven Years, but Now My Elder Sister-in-Law, the Lady Fengyi, Will Take Her to Shengjing [Shenyang], So I Wrote These Twenty Lines as a Present.

Congregation and dispersal are not fixed,
Close and far all have their karmic bonds.
Grieving over separation does no good at all,
But alas, we are still tied by our emotions.
  My thoughts follow the rivers of Liaodong,
My yearning encircles the mists of Jizhou:
You will follow her for a thousand miles,
After keeping me company for ten years.
  When sewing, you helped me sort the threads,
When doing my hair, you put in the pins.
This happy past I will keep in my mind,
But I am worried now you're set to leave.
  Your clothes are all packed in the cases,
Send us a letter when you have arrived—
Feelings at parting: traces of flying birds,
A flood of emotions: days of falling petals.
  Don't think too much about your old mistress,
Please serve your new friend with devotion.
The city of Shengjing is our old homeland,
So tell me all the sights when you return.

Late Spring, on the Spur of the Moment

The day is still: in inner chambers dreams at noon last long,
This is the time of year the weather really tires one out.
A green shade moved by sunlight covers now my writing desk,
Red petals tossed by the breezes drop into the inkstone well.
  There's a method to shrink the earth: you must make a painting;
But no technique will tie down spring: one just writes a poem.
Outside the light curtains I will spread a pure mat, and invite
All my elder and younger sisters and cousins for a game of go.

Sent to My Elder Sister-in-Law Fengyi as a Letter

It's hard to say "separation" at parting—
How could my heart bear to see you leave?
I am alone and do not find you anymore,
So I am filled now with a constant longing.

The sinking moon reminds me of your brows,
The halting cloud makes me think of your hair,
I tried to compute the day of your arrival,
So now again I am waiting for a letter.
By sleeping and eating I have recovered,
So I can let you know I'm doing well.
At leisure, putting my embroidery aside,
I rely on verse to make it through the summer.
Dealing with others, I don't try to be smart,
Telling my feelings, I always sound foolish.
So I send you this letter with all my wishes—
Misty trees lower their green to the ground.

Haidian

In the dim light of early morning the rain in the suburbs clears,
At the crack of dawn a light carriage carting dreams left the city.
The one stretch of lighted hills differentiates near and distant,
And the myriad patches of clouds demarcate shady and clear.
In the sound of threshing grain is the joy of a bountiful harvest,
Between the rows of sparse willows the imperial road runs level.
From where that overwhelming fragrance of osmanthus flowers?
The pavilions and towers of noble mansions all tower and soar.

On the Poetry Collection of the Hall of Ice and Snow

In the *Airs of the States* the Songs of Zhou top the Four Beginnings:
From ancient times chanting and singing start in the inner quarters.[13]
Don't dare to say that it's a virtue for a woman to have no talent at all,
As since antiquity women have been amongst the writers of odes.[14]

The world tends to state that poets are bound to suffer adversity,
But I say that in adversity poetry often becomes more skillful.
Just have a look at those poems that are transmitted to later times:
Most of them originate in sorrow and grief and great frustration.

My teacher owes her superior intelligence to her innate wisdom,
She knew her characters while still a toddler, at the age of three!
Her family was poor, her mother sickly, she suffered misfortune,
But in the spare time left by her needlework, she loved the arts.

When she married, her husband was a member of the secretariat,
So by good luck she had found her place in a house that loved books.
In the inner chambers they linked verses, as spring turned warmer;
At dawn he hastened to court, leaving her alone all the long day.

But a jealous wind suddenly snapped that mandarin-ducks weed,
And the sprouting orchid shriveled because of the freezing cold.
Out of all persons she was the one to suffer such a poor fate,
This without cause made her pink cheeks age before their time.

This grief is unending, lasting as long as both heaven and earth—
Her great chastity, like pine and bamboo, is quite conspicuous.
Calling her works "Ice and Snow," she is comparable in purity,
Taking the name of "Return to Truth," her aim is transcendence.

Moved to feelings by experiences, she formulates her ambition,
In this collection she gives expression to her lifetime's thought.
She has no verses on breeze and clouds, or moonlight and dew,
She pursues poetry purely on the basis of nature and inspiration.

It is my good fortune to be counted amongst her disciples,
Carrying a sutra, asking an explanation, I'm filled with devotion.
When I close this book after having read her pure poems at night,
The shining moon illuminates the dark vault of the autumn sky.

Sudden Feelings in Our Little Garden

Taking small steps I linger deliberately,
But a few gusts of western wind urge me on.
A light mist rises with the onset of dusk,
The sinking sun hastens the arrival of fall.
Red leaves start to dot the high trees, and
Chrysanthemums suppress the green moss.
How great this evening's clear feeling—
Leisurely I walk across the level terrace.

My Second Elder Brother Yingjun Was Posted to Kulun, Which Is Our Old Hometown. On the Day I Saw Him Off, I Dashed Off This Poem.

At the age of four I came here to the capital,
Thirty years I've been away from our hometown.
What is the location of our hometown?
North of the passes, lost in the clouds.
We are descendants of Chinggis Khan,
And Kulun has always been our fief.
A hundred thousand who draw the bow—
We, "proud sons of heaven," are strong!
At night we're used to sleep in felt tents,
For breakfast we'll happily have frozen milk.
Fortunately, we are living in a unified world,
Without borders between middle and outside.
Carrying your sword, you served in the guard,
And were ennobled with an inherited rank.
Too bad I am only inner quarters material,
From early on I donned the current fashion.
I've never dreamed of riding a saddled horse,
All my ambition is focused on fine literature.
By the window I busy myself with cosmetics,
And at night I devote myself to my books.
Floriate and barbarian are different in style:
My old hometown is now a foreign region![15]
When you speak to me in that weird language,
I have to confess I have completely forgotten all of it!
Now you have received this appointment,
And you will return home, covered in glory.
But we look upon the place as a strange land
And the whole family is filled with fear.
But I have something I want to say to you,
As I offer you this parting drink now you leave.
The Son of Heaven rules the four barbarians,
So they may protect us against the Wastelands.[16]
Recently, I hear, they are very docile and meek,
And their honest customs are better than normal.
To my regret, I am not a man, so my desire
To go back there will never be fulfilled.
I hope that you, brother, will make an extra effort

To restore our inheritance to its former glory.
  Let's not cry sentimental tears like lovers
And vainly indulge in sadness and grief.

Thanking Lady Zhang Mengti for Being So Kind as to Inscribe My Small Portrait; Promptly Sent[17]

When inner quarter poets are discussed,
You are at present counted number one.
My day of birth was late but not too late,
So I could meet you in this sea of dust.
  The dreams of southern lands are shrimps and greens;
The nation's capital in spring is birds and flowers.
In a high room you write your lofty verse;
Disconsolate you often fix your mind.

Harmonizing with the Departure Poem of Third Sister Youlan[18]

1.

How I fear that moment your carriage will depart from our gate!
I grasp your hands and cannot let go, pained by this separation.
Of course you'll enter my dreams in the future because of love,
But I am worried that once I'll wake up not a trace will be left!

2.

While together we were like threads of silk mingled with hemp,
When you leave in a moment we'll each be at one end of the earth.
I know very well that congregation and dispersal are normal affairs,
But I'm so jealous of those intertwined flowers on a single branch.

From *Following the Original Rhyme-Words of Third Sister Youlan's Memories of Me in Hangzhou*

1.

In the Sixth Month, I learned, you crossed the Yellow River,
In clear autumn you then forded the waves of the Yangzi.
Longing for home you must shed "tears climbing the tower,"
Hating this separation in vain I write "a song drinking wine."
  As soon as your letter had been sent from the West Lake,
I feared that the Yellow Turbans had increased in Zhejiang.[19]
Shield and spear filling the earth—far apart from each other,
So I scratch my head in desperation, asking Heaven for help.

Sent to My Husband in the Winter of Gengshen *[1860], When He Was Staying in Luanyang*[20]

Let's not talk of the suffering of longing,
Of no use any sadness over the hard road.
The alarums of war approach the capital,
In snowstorms you shiver in a single coat.
 There is no news about going or staying,
Floating or sinking depends on your office.
In my own hand I write you this letter
To let you know we are all doing well.

Sent to Seventh Sister Heyou in Tianjin

High lofts and rising pavilions: summer scenes aplenty!
What are the pleasures of Tianjin at this time of the year?
Having chanted one's words, writing them on a banana leaf,
Having done one's toilette, a passing scent of lotus flowers.
 In your fine pavilion you must have added many new works,
In this desolate garden I often try to avoid the old misty vines.
On the Western Hills the walnuts have ripened last night,
I'm sending you a box of them to bolster your tipsy song!

From *My Seventh Sister Heyou Has Been Living in Tianjin Now for Many Years, and Whenever She Finds Fresh Fruits and Delicacies, She Sends Them to Us by Mail. When She Recently Came to the Capital She Once Again Bragged to Me in Her Poems about the Foodstuffs She Remembered from Tianjin. When, Long Ago, Su Shi Was Living on Hainan, He Developed a Taste for Oysters, and Afraid That Others Might Also Come to Like Them, He Gave Instructions to Keep It a Secret. Now if I Read My Sister's Poems, Her Intention Even Surpasses That of Su Shi. So I Improvised Four Poems Employing Her Original Rhyme-Words, as a Small Token of Gratitude for Her Tasty Tidbits.*[21]

3.
Do not brag that your special treats outdo the court of the Tang,
When a single horseman raced through the dust to deliver lychees.[22]
Now the ocean boats from Fujian arrive in only three days:
You buy those red fruits wholesale, then write your own poem.

From *Ink Princess Was Seventh Sister Heyou's Younger Sister-in-Law. It's Now Ten Years Since She Passed Away. I Had This One Sheet of Paper with Poems Written in Her Own Hand That I Kept at My Place. These Poems Were Written When She Thought of Heyou. For Years I Carefully Stored Them in a Bamboo Box. When Heyou Last Year Came to the Capital, She Begged Insistently for It. Despite My Old Love for a Former Friend, I Was Led by My Feelings of Attachment for Heyou, So I Composed Four Poems Following the Original Rhymes That I Had Mounted Together [with the Original Poems] and in This Way I Returned Them to Heyou.*[23]

1.

Revisiting that former dream I reach a springtime city:
As soon as I recite one line, a hundred sad emotions.
In vain remains a single ringlet of this Lucky Luster—[24]
I have, when I compare our poems, to admit defeat.

In Celebration of the Eightieth Birthday of My Teacher Guizhen

True practice originating from the Isle of Penglai,[25]
A high age approaching that of the Maiqiu Elder:[26]
Your nature flourishes like the pine and cypress,
Your body wanders with the rivers and clouds.
Your great virtue is fixed for a thousand years,
Your new poems will survive into the future.
Calling myself one of Your Ladyship's disciples
I am filled with shame as I tally your years.

12

From Hengyang to Beijing

Lingwen Zhuyou

WHEN ZHUYOU'S FATHER, A MANCHU OFFICER, WAS POSTED TO the Hengyang garrison in Hunan when Zhuyou was a young girl, he engaged the services of a young local boy as tutor for his children. This impecunious young man, only a few years older than Zhuyou, was Peng Yulin (Xueqin; 1816–1890), who would go on to play a major role in the suppression of the Taiping rebellion by organizing the government's river fleet.[1] Until his death he would be one of the most respected Qing officials.

After Zhuyou's father died at Hengyang, the family accompanied his coffin back to Beijing. There she was married, and when her husband died without issue, she adopted a son of his elder brother as heir. This young man, Ji-shun Rong-fan (d. 1900), served his adoptive mother most filially. After Ji-shun had become an official he befriended one of Peng Yulin's sons, further cementing the relation between the two families. On at least one occasion Lingwen Zhuyou met with Peng Yulin during one of his visits to Beijing and used the opportunity to share memories of their happy days down south. When Ji-shun in 1884 wanted to have his mother's collection of poetry printed, he of course requested a preface from Peng Yulin.[2] The latter complied and sketched an engaging portrait of his former pupil as a young girl before praising her chastity as a widow:

Preface to *Poetic Drafts of Floss Fragrance*

> *Poetic Drafts of Floss Fragrance* are the work of the female scholar Zhuyou of the Kuyale clan of Changbai, who has been recognized for her chastity and filial piety and was ennobled as Tai Gongren.
>
> In the reign period Daoguang she followed her father, the noble of the imperial lineage of the ninth rank Song-zhong-feng, on his official postings in Chu [Hubei/Hunan] and Wan [Anhui]. At one moment the noble of the imperial lineage was appointed in my native prefecture as the regimental

commander for Hengzhou, and he invited me to head the household school. At that time Zhuyou was still a child. She attended classes for a few years, and manifested great native intelligence, and liked to recite and sing. She widely read all kinds of books and loved to discuss loyalty and filial piety, chastity and righteousness, and such stories of as those of Nie Yinniang and Hongxian.[3] Her eyebrows would fly, her colors would dance, and she jumped up and down to try these things out for herself. How she hated the fact that she was not a man who could rely on his sword to travel a myriad of miles and obtain the seal of high office! Despite the fact that she was a daughter of a noble family, she had all the basic qualities to be a brave knight!

She served her parents most filially and married the antechamber guard Zhong-shan-ting, but within a year she became a widow. Her house consisted only of the four bare walls. Ji-shun Rong-fan, a son of her husband's elder brother Lord Jin-zhai, was established as her husband's heir, but at the time he was only an infant. She fed and raised him and brought him up. Twice she arranged a marriage for him, and she never borrowed a thing to defray the costs, because she relied on her needlework to provide for everything. She fully tasted deprivation and poverty! But Rong-fan served his mother also in a most filial way, and was capable of fully understanding his mother's heart. He exerted himself at his studies. He started out as clerk, and upon recommendation was appointed as department director in the Ministry of Justice. Being on duty inside the palace for days on end, he served together with my late son Yongzhao, and they became inseparable friends. So the friendship between our two families has existed already for two generations.

When Zhuyou became fifty, her gate was decorated by imperial decree.[4] Soon afterward Rong-fan was promoted to the position of military-administrative circuit intendant for Koubei in Zhili, and obtained her ennoblement as lady. Master Ouyang[5] once remarked, "The practice of goodness is always rewarded, but slow and fast have their time." If I now observe how Rong-fan and his mother enjoy their reward even faster and quicker than the beat of a drum, it must have been brought about by the bitter chastity she endured while raising her son and suffering deprivation!

In the spring of the *jiashen* year of the Guangxu reign period (1884), when I was serving in the military in Lingnan, Rong-fan sent me letter from the northern border. He wanted to print the *Poetic Drafts of Floss Fragrance* and publish them, and begged me for a preface. Now, one half of the three hundred odes have, in my opinion, been written by women.[6] From ancient times until the present those women who excel in poetry have been called talented women. But many of them show talent but no chastity, such as Zhuo Wenjun, Cai Yan, and Zhu Shuzhen.[7] Even though they excel in poetry, what is to be revered in them? Those who were renowned in the period of Spring and Autumn for their chastity were Gong Jiang of Wei,[8] Boji of Song,[9] and Shuji of Ji.[10] Even rarer are those who combined chastity and talent. There are only the two stanzas of "The Cypress Boat." These were written by Gong Jiang. This is a poem by a chaste wife who also was a talented woman. In later times only "The Chant of the Yellow Goose" by Tao Ying from Lu could continue that sound.[11] The collection of this writer may be read as the odes of "The Cypress Boat" and "The Yellow Goose."

I am already advanced in years and hurry about amidst the war horses.[12] Because I had some respite from my many duties, I did not refuse to write a preface at the beginning. When I think back to forty years ago, it is still like yesterday, but alas, Master Zhong-feng is not among the living anymore. So while holding the brush I could not help myself from heaving a heavy sigh.

By Grand Master for Splendid Happiness by Imperial Decree, Imperial Commissioner for the Organization of the Coastal Defense of Guangdong, Junior Guardian of the Heir Apparent, President of the Ministry of Defense, Granted the Privilege of Wearing the Yellow Riding Jacket, Granted the Privilege of Wearing the Peacock Feather First Class, Commandant of Light Chariots, Meticulous and Brave Baturu[13] Peng Yulin from Hengyang

Lingwen Zhuyou's collection is of modest size. The poems are arranged in chronological order and start with her early poems from Anhui and Hunan and her trip back home. In her poems of later years she would often remember her happy youth in Hunan, on the banks of the Xiang and in the shade of Mount Heng. Probably the most remarkable work in her collection is a series of twenty quatrains entitled "On Widowhood," which ends on the happy note of her son's marriage. As may be expected, the second part of the collection also contains several poems addressed to Peng Yulin. The collection is concluded by several poems in praise of chaste women.[14]

LINGWEN ZHUYOU

Learning to Write Poetry

What is it in which I can lodge my heart?
That's why I rashly study writing verse.
I know to find the fragrant lines of Ban

But lack alas lush lyrics of the Song.[15]

The autumn insects chirp their song of sorrow;
The grasses in the field are one wild mess:
So let me put aside my needlework
To rein in tight all these unbridled thoughts.

Accompanying My Father I Arrived from Xin'an in the Capital of Anhui, and on the Road We Passed Seventy-Two Mountain Ridges, So I Improvised the Following Quatrain in Jest

As I look back, White Marchmount's clouds still follow in my trail;
Along the road the rivers doubled, mountains multiplied!
Don't dare to call this pretty face an inner-chamber weakling:
I crossed the peaks of Southern Anhui, seventy and two!

From *Waiting on My Teacher Xueqin as He Made a Painting, Two Poems*

2.

In paintings there's a poem and in poems there's a painting—
My Classics teacher, virtue teacher, and now painting teacher!
I am your pupil, your disciple, from the inner chambers,
And will not shrink from looking on while standing all the time.

Weeping for My Father

Stern Lord, what was the cause you left us for the Yellow Springs?
Now you are gone it wounds my heart you never will return.
Ten thousand miles away from home I'm overcome by grief
As blowing springs winds cool the ashes of the spirit money.

Written While Overcome by Emotion on Board the Boat Leaving from Hengzhou with My Mother and Younger Brother to Take My Father's Coffin Back to Our Banner

Most pitiable is my mother who is frail with age—
Her hair in buns, her clothes of hemp, she boards the coffin boat.
Burned spirit money whirls about, like butterflies so white;
Dyed bright red, like azaleas, new streaks of tears appear.

This sorrow seals the mighty Heng with many layers of clouds;
Our dreaming chills the Xiao and Xiang, the moonlit one expanse.
Ten thousand miles away from home, those passes to the north—
Sleeping on straw my little brother is still in his teenage years.

Crossing Dongting Lake

The double lake: one watery expanse to the horizon;
In flocks of thousands sacred crows all circle round and round.
When the boat crossed [the lake], a limitless number of black crows came flying and roosted on the mast and sweep, and the boatmen fed them with food. According to legend these are the three thousand black crow soldiers of the goddesses of Dongting. It is a lucky sign if they protect the passing passenger ships. They are not found in other places.
The silver waves—ten thousand acres—really have no limit;
The Mountain of the Goddesses? One dot in blue dusk haze!

Traveling by Boat and Enjoying the Moon

The breeze so light, the single boat so stable;
The tide is level and both banks are wide.
Right in the middle, seated, I, alone—
Above, below: the fully rounded moon.

When Our Boat Reached Yangzhou It Was the Lantern Festival, and the Crowds of Men and Women Resembled Clouds. I Improvised Two Quatrains to Record My Elation.

1.

The sound of laughter flies beyond green-willow city walls;
In simple clothes with light makeup they walk around in groups.
Lanterns on storied boats of pipes and drums amass, disperse:
In this one hazy mist of flowers no one can see clearly.

2.

In every house the upper rooms have opened every window;
The golden beasts of precious burners burn the scent of musk.
And in their locks three hundred sprigs of an unblemished fragrance:
Outside the curtain you are startled by the smell of flowers.

Widowhood, Twenty Poems

1.

What hurts one most is separation—while alive, through death:
One moment of togetherness turns out to be a dream.
What is the reason that that little boy Creation
Plays with us human beings in this reckless manner?

2.
The joy and laughter of old days belongs now to the past;
To all affairs my heart is ashes, leaving but this body.
Who keeps me company when hauling water, hulling rice?
When evening comes, my closest friend is now a single lamp.

3.
Despite all efforts of Nüwa to set the heavens straight,[16]
That Separation Heaven still exists here in our grief.
How come the moon at first is round, and then again defective?
For all eternity the reason can't be fully fathomed.

4.
I make great efforts to keep up the proper social forms,
But who is there to understand my suffering and toil?
Our human feelings are the same, but cold and warm do change.[17]
And then I have to be concerned suspicions may arise.

5.
The floss of willows drifting and the mournful cuckoo's cries—
It's long ago that I awoke from that one springtime dream.
Bereft of feeling you abandoned chilly, cheerless me—
The rain so cold, a single lamp, and none to show me pity.

6.
My sorrows are like little weeds that reemerge in spring,
Day upon day more numerous, and tangled just like hemp.
They then turn into streaks of tears, a thousand and a million,
Enough to dye the flowers of azaleas all red.

7.
When I recall those past events, they are completely gone—
Because I fear the springtime chill, I close the patterned curtains.
The pairs of swallows do not know my lack of interest:
Outside the screen they chirp and twitter in the setting sun.

8.
Too listless to pick up the needle and to fix my eye—
With storm and rain and rain and storm this spring looks more like autumn.

And ever since the one who used to paint my eyebrows on is gone,[18]
The fallen petals on the ground spell grief beyond endurance.

9.
The fragrant gauze like piled-up snow I still refuse to cut;
Brocade embroideries are to my eyes like dust and dirt.
However hot the summer heat, my heart is not rekindled;
Those past events—when I look back, all thought has turned to ashes.

10.
Discarded are my hairpins, idle; cold my toilet-case—
I've come to hate the noisy crowds, all luxury and wealth.
The little cup of medicine is now my dearest friend:
It stays with me throughout the year, I never get fed up.

11.
To love a boy is not so light, to raise a boy is hard:
In hunger, hardship, heat, or cold you want to see him happy.
How often will you late at night, unable to doze off,
Request a lamp and have a look, afraid he is awake?

12.
What is the thing that through the years has hurt my heart the most?
This body haunted by the ghost of sickness, fiend of sorrow.
And when I saw this sack of bones reflected in the mirror,
The only one to pity me was that reflected image.

13.
Each time it was a festive day, I'd be awash in tears,
By many kinds of limitless emotions overcome.
And even though my sisters all were filled with deep concern,
I could not tell my closest kin the sorrow in my heart.

14.
A fiery sun, a roasted window, and the curtains drawn:
The kind of drowsy weather that you only want to sleep.
And when you feel most desolate, most awkward, and most bored,
You hear outside the window once again the crying cuckoo.

15.

In idleness I raise the lamp and read "The Cypress Boat,"
The window filled with crickets chirping and the cold of autumn.
How often did I, when preparing for the orphan's lessons,
Forget how late it was at night, how low the moon had sunk!

16.

The face reflected in the mirror now would only hurt me—
The eyebrow-brush I didn't use, not caring for makeup.
To no avail I had been left with these heart-rending tears:
Crab apples bloom when they are shed in front of autumn steps.

17.

My heart grew even colder when the year again turned cold:
A bronze jar dripped to pieces as the water clock fell silent.[19]
I set aside what filled my heart and thought about this house:
An orphan son, a freezing yard—my tears would never dry.

18.

Unlike Meng Liang I had no chance to soar and fly together,[20]
So springtime flower, autumn moon would hurt me in my guts.
As a result, all tastes now are present in my heart,
As I have tasted hot and bitter, sour and sweet in turn.

19.

Who knows how many kinds of bitter suffering and pain—
The swallow and the orioles have just brought up their chicks.
But only when their coat of feathers is full-grown and gleaming,
Their parents have, as they soar high, achieved their life's ambition.

20.

Through twenty years of bitter toil, all problems I have seen,
But now the son has found a wife, the mother too is pleased.
How often did the moon of olden times, there in the window,
Shine on a chilly, cheerless life, and on what poverty?

Memories of the Past, Two Poems

1\.

On Xiao and Xiang our light boat sailed—the final month of spring;
And as we traveled I would chant—unfailing inspiration!
I still remember how one moonlit night on Dongting Lake
I watched the flying crows while leaning out the cabin's window.

2\.

Teacher and pupil—tears of parting, shed upon the bridge:
These even after twenty years I still can not forget.
And how I envy in late autumn geese at heaven's edge
That make each year one time the journey to Hengyang.

An Intercalary Seventh Night, Two Poems Written in Jest[21]

1\.

The magpies build their bridge again high up in the blue heavens:
Oxherd and Weaving Maiden cross the bridge once more.
Meeting like this now for one hundred twenty thousand years—
Who knows how often they enjoyed a night like this?

2\.

O how I hate the many separations in this life!
Reunion and dispersal: all are always fixed by fate.
Oxherd and Weaving Maiden are in luck this year:
They meet again after one single month of separation.

Lamenting the Fall of Yangzhou[22]

For wealth and luxury it has been famed since ancient times,
I too once used to roam across its bridges, twenty-four!
In days bygone the misty flowers charmed the painted boats;
But ruined rubble now surrounds the singsong houses there.
It stabs my heart, how past events have all become a dream,
And in a blink this floating light again is final autumn.
How sad it is to think that on the road by Flat Hill Hall
The fighting has gone on for years—it fills the heart with grief!

From *Moved When Pawning My Clothes; for Ji'er. Two Poems*[23]

2.

I now have pawned my new coat and I also pawned my old one,
And I recite short verses to dispel my gloomy sorrow.
"Eventually one finds in books a thousand sacks of grain":[24]
My son, you'll have to study hard, search every nook and cranny!

On My Fortieth Birthday

How quickly spent, those years and months, betraying spring and fall!
The brilliant light of forty years has chased the flowing stream.
But my proud bones still love to ask the plum to be my friend;
My empty heart prefers to have bamboo as her companion.
Running this house I've long accumulated red salt problems,[25]
Which in the mirror newly have increased my white hair worries.
What can be done? I deeply sigh, feel pity for myself—
Follow the times, accept your fate—what sorrow can there be?

Self-Consolation

Success and failure are at birth determined:
What can one do about one's life on earth?
As far as I can see toward the horizon
The fragrant grasses flourish green and dark.
A somber sorrow rises from inside me;
But I voice strong emotions in a song:
Accept your fate and you'll be filled with joy—
Why should I sigh about the fleeting waves?

Sleepless on a Winter Night

The night is still: I hear the drums[26] resound;
A fading candle shows one bean of fire.
My deepest feelings follow fleeting streams;
My body most resembles floating flotsam.
The moon pierces the window with chill beams;
With freezing noise a storm takes down the leaves.
Beset with sorrows I cannot find sleep—
A lonely honking goose at heaven's edge.

13

The Modest Pursuit of a Minor Way

Duomin Huiru

DUOMIN HUIRU WAS A MANCHU WOMAN OF THE XITALA CLAN. She was married to the Manchu official Song-chun, who passed the metropolitan examinations in 1869, and in 1889 succeeded the famous statesman Li Hongzhang (1823–1901) as director-general of grain transport after having served earlier in places as far apart as Nanjing, Taiyuan, Baoding, and Qinghe. Upon Duomin Huiru's death, her poems were collected and published by her son Bao-kang, who also provided a postface:

Postface

> My late mother, while still alive, once said, "Poetry is a minor pursuit for men of learning and high dignitaries. It is not something that holds a high position in a woman's tasks. If you practice it, it is not easy to become skilled. Even if you are skilled, your works will not necessarily be transmitted. Even if your works are transmitted, it will only be a few stanzas, which are placed together with monks and priests.[1] Only in one or two cases out of hundreds and thousands do complete collections circulate in this world." For this reason she threw away her poems as soon as she had finished a draft, or hid them and did not show them to others. Even those such as I who waited on her from early till late did not often see them.
>
> Only after my late mother had passed away did we find collections of autographs in her boxes for a certain number of poems. I wanted to have them printed so as to publish them, but I was afraid that I would in that way go against my late mother's intention. But if I kept them hidden and did not publicize them, my crime would be even greater. My father said, "This was your mother's favorite practice, and it is all that is left of her. So it is

your responsibility to collect them and print them." I thereupon had them printed, and respectfully made the above record.

Respectfully written by her son Bao-kang

The collection comes with a preface by Liu Keyi (d. 1900), who passed the metropolitan examinations in 1892. He was a well-known poet and served in the Hanlin Academy, going on to become one of the first professors at Peking University, but his preface is mostly in praise of Bao-kang.[2]

Duomin Huiru may have expressed her feelings about poetry in modest terms, but her husband's comments as quoted by her son reveal that she took her writing activities very seriously. Many of her poems describe the scenes she encountered while traveling with her husband to his various posts all over China. Her collection also contains two poems inscribed on the poetry collections of other women writers. In one poem, titled "Discussing Poetry with My Female Disciple Sufang" (quoted in this volume's introduction), Duomin Huiru argues that what matters is not imitation of the style of the poets of the Tang or the Song, but the direct expression of emotions.[3]

DUOMIN HUIRU

Sitting Late in Green Stream Pavilion

Between the evening hills returning sunlight:
This scenery expands so wide and far!
I sit and watch and love the somber woods—
A freezing bird returning late, alone.

A Spring Walk in Spoon Garden[4]

The nine-fold curving springtime banks and then the sunrise clouds—
Around the house the freezing birds that wake me from my dreams.
Still here and there a hazy mist on paths with remnant snow:
Despite the cold and all alone I pluck a sprig of plum.

The Fifteenth of the Third Month

The color of the night as cool as water:
The blossoms of the apricot are freezing.
Poetry's demon leads me by a string

To make the rounds of winding balustrades.
My clothes feel thin just like they do in fall;
We watch the moon together through a window.
From what the little servant girl is saying,
She too seems saddened by spring's wreck.

From *Leaving the Capital; Impromptu Poems*

1.

Transporting dreams, a light cart leaves the phoenix city,
Lightly the morning breeze oft touches a traveler's clothes.
Cooking smoke from some farm: we see the breakfasts brought;
Shade of a hat as a whip is cracked: hurrying on at clear-sky noon.
The color of grass that halfway hides the distant road;
Blossoming branches, bending down, scoff at our long march.
It's more than two thousand miles to the River's Southland,[5]
And we've barely finished the first stretch south of Beijing.

At Jining, on Our Boat

This far and distant watery land, stretching thousands of miles:
My dreams pursue the freezing clouds crossing the river's flow.
An easterly wind, so rain and sleet come drizzling down at dawn—
A single leaf scuttles back and forth amidst a soaking mist.

Suffering from the Heat

Lotuses in the pond send us a whiff of fragrance;
The dew on seats is judged an imperceptible cool.
Returning birds hurry toward the lofty trees, and
Silent flowers are a bright show in the setting sun.
The mold inside attacks the worm-eaten books;
Cnidium loved by snakes spreads its tender stalks.
To my sorrow I have no clue how to avoid this heat—
There's no recipe to be found for ice and snow.

The Artificial Hill

Stones from a somber wood were here amassed,
And then piled up to form some rising peaks.
High buildings now are hidden by their curves;
Flowering trees provide their ample shade.
The morning dew moistens the dark-green moss,

The setting sun hangs from a verdant pine.
When I look back I see below the hill
The pond, one vast expanse of limpid water.

On the Road Past Haidian

1.

I left the city on a westward journey—
Oh how we hurry on this springtime trip!
The flowers blossom as the Third Month ends;
All air is scented by the waves of wheat.
Encircling fields the mountain mists are blue;
Around the village grass and trees turn darker.
The softest breeze is blowing oh so gently;
I turn my head—again the setting sun.

2.

My sleeves are touched by soaking emerald,
As glowing mountains are stretched out in curves:
The road starts winding once the woods begin,
And people seem to travel in a mirror.
A shallow stream leaks from a waterfall,
And ancient trees support a lofty bridge.
Poetic innards match the drum and fife;
I hear the oriole—a hundred trills!

From Numinous Light Monastery to Secret Demon Cliff

The carrying chair progresses like a snake:
So I arrive here halfway up the mountain.
It is one peak and then again one peak,
Which, clad in green, now bow, now rise again.
When broad, the path is flatter than one's palm;
Where steep, the space will barely hold a heel.
One moment we arrive inside the clouds,
One moment we go through a deep ravine.
The road around the Secret Demon Cliff
Is even more a row of rocky ledges.
They seem to be competing with the sky:
These many peaks here are beyond description!
When I look down, the city and the suburbs

Are all arrayed like screens and little desks.
I pour some wine and tell the mountain god:
My travels here are really not yet done!

From *Impromptu Poems from the Western Garden; Shown to My Son Kang and Others*

2.

I teach my girl to sort the silks
    And diligently embroider their Buddhas;
I tell my son to grasp his brush
    And correct his most recent poem.
Our little Yan (*my infant daughter Baoyan*), still a toddler,
    Has no work assignment at all,
So she gathers flower petals
    And puts them in an inkstone's pond.

14

A Poet from the Homeland

Lady Husihali

THE MANCHUS WHO HAD MOVED INSIDE THE GREAT WALL after 1644 considered Beijing their home, and the women poets discussed so far spent all or part of their lives there. Over the course of decades, Manchus who had been settled in garrisons elsewhere came to see those locales as their hometown. Records from the end of the nineteenth century mention Manchu women poets from Hangzhou, but their collections appear to have been lost. Some Manchus, however, remained in Manchuria, guarding the Manchu homeland and serving in the government bureaus of the secondary Qing capital at Shenyang (Shengjing, Mukden). Lady Husihali was born in one such family, and while her husband and eldest son visited Beijing on occasion, she most likely never visited that city throughout her well-documented life. Until she followed her husband to Jiangxi much later, she spent her life in various places on the Liaodong Peninsula and in Shenyang.[1]

Lady Husihali was not only a very prolific poet, she also was a very precocious one. Her two collections, *Small Drafts from Leisure after Needlework* (Xiuyu xiaocao) and *A Record of Accompanying My Husband to His Official Posting in Jiangxi* (Jiangyou suihuan jishi), are both arranged chronologically year by year. The earliest poems in the first collection date from 1858, when she was only eleven (by Chinese count, so likely one year younger). Starting from that year we have poems from almost every year of her life. Many poems come with detailed prefaces that provide more details on her circumstances. Her first teachers were her mother and her uncle. Her father was a lowly official, who never advanced beyond the rank of clerk. Her mother died when she was a teenager, after which her maternal relatives took her in. A childless uncle later paid for her dowry. Her father, we learn from a later poem, spent his money recklessly and married a second wife who developed mental problems.[2]

Lady Husihali's husband, Hui-ge (also known as Shitang; ca. 1845–ca. 1910), hailed from a local family as well. Like her father, he started out as a clerk in one of the government departments in Shenyang, but his career proceeded smoothly as he was repeatedly promoted. He may well have been indebted to his father, A-er-jing-a, who was rising in rank in the military in these years, as we learn from his short biography in the local gazetteer of Liaoyang:

> A-er-jing-a had the surname Gua'erjia and belonged to the Manzhou Bordered Red Banner. His ancestors followed the conquest starting out from Changbai, and were garrisoned in Liaoyang. They settled to the north of the city in Zhongbao where the family continued to live. Starting out from the rank of cavalry lieutenant, A-er-jing-a was eventually promoted to the position of post commandant for Xiongyue and assistant commandant for Jinzhou. For his merits during the battle of Sanzuota he was awarded the privilege of wearing the peacock feather. He was listed for appointment as vice commander-in-chief. He had two sons: Hui-ge and De-yong.[3]

While Hui-ge's career developed, the couple had a number of children. The oldest son, Rong-yin, survived, but in 1877 a younger son died at the age of six, and for a number of years the works composed by the grief-struck mother were poems lamenting her darling. Only in the 1880s did she return to other topics, in many poems describing herself as devoting her time to study and writing. In the early 1890s she started to suffer from deafness.

In 1893, Lady Husihali's husband Hui-ge was appointed as prefect of Yuanzhou in the western part of Jiangxi. The couple traveled first by steamboat from Niuzhuang to Shanghai, stayed for more than a month in Shanghai taking in the sights, and then traveled on by boat to Yuanzhou. Here, and in later postings as prefect, Hui-ge distinguished himself as a capable administrator:

> Hui-ge's style name was Shitang. Starting out as a clerk he reached after three promotions the rank of director. He subsequently served as prefect of Yuanzhou in Jiangxi, of Puzhou in Shanxi, of Jiaxing and Quzhou in Zhejiang, and of Pingyang in Shanxi. During his term in Yuanzhou he defeated the Eight Trigrams Sect and was allowed to wear on his cap the peacock feather of the second class. He was an expectant circuit intendant. At the age of sixty-five he died in Gaoyou in Jiangsu. His son Rong-yin was an expectant district magistrate.[4]

Hui-ge not only dealt with local banditry and other social problems through military means, but also through poetry, composing moral songs that he had printed and distributed.[5] He made a good impression on the local population and his superiors by the way he handled a severe drought that hit Yuanzhou in 1895. He not only prayed for rain, as was expected of officials in such cases, but also took more practical measures:

> Hui-ge's social name was Shitang. He was a bannerman of the Gua'erjia lineage. In the winter of the year *kuisi* [1893] he was promoted from his post in one of the departments to prefect of Yuanzhou. His character was honest and daring and in his administration he was strict and clear. As soon as he stepped down from his carriage, he made it his task to rectify men's hearts and improve the local customs. He especially strictly prohibited gambling. Each night he would personally go out for an inspection and make the rounds. The common people all changed their behavior. He also composed songs and ditties to instruct the people in loyalty and honesty, filial piety and brotherly love. In the year *yiwei* [1895] when the harvest failed because of a terrible drought throughout Jiangxi, he urged the gentry and the merchants and all rich people to buy grain and sell it at equitable prices. As a result the famine of the next year did not bring too much damage.[6]

Lady Husihali was fascinated by the ritual and practical aspects of her husband's function as prefect. When her husband wrote his poems warning against gambling and whoring, she composed a set of twelve eight-line poems instructing the local female population in morality. And when her husband prayed for rain, Lady Husihali joined her prayers to his by setting up an altar in the inner apartment, as we learn from one of the prefaces to her collection by a certain Wen Huacheng:[7]

> Poetry is the voice of the heart. It is just like playing the zither: when you are at peace, the sound is mild; when you are agitated, the sound is strident. That is why its way with respect to the inner chambers gives highest priority to natural emotions. This applied already to Xie Lingyun and Bao Linghui in ancient times.[8] But among the works that have been transmitted, the majority chant of moonlight and breeze. You will not really find that many that are concerned with moral education and follow in the footsteps of Ban Zhao to write books that provide instruction.[9]
>
> I, Huacheng, am shallow and ignorant and was without any reason invited by the prefect Lord Hui to preside over explanation sessions.[10] I have long been impressed by his teaching by personal example and his teaching by words. This summer, in the Fifth Month, we suffered from a drought. At midnight His Lordship, barefooted and in tears, prayed to the gods, asking them to save

the people's lives. Her Ladyship had established an altar in the inner apartments; she observed the fast and purified herself, and before the morning was announced she would kowtow and call on Heaven, and she would not rest even in the slightest until the sun had gone down. This they continued to do for a ten-day period, when sweet rains came down profusely and the grains completely revived. The people of the prefecture happily praised His Lordship's virtue and also included Her Ladyship.

In this way I was well acquainted with Her Ladyship's moral stature but I did not yet know that she also was an expert poet. Later, His Lordship produced poems for educating the people, which he showed to me. Appended to these were some poems of instructions for the inner quarters by Her Ladyship. Her sharp words and loving intention seemed to be from the same hand as the works of His Lordship. If you would place them in the *Precepts for My Daughters* of Ban Zhao, they would make up for the deficiencies of that work. I very much wanted to see all of her works but it would not be proper to ask for them, but it so happened that His Lordship asked me for a preface. So finally I had the privilege of reading the complete collection. The meanings of her poems are strict and their wording is brilliant. When I had recited them several times I could readily imagine the stillness of her heart and the mildness of her voice. They approached the intent of the Sweet Zither.[11]

Her Ladyship was the descendant of an illustrious family. From her earliest youth she was addicted to reciting and chanting, never letting go during her several decades of wifely duties. She moreover grew up in the Complementary Capital and repeatedly followed her elders to their official postings. She widely observed famous mountains and large rivers. That is why her bosom became wide and large, and her words were clear and florid. But her main intent was to provide people with a mental recipe for doing good. In this she was very similar to Ban Zhao. How could Xie Daoyun and Bao Linghui be mentioned in one breath?

I have yet another comment. When in the past people had established order and achieved merit, this would find expression in songs. This is why one could observe the morals of the people by collecting their poems. From the poems recited one could deduce the quality of the administration of a country. Now Her Ladyship's poems are a means by which she manifested her domestic order to aid His Lordship. From there one can know His Lordship's poems. And one can even know His Lordship's administration.

Written in the First Month of summer of the twenty-third year (a *bingshen* year) [1896] of the Guangxu reign period by Wen Huacheng of Zhaoping

Lady Husihali most likely died late in 1895.[12] From another preface, dated 1896, we learn that Hui-ge had ordered his son Rong-yin to prepare her collected poems for publication. Following a woodblock printed edition of 1896, the collection was reprinted lithographically in Shanghai in 1903.

Lady Husihali may have been a mediocre poet at best in most of her works, but her interests ranged widely. She wrote not only about her own family, but also about social issues like opium smoking. We find poems on the famous novel *Dream of the Red Chamber* alongside poems on local customs and beliefs. While she enjoys her new life as the wife of a prefect, she is also worried by Japan's destructive inroads in Manchuria in 1894. She describes earthquakes and steamboats, and is impressed by Shenyang and Shanghai. She writes about her little kitten as well as the Bodhisattva Guanyin.

LADY HUSIHALI

Poems from *Small Drafts from Leisure after Needlework*

1858

New Year's Day, an Improvisation

Now time returns to the First Month, it is a lucky moment:
Firecrackers are exploding and all things today are new.
The streets are filled by bustling crowds in carriages, on horseback—
All people on their way to wish their friends a happy year.

The Little Cat

Most passionate of all creation is my little cat:
It leaps onto the fence trying to catch the drifting petals.
It feels unhappy when its food is lacking fish and shrimp;
Its eyes betray when it observes approaching *zi* and *wu*.[13]
Here on the couch it sleeps and snores, dozing throughout the day;
Next to the hole it sits in silence when it's catching mice.
But when in trees the birds are loudly fighting over nests,
It reaches in one single jump the highest branch of all.

1859

From *On Divine Immortals*

1.

Freed from attachments to this world for myriads of years;
Moving on clouds, riding on cranes, ascending to the heavens.
When gazing downward from the highest peak on Penglai Island,[14]
They only wish that each of us will quickly be enlightened.

From *On Ghosts*

3.

Their lifetime is but bitter toil for glory and for profit;
But when they die it all turns out to be a single dream.
Only upon arrival down below are souls enlightened
And realize that sins and merits get their just reward.

1860

From *Emotions on Reading* Dream of the Red Chamber

2.

The single dream of these red chambers wakes up the deluded:
Don't take the field of fame and profit for the final truth.
Those dozen beauties—golden hairpins—now have disappeared:
They are but heaps of sun-bleached bones hidden by fragrant dust.

4.

Illusion's realm in vain resulted in one deep attachment:
The strange romance of the red chambers will be told forever:
She spent her life in shedding tears because of love and longing
And still her soul left for the paradise of parting's pain.[15]

The Earthquake

It took place in the fourth watch of the night of the twenty-fourth day of the Eighth Month, in Gaizhou, in the tenth year of the Xianfeng reign period [1860].

Because the energy of *qian* and *kun* went in reverse,[16]
It brought about an earthquake that was roaring like the thunder.
A single moment of great shaking scared a thousand miles;

It was the end of the Eighth Month, the fourth watch of the night.
No simple dwelling could support this: roofs came crashing down;
It was the poor who were alas the first to lose their lives.
But how ridiculous are all those country simpletons
Who spread the rumor that the giant turtle blinked an eye.[17]

Self-Characterization

From birth I lack all talent but I do not know myself;
In vain I ply the brush and wrack my brain.
Even the winter plum is apt to give me inspiration:
One twig is blooming right before my window.

1868

Returning from Xiongyue to Shenyang[18]

In the year *maochen* [1868] of the Tongzhi reign period, my husband, Shitang, was appointed as clerk in the Ministry of Finance, so he went to the capital to take up his position. This was in the Third Month, when the soaked roads made travel difficult, so I improvised a regulated poem.

The carts and horses wind their way, returning to our hometown:
Only today I realize that travel may be tough.
The blustering storms blow wildly through the grasses on the field;
The greening willows are too weak to wear this springtime cold.
The dust on travel jackets is still there when wiped away;
No sun can dry the wet and muddy surface of the road.
At such a time you had to leave your parents and return—
"We wish you lucky man a safe and pleasant journey!"

Bamboo Branch Lyrics on Opium Smoking[19]

1.

One lamp that has been finely wrought, one plate that's square in shape;
Bamboo was used to make the pipe—why is it called a gun?[20]
The weapon is concealed inside so people will not notice,
But once you start to smoke, your inner organs all decay.

2.

Before the lamp they lie at ease, a pleasure without limit;
They hold the long gun in their hands, their mouths puff out the smoke.

When they inhale, when they exhale, they're truly satisfied—
Never develop, I beseech you, this addiction.

3.
They're living in a haze and do not know the time of year;
Stretched out like dead before the lamp they're roaming in their dreams.
They mix up break of dawn and dusk, neglect their needlework,
And when the sun is setting, they sit down to do their hair.

4.
It is no sleep, it is no illness, but they lie in bed
And lazily observe their lamp, that single speck of red.
With double energy they keep on talking through the night
But when the sun stands high at noon their mind is all a haze.

5.
By smoking on their cushion they enjoy it even better;
The room is filled by clouds of smoke that smell like fragrant orchids.
All thoughts of fame and profit have been left behind completely:
They look like fools, they look like drunks, they're such a sorry sight!

6.
How are they different in shape from beasts that spit out smoke?[21]
Stretched out there on their couch they have a mind that's empty.
Yet they insist this is the salve that cures all their disease—
Who realizes it will shorten their apportioned lifespan?

7.
Who is the person who designed this trap that is so strange?
Once people have been sucked inside, there's none who can escape!
Your lively energy in speaking up in your defense
Is all due to the clouds of smoke that fill your empty stomach.

8.
In recent times more and more people start to take this drug,
But it's the drug that takes the people and it shows no mercy.
As soon as one goes down this road, one never will wake up
And all one's vital energy will be completely wasted.

In Praise of the Complementary Capital

Divinely blessed this River Shen: a home of emperors;
Surrounded by both seas and hills: an energy that lasts.
The bannermen and common people live in their own wards;
The bureaucrats and officers have their divided tasks.
   A thousand miles link this location to a pair of islands;[22]
The city wall with its eight gates follows the four directions.
Most beautiful are the high buildings of the golden dragon:
A heaven-sent inheritance that will endure forever!

1871

For My Younger Brother Xin-shao-yuan on the Occasion of My Mother's Burial

My younger brother was adopted by my parents at the age of thirteen as their heir. Later the family became exceedingly poor. Still, he made sure to go to Xiaxiahe to bury our mother near the ancestral graves. This was in the Eleventh Month of the tenth year of the Tongzhi reign period [1871]. Filled with emotions on account of this I wrote these poems for him.

1.

You went to the ancestral graves while traveling at night,
You never could forget the love with which you had been raised.
Now I believe that filial sons are found in poorest homes;
A good child does not have to be his mother's baby boy.

2.

The greatest virtue since all times is filial piety:
How laudable that you escorted our dear mother's coffin.
On ancient roads late in the day you had to find an inn;
At shabby hamlets aging trees were locked in somber mists.
   Near winding streams the narrow ledges seemed without a road;
The weirdest rocks and strangest peaks rose high, piercing the sky.
But if one is sincere at heart, the gods are bound to help,
So be assured that in the future you will be rewarded.

1875

Teaching My Eldest Daughter Her Reading Lessons at the Window

When you get up at break of dawn, when you have combed your hair,
It's time to memorize some lines of text below the window.
When practicing arithmetic one has to be precise,
When copying one's characters one must be circumspect.
  Refrain from reading songs and lyrics so your heart stays pure;
Recite the odes repeatedly and let their flavor grow.
Each moment's worth a thousand gold, so cherish every minute:
Recite your lessons loud and clear until the sunlight fades.

1877

From *Lamenting My Deceased Son San-yin*

My son was six years old and studying the books with a teacher. In his intelligence he surpassed all others. Suddenly he was infected by a winter epidemic and he died within two days. This happened in the middle decade of the Tenth Month of the third year of the Guangxu reign period [1877].

2.

Infected by a sudden illness that was hard to cure
He still recited poems with his final failing breath.
From now on he and I will be forever separated,
I wait for him but when will be the day of his return?
  The only time to meet with him will be in midnight dreams;
This bitter pain cannot dissolve its thousand kinds of longing.
The many things of these six years have all become the past
And filled with feelings I shed tears below the full round moon.

From *Emotions While Lamenting My Son*

2.

Diseased for one day and a half, and then he passed away:
These six years now in truth resemble just one single dream.
But still I call to mind his voice and face—but all in vain:
Where do I find on the nine plains my little darling boy?

4.

The withered grass, the setting sun, the single earthen mound:
The paper cash is burned to ashes and my tears flow freely.
My silly heart is still convinced my baby is around—
Where may the little boy now be, where is he to be found?

5.

The pearl has sunk, the jade is shattered: sadness without end;
All things come down to this one single little mound of earth.
I have collected all his books and burned them in a fire:
Can he still read them and recite them like he did alive?

1880

On Myself

One half of me is without work, one half is busy.
When I'm depressed I grasp my brush and ask Blue Heaven:
You have me all day long in vain recite my verses
But to my shame I lack the skills to aid the world.

An Idle Chant

My brush and ink and classic books are spread out on the couch:
For whom am I in such a hurry, busy all day long?
My love for flowers is an obsession as I plant so many;
I have no bond with alcohol—don't dare to take a sip.
  When reading histories I like the pre-Han writings;
In writing verse I hate what comes after the Tang.
When idly I pick up a book, but rarely understand it,
And seated at the window I recite some of the *Odes*.

1882

Hua Mulan[23]

For twelve years serving as a soldier she replaced her father
And in the army no one knew she was a pretty girl.
A sword hung from her willow waist and spat out a cold brilliance;
With jade-white arms she drew the bow as round as the full moon.
  She was not given a high office as she was a woman;
Escorted back to her old town she knelt before her parents.

This hero in the end turned out to be a tender female:
She put to shame the men who lacked her filial sense of duty.

1892

Improvisations While Overcome by Depression Because of My Deafness

1.

I'm sitting here all filled with gloom and don't know what to do:
Before my old disease is cured, a new complaint is here.
It's not the fault of my physician that he lacks a drug—
It's due to my exhausted mind and to my many worries.

2.

Whenever people talk to me I act as if I'm simple:
It seems as if I'm meditating, way off in a trance.
But day and night a roaring rumble fills my mind with gloom—
Who understands the racket in my ears?

A Song on My Deafness

All of a sudden deaf in both my ears—it's way too cruel:
When people talk it is a mumbling that I fail to grasp.
But in my ears the sounds of nature will reverberate
As fiercely as a thunderstorm or as the crashing waves.
   Or softly like a flute that's played without a distinct tune—
And then again it's like a gong that's someplace loudly rung.
My heart unable to find peace, my soul bereft of quiet,
I feel depressed and am beset by thousands of vexations.
   It may not be a stabbing pain but still it is a nuisance
And even the best medicine will not achieve a cure.
But there's no point to fight with fate over each thing that happens
And in a misty haze I'll spend the years that still remain.

1893

Sent to My Eldest Son, Rong-yin

At that time he was in the capital for the provincial examination, while I was about to follow my husband to his posting in Jiangxi. I sent him this letter just before leaving.

1.

You, son, are in the capital, your mother leaves her birthplace:
By streams and mountains separated and a long, long road.
Why don't we both in dreams return to our old hometown?
Then we can be together in one hall and talk at will.

2.

Alas, most bitter is the separation from one's own:
The capital and southern Jiangxi are so far apart!
When will the thousand branches all return to the one root?
Parting and meeting in this life resemble floating clouds.

Poems from *A Record of Accompanying My Husband to His Official Posting in Jiangxi*

From *Impressions on a Steamboat*

On the eleventh day of the Eighth Month we boarded the boat at Niuzhuang.

1.

The sounds of winds, the sounds of waves: they cannot be distinguished;
The black smoke billows forth and frees the whole ship from its weight.
In moving it does not require the labor of the boatmen:
Now I believe the marvelous construction of the steamboat!

2.

The black smoke rises straight into the cover of white clouds;
The steamboat moves across the sea but does not use a sail.
Yet on the surface of the main it cuts a path through waves
As if it crashed the billows through the force of a great storm.

3.

Unbounded is my view until the water meets the sky;
The engine's roar is like the raging of a seething cauldron.
Here at this spot we are beyond the common world of dust;
The huge expanse of *qian* and *kun* is all too true indeed!

4.

The steamboat cuts through this expanse of water as if flying;
One clearly hears the engine's roar, the crashing of the waves.

Open the porthole and one sees a vista without end
Of the blue sea, of the clear sky, and of white floating clouds.

Shanghai Impressions

From all directions congregating: travelers galore!
The wealth and splendor of Shanghai do make it quite a sight.
When night arrives the lamps are lit: the theaters are opened;
Dazzling the eyes, the foreign buildings range along the sky.
Electric bulbs are strung up high: their light is without limit;
From everywhere music and song resound without a pause.
And best of all, the streets are smooth so carriages run fast
And come and go, I notice, without raising any dust.

Shanghai Bamboo Branch Lyrics

1.
Along the street all one observes is only wealth and splendor;
The light of the electric lamps shines on ten thousand houses.
Now human voices fill the air, and carriages the streets:
Here people only come to life when deepest night has fallen.

2.
The oriental rickshaws[24] race with an unending racket;
When night has fallen even women roam along the streets.
One finds here little of the hallowed culture of the Classics:
The people only care here for great pleasure without worry.

3.
The lamps shine bright and so this city never knows the night:
The pleasure seekers come and go; the streets are filled with crowds.
The noise of rickshaws shakes your ears, the sounds of songs are seething:
This is one long-term Lantern Festival in years of peace.[25]

4.
There is no single place in Shanghai that's not wealth and splendor:
The theaters and sing-song houses number in the thousands!
The arias and melodies are all the latest tunes
And courtesans perform their songs while strumming on a lute.

5\.
Even at night the sounds of lutes have not yet fallen silent
And the carousal still continues in the sing-song houses.
But luxury that is excessive cannot last forever—
The sea, the moon, the creek, the clouds: a sorrow without bounds!

6\.
Prosperity: in past and present how long will it last?
The moon that's full is bound to wane: such is the rule always.
So do not say that wealth and splendor are to be admired;
But realize that only simple honesty endures.

Improvised When Departing from Shanghai on the River Steamer

1\.
When we arrived it was mid-autumn, now it is late fall,
More than a month we stayed and tarried here in a hotel.
Today we once again become two "drifters on a raft"
And roam as far as the horizon, edge of sea and sky!

2\.
Departing here we move still farther from our land of birth;
Once on the boat it is as if we left the common bustle.
We do not know where we will go or when we will return—
How different we are from tides that are the same each day.

3\.
Two months have passed already now I count the time that's gone,
And setting out we once again are friends with clouds and streams.
This journey to my husband's post became a Handan dream:
What day will be the year the yellow millet will be cooked?[26]

4\.
Who now will sing a parting song when we pursue our journey?
It may not be our hometown here but parting's pain is greater.
The streams are green, the hills are gray: they open a new vista—
The region of the Yangzi River sports fine mists and waves.

From *Improvised Poems on Moving into the Yuanzhou Prefecture*

We moved in during the Tenth Month of the nineteenth year [1893]

1.

Proliferating mosses grow throughout the corridors
And broken tiles and piles of rubble damage quiet rooms.
Both hall and study are quite simple without much adornment
But everywhere throughout the house red lanterns have been raised.

2.

The double gates and massive roof are overgrown by weeds;
The hundred curves of corridors connect to endless places.
I call to mind Yuanzhou's prefecture in its glory days[27]
But now at present half the buildings have collapsed in ruin.

3.

The courtyard trees grow close together, offering green shade;
One often hears the mountain birds that spit out lucid notes.
The high hall is as quiet as a meditation cell,
So who arrives here must desire to sit and sink in stillness.

4.

From the beginning of winter it rained incessantly.

The somber clouds will never break and float below the sky;
The chilly air is quite oppressive even at one's desk.
The midnight rain outside the window, bleak and desolate,
Drips vainly on the courtyard steps as if it was late fall.

From *Evening Prospect from the Eastern Ridge*

Near the small courtyard to the east of the prefectural office is an earthen hill from which one has a wide view. When I went there for a walk with our children, our youngest daughter suddenly asked: "Can you see our hometown when you climb to the top?" I thereupon improvised these poems.

1.

When walking on the Eastern Ridge we lift our heads and gaze:
The verdant mountains far and near reflect the setting sun.

The one word of our infant daughter moves us all to sighs:
"Will we there on the highest spot then see our hometown too?"

1894

From *In Yuanzhou during the Spring Rains the Skies Will Not Clear for Many Days, So I Wrote This as a Record*

1.

The somber clouds here last for months—what can one do about it?
They don't allow a single speck of balmy sun to pass.
The earth may have returned to spring, but heaven still is cold;
The winds do not yet have the strength to blow away the rains.
  The roads are overgrown by moss which makes for slipp'ry going;
The humid air invades the body so one is not well.
One only feels much better when the sun comes through a little
And hears birds on the branches that then sing their songs.

Welcoming the Prefectural God of Walls and Moats

The god goes out on an inspection tour each year on the twenty-seventh day of the Fifth Month.

1.

The many gates, one after one, have all been fully opened;
The canons roar and a loud voice reports a guest's arrival.
It is as if a high official visits the prefecture,
But like a Bodhisattva he is seated on a lotus.
  A dragon robe, a belt of jade: his cap and gown antique;
To drums and pipes, with flags and banners the god's chair returns.
The two of them, one yin, one yang, were both appointed here—
Is it a karmic bond that fates this meeting far from home?

2.

The flags and banners line the road to greet the city god;
He passes through the double gates and comes into the hall.
The fame of his divinity is truly great and awesome;
Now who on earth can say that yin and yang are far apart?
  He pays a visit just as if renewing an old friendship;

He is received with all due honor: incense scents his way.
When the protectors of the people come outside together,
The common crowd below the steps kneels down in great confusion.

From *I Heard That Several Cities South of Fengtian Had Been Lost and Was Therefore Filled by Emotion*

1.

The long-haired rebels at Gold Hilltops[28] raged for many years:
How to be pitied are the people in that struggle killed!
But southern provinces had barely been reduced to order,
Now eastern ocean savage demons start the fires of war.
  Our soldiers are afraid to fight, the officers are useless,
While the barbarians advance—their power is immense.
When I look north, I wonder when this warfare will subside;
Time and again I scratch my head and call out to Blue Heaven!

From *Written While Depressed*

Because the Japanese were wreaking havoc in the border regions.

1.

My ears are filled with a loud racket, an unending noise:
It's partly due to an old illness, partly to new worries.
The Japanese, I hear so often, penetrate the border:
Our relatives, our hometown too, these occupy my mind.

2.

Out of the blue, all of the sudden has this warfare started.
Alas, it is impossible to hear about our hometown.
Whenever I return a letter, feelings are too strong:
The characters are not as many as the teardrop stains.

8.

Year after year the troops were trained but it was all in vain:
The soldiers of the enemy are riding on the wind!
Alas for all the favors that the dynasty bestowed:
Our officers don't do a thing and have no single plan.

At Night I Dreamed That the Bodhisattva Manifested Herself amidst Ten Thousands Rays of Gold and Imparted Me Many Startling Words[29]

This happened on the sixteenth of the winter month of the *jiawu* year [1894]. When I awoke I still seemed to see her before my eyes, so I wrote these poems as a record.

1.

Amidst ten thousand rays of gold appeared her golden body:
I met the Buddha in a dream as proof of former karma.
A single word disclosed the truth and so I was enlightened;
Now I call out to all those people who are still deluded.

2.

It may have been a vision but a miracle it was:
In no way any different from the famous Handan dream!
She showed herself to preach the law: to emptiness enlightened;
The words she taught I still remember, grateful for her mercy.

1895

From *Hoping for Rain*

In the Fifth Month of the *yiwei* year [1895] of the Guangxu reign period, we were hit by a drought, so Shitang as prefect prayed for rain. Moved by this I wrote these poems.

1.

Whenever we see floating clouds, they pass and pass again.
Why does Blue Heaven visit us with this long-lasting drought?
Inside the woods I hear the doves calling repeatedly,
Hoping so much that the next day plenty of rain will fall.

2.

The farmers hope with all their heart but still no sprouts will grow:
The rice fields and the garden pads are scorched by burning suns.
If I would only have the gift to travel with the thunder,
I'd happily among the clouds pour out the gourds of heaven.

From *Rejoicing over Rain*

The prefect had twice set up an altar, but he had not yet brought down a major shower. When he set up an altar for the third time, he dispatched officials to fetch water from the holy spring in the region of Southern Temple (Nan Miao). The next day a sweet rain fell all over the prefecture and the people were very happy. Thereupon I wrote these poems entitled *Rejoicing over Rain* as a record.

1.

The people's livelihood depends on farming and on silk,
A bumper harvest of the grains is every year their hope.
During the drought all the officials prayed for rain together;
The prefect led the civil officials and military officers in praying for rain from early till late.
They kept the fast for ten days long, repeatedly burned incense.
When the prefect had set up an altar, he each day kept the fast and recited the sutras.
So their devotion had the strength to change the mind of heaven;
To fetch the water was a means to satisfy the crowd.
Because they had repeatedly prayed for rain but without bringing down sweet showers, he dispatched officials to the holy spring in the regions of Southern Temple to fetch water from there. The next day it rained all over.
Indeed sweet showers then came down in a sufficient measure
And villagers throughout the fields were grateful to Old Heaven.

From *On Myself*

1.

When nine years old I studied couplets, I was still a child,
My uncle was my teacher and he taught me very well.
I had to my good fortune a strong karmic bond with books:
I loved to read them at all times—but memorized them poorly.

2.

Before I could discriminate my nature was quite simple
But I had a good teacher in the person of my uncle.
And from the age that I was three, my father taught me too—
Alas, my talent failed me and I loved to chant but poems.

3.
I traveled with my father and my in-laws to their postings,
And now I traveled with my husband here to Yuanzhou city.
In all these places I amused myself with writing poems—
As long as one can live at ease, what else should one desire?

From *Twelve Instructions for the Inner Chambers*

1.
Admonishing Women in the Inner Chambers to Maintain Strict Discipline in Order to Complete Womanly Virtue

Recite the *Odes* and learn by heart the "Two Souths" in the Airs:[30]
In past and present all comes down to transformation by virtue.
Respectfully serve your father and mother with utmost filial piety;
Establish accord between sisters-in-law by stressing harmony.
 Be circumspect in speaking, know when to shut your mouth;
Work hard at weaving and spinning, don't resent your poverty.
Rise early, at your toilet table neatly wash your face—
Don't walk around all day with a disheveled head of hair!

2.
Admonishing Women in the Inner Chambers to Exhaust Filial Piety in the Service of Their Parents-in-Law

Men and women have to know that filial piety comes first;
This is the long-transmitted Way to order the family well.
As an infant one obeys one's parents with a respectful heart;
As an adult one's parents-in-law, admiring their experience.
 Simple food will gain their pleasure when served in person;
Medicine will heal their diseases when diligently prepared.
Your children will imitate you if you set an example
And treat you in the same manner until your dying days.

5.
Admonishing Women in the Inner Chambers to Read Books in Order to Understand the Rites and Their Duties

The rites and your duties are clearly expounded in books:
Even in the inner chambers you have to study the Classics.
In the biographies of the chaste and filial are many girls;
Among those in skirts are many who are wise and good.

To follow the rules and norms you must grasp principle.
When you pay attention from page one you'll understand.
Don't read lecherous lyrics or listen to lascivious songs—
Quiet modesty and chaste stillness will make your name.

7.

Admonishing Widows to Maintain Their Chastity to Display Their Lasting Loyalty

A mirror broken, love birds parted: the greatest misery of all—
Because of the oath of the cypress boat one admires the young!
To maintain chastity actually does not depend on rich or poor;
To make up one's mind requires perseverance in suffering.
How shameful was Wenjun's behavior—an eternal regret![31]
Let's remember Lady Fan, acting wisely throughout her life:
As clear as ice, as pure as jade she earned state recognition
Leaving a fine reputation for ten thousands of generations.[32]

11.

Admonishing Women to Accept Poverty and Trust in Fate

All events in this world depend on fate, that's the truth,
So don't complain about poverty, blaming your parents.
Meng Guang lifted the tray, always showing respect;
Madam Huan worked hard at farming because of want.[33]
Those who are wise and filial must seek future results
As riches and glory all have their causes in prior karma:
All your actions and deeds have to conform to principle—
Supporting virtue, Blue Heaven aids those who are good.

12.

Admonishing Women to Attend to Washing and Sewing in Order to Finish the Winter Clothes

If winter clothes are well prepared one can get through the year:
Shake up the old floss once again and make sure it doesn't stick.
If there is much dirt where you're washing, change water often;
If the textile is thin when you're sewing, add some more cotton.
If things are torn or worn, repair them with careful deliberation;
Whether it is cold or warm, the body should feel naturally at ease.

When fine or coarse linen are finished they're fit for the summer;
In all four seasons clothes and shoes should be without any holes.

Postface of *Twelve Instructions for the Inner Chambers*

Ban Zhao wrote her *Precepts for My Daughters* in seven sections, while Song Ruozhao wrote the *Analects for Women* in twelve chapters. Their fine words and pure norms are equal in beauty despite the difference in period, and they have been revered as imperishable rules in past and present. I may not be clever, but from my earliest youth I have received my mother's instruction, and always when reading books and histories I have felt that I learned something. When I grew up, I held dustpan and duster in the Gua'erjia family. Provided with unfailing instructions I preserved an obedient disposition; serving my elders and caring for the young I was always respectful and circumspect, so I would not bring shame on the family.

In the autumn of the *kuisi* year [1893], my husband was appointed as prefect of Yuanzhou. From the moment he arrived at his post, he made every effort to bring about order. He once said: "Customs depend on honesty as their basis, and the administration gives priority to transformation by teaching." So he wrote forty bamboo branch lyrics that warned against whoring and gambling, which he had printed and spread through the villages and distributed for free to the common people, who all were moved by them and improved their behavior. This shows that there are no people who cannot be taught and that it all depends on the teaching by their officials and superiors.

The prefect now has written another twenty-four lyrics on repenting one's mistakes and practicing goodness, because he wishes that each and every one may repent his earlier mistakes so they all might share in a life of comfort and ease. His aim is to bring peace to the people, and his whole administration is infused by that intense desire. Thinking thereupon that order in society should be accompanied by order in the family, I have, disregarding my vulgar coarseness, dashed off twelve pieces of instructions for the inner chambers as admonitions for those women who are not diligent and not filial. How would I be able to contain my joy if these poems would be able to improve morals and change customs—that is my sincere hope.

Written by Husihali from Changbai

ABBREVIATIONS

DMB	Goodrich, L. Carrington, and Chaoying Fang, eds. 1976. *Dictionary of Ming Biography*. 2 vols. New York: Columbia University Press.
ECCP	Hummel, Arthur W., ed. 1943–1944. *Eminent Chinese of the Ch'ing Period (1644–1911)*. 2 vols. Washington, D.C.: United States Government Printing Office.
QSG	Zhao Erxun 趙爾巽, ed. 1976. *Qingshi gao* 清史稿. 48 vols. Beijing: Zhonghua shuju.
QSLZ	Wang Zhonghan 王鍾翰, ed. 1987. *Qingshi liezhuan* 清史列傳. 20 vols. Beijing: Zhonghua shuju.

NOTES

DATES AND NAMES

1 The clan names that end with *jia* derive from Chinese family names that were given a Manchu form when the whole family was reclassified as Manchu, or when a woman from a Han-banner family married into a Manchu family.

INTRODUCTION

1 For a full translation of this preface, see chapter 8.

2 On the role of the Manchu language in Qing history, see Crossley and Rawski (1993) and Elliott (2001a, esp. 290–304).

3 One of the women who had mastered written Manchu was the wife of the famous official Ming-zhu (1635–1708), who herself lived from 1637 to 1695. Another was Lady Geng, the wife of Ming-zhu's son Kui-xu (1674?–1717), who is also said to have been "conversant with the national script."

4 Chang (1997, 165–66).

5 Gao Chunhua (2014); Ho (1998, 281–85); Xiaorong Li (2009); Xiaorong Li (2012, 52–82); Mann (1997, 94–117). Yun Zhu is also often referred to as Wanyan Yun Zhu. A sequel to her anthology, the *Guochao guixiu zhengshi xuji,* was published by her granddaughter Miaolianbao in 1836. This work contained 919 poems by 459 women poets.

6 ECCP, 955–57; Liuxi Meng (2007, 63–76); Schmidt (2008). Yuan Mei was far from the only male teacher to accept female pupils. See Zhong Huiling (2000, 206–57). Yuan Mei's conspicuous support of women's poetry stimulated Zhang Xuecheng (1738–1801) to write his *Fuxue* (Women's study) in which he criticized the fashion of women's poetry he observed around him. See Mann (1992; 1997, 83–94). I have found no explicit references to Zhang's treatise in the works of Naxun Lanbao or any Manchu women writer.

7 ECCP, 717–18.

8 Cai Wan (1695–1755) is the author of a collection of poetry entitled *Yunzhenxuan xiaocao,* which was printed in a very fine edition in 1779. She was the daughter of Cai Yurong (1633–1699). Cai Yurong's father had surrendered to the Manchus in 1642, and the family later belonged to the Chinese Plain White Banner. Cai Yurong held a series of high provincial and metropolitan posts. Cai Wan married Gao Qizhuo (1676–1738), who from 1723 on served either as governor or governor-general in Southern China. See ECCP (734–36); and Hu Wenkai (1985, 731–32).

Gao Jingfang's family belonged to the Chinese Plain Red Banner. Her father Gao Qi reached the rank of governor-general of Zhejiang and Fujian; her husband was a certain Zhang Zongyuan. Her collected works, both *fu* and *shi,* were printed in 1719 as *Hongxuexuan shiwenji.* See Hu Wenkai (1985, 499).

9 Elliot (2001a).

10 Crossley (1999, 281–336).

11 On the privileged and problematical status of the Manchus during the last five decades of the Qing, see Rhoads (2000, 11–69).

12 ECCP, 386–87. Also see the entry in Ho (1998, 52–55). The dominant current understanding is that Gu Taiqing was a granddaughter of Ochang (d. 1755), a nephew of the high Manchu official Ortai (1680–1745), who was posthumously stripped of all his titles in 1755. On that occasion Ochang was allowed to commit suicide (ECCP, 601–3). This would make her a Manchu of the Silin Gioro clan. Gu Taiqing's father survived as a private secretary, and several scholars are convinced that she spent a large part of her youth in the Jiangnan area (it has also been claimed that she hailed from Suzhou). When Yi-hui married her as a concubine, she was registered as a daughter of a soldier surnamed Gu, because Yi-hui as a member of the imperial family was not allowed to marry a member of a "criminal family." See Lu Xingji (2005, "Qianyan," 2). Also see Chen Shuiyun (2005, 104–11). This article provides a survey of the printing history of Gu Taiqing's poetry, of the various accounts of her life, of the changing evaluation of her lyrics, and of the study of her novel *Hongloumeng ying*.

13 See "Gu Taiqing Yihui shehui jiaowang zhuyao renwu biao," in Zhang Zhang (1998, 788–89); Widmer (2006, 181–200); Zhan Song (2009).

14 For recent editions of her works, see Zhang Zhang (1998); and Lu Xingji (2005). For recent evaluations of her work, see Deng Hongmei (2000, 452–88); Huang Yanli (2002, 22–66); Ma Qingfu (2012, 467–82); Zhang Juling (1990, 231–45). For selected works in English translation, see Chang and Saussy (1999, 589–600); Idema and Grant (2004, 630–52); Grant (2009).

15 On Gu Taiqing as a novelist, see Widmer (2006, 200–216). For a modern edition of *Hongloumeng ying*, see Yuncha Waishi (1988). Gu's two surviving plays are *Taoyuan ji* and *Meihuayin*. See Huang Shizhong (2006, 88–160).

16 ECCP, 227–28.

17 Lady Han is said to have started reading the Neo-Confucian philosophers at the age of five and to have mastered the Classics at the age of thirteen. She loved to read the stories of loyal ministers and chaste women, and was also widely acquainted with fiction. She authored a poetry collection titled *Dailü caotang yishi* (Remaining poems from the thatched cottage surrounded by green). Her best known work is a series of thirty regulated poems on "Flocks of Geese" (*yanzi*; i.e., migrating geese flying in formation like the character "one" [*yi*, a straight line] or "man" [*ren*, an inverted V]). Xu Shichang (1995, 185:53b–58b [3070–73]). See Fashishan (2015, 2:1135–36) for a brief account of the life of Lady Han as "Xianbi Han Taishuren xingzhuang."

18 Fashishan (2005, 528–31).

19 Zhan Song (2009).

20 Zhenjun (1991).

21 Zhenjun (1973, 4:36a–44a).

22 Enhua (2006, 156–61).

23 Hu Wenkai (1985, 813–19).

24 Du Xun (2012, 465–73). Du Xun does not include Gu Taiqing among the Manchu and Mongol poets, but lists her with the Han Chinese authors. Both Hu Wenkai and Du Xun list Chinese banner women with Han Chinese authors. Modern survey articles such as Zhang Jiasheng 1989 and Zhu Zhuxian 1997 tend to be very incomplete in their coverage.

General surveys of Chinese-language Manchu literature of the Qing dynasty discuss at best a few female poets.

25 For a full list of the poetry collections by Manchu women used in this volume, see the bibliography.

26 Xiangcen's small collection *Poetry Drafts from the Dream Flower Pavilion* (Menghuage shigao), printed around the middle of the nineteenth century, would appear to be a typeset edition. Xiangcen had died at the age of twenty-four and her husband Su-wan Duo-ling eventually ordered a son from his second marriage to see to the printing of her surviving forty-one poems (many of them on sickness).

27 I have not encountered examples of collections that were printed at the initiative of, and financed by, non-kin males such as teachers and bibliophiles. Such editions appear to have been quite common in the Jiangnan region. See Zhang Lingyu (2012, 153–60).

28 Gao Chunhua (2014, 133). For modern reprints of Yun Zhu's collection see, e.g., Yun Zhu [1994?], Yun Zhu (2010).

29 Cf. Zhang Lingyu (2012, 160–63).

30 The collection that contains her early poems up to 1768, titled *Green Window Chanting Drafts* (Lüchuang yingao), has only been preserved in manuscript.

31 For a general discussion of the paratextual materials that are commonly found in women's collections of poetry and their biographical value, see Fong (2012).

32 *The Book of Odes* was used in defense of women's poetry in male-authored prefaces to collections by female authors from the 11th century on (Xu 2006).

33 Crossley (1990, 169).

34 On long autobiographical poems by Chinese women of the eighteenth century, see Fong (2008, 9–53; 161–65).

35 One example is "The Scenery at Xiyang Ridge" in Baibao Youlan's collection.

36 Ko (1994) has been a trail-blazing study in this respect.

37 Mengyue, *Zhuwu shichao*, 4b.

38 Both Shen Shanbao and Gu Taiqing mention a poetry club to which they belonged, along with several other Manchu women, for instance the daughters of Gu Taiqing and Yun Zhu. See Zhan Song (2009, 125–26).

39 Yun Zhu's granddaughter Foyunbao (d. 1856), a well-established Manchu woman writer in her own name, contributed an endorsement poem (*tici*) to the 1857 edition of Baibao Youlan's collection (the only endorsement verse by a Manchu woman in Yun Zhu's *Guochao guixiu zhengshi ji* was written by the wife of a classmate of her son Linqing). Foyunbao was a good friend of Naxun Lanbao, who also was acquainted with the wife of one of Yun Zhu's grandsons.

40 This text is also included by Cao Zhenxiu in her *Xieyunlou xiaogao* 2:5a–b. Cao Zhenxiu was the wife of the well-known poet Wang Qisun (1755–1818). Her husband served on the private staff of Lady Tongjia's son Chun-ying (1761–1800) in 1790 and 1791.

41 Bingyue, "He Luo jiefu Peixiang yuanyun," *Lengzhaiyin chubian* 3:10a–11a; Tongjiashi, "Fuzeng Luo Shilan nüshi" and "Ci Shilan nüshi jianzeng yuanyun," *Xuchuang yake* 2:14a–b. In view of Lady Tongjia's fulsome praise for "Luo Shilan" I assume "Luo Qilan" is intended here. This probability is strengthened, in my view, by the fact that Lady Tongjia's son Chun-ying at about the same time composed a poem on the subject of Luo Qilan's famous "Painting of Teaching my Daughter in Autumn by Lamplight" (Qiudeng jiaonü tu), which

is included in his *Xubaiting shichao* (2:25b–26a). While Luo Qilan's poetry collection contains no indication that she ever visited Beijing, Lady Tongjia's first poem would suggest she did so not only once but twice, as it contains the lines "Even though I met you only twice in these four years / All my worries are removed on seeing you." The poems by Lady Tongjia and Bingyue are not included in Luo Qilan's *Tingqiuxuan guizhong tongren ji*, in which she collected endorsements by fellow women writers. On the Manchu grandees and court officials included in her *Tingqiuxuan zengyan*, in which she collected endorsements by male literati, see Hamilton (2010, 116–20). Among the names included is Fashishan, but Ying-he should be added to the list. Chun-ying's poem is not included in *Tingqiuxuan zengyan*. Luo's painting was not unique in showing a woman teaching, but in showing her teaching an adopted daughter instead of sons (Wang Weiping 2014). Luo Qilan's collections are conveniently available in Cha Zhengxian (2010, 1:577–799). Fashishan in 1811 also contributed a preface to the collection of Luo Qilan's good friend Bao Zhihui.

42 Cui Xiujing (2010); Hamilton (1997); Hamilton (2010). Idema and Grant (2004, 612–20).

43 Zhang Qieying was widely regarded as one of the finest female poets of her generation. She hailed from Changzhou but joined her husband in Beijing in the years 1829–1844 and 1847–1853. See Mann (2007, 62–129).

44 Zhenjun (1973, 4:40a–b).

45 Fashishan (2005, 529–30). On the complex motivations behind the act of burning one's poetry see Yanning Wang (2012): the public display of female modesty also served as self-advertisement, enhancing the value of the poems that survived.

46 Yun Zhu accompanied her son Lin-qing (1791–1846) on his travels once he had entered the bureaucracy as becomes clear from his illustrated autobiography *Hongxue yinyuan tuji*. For a general discussion of women's poetry and travel see Fong (2008a, 85–120), and Yanning Wang (2014, 69–114). For Lin-qing see ECCP 506–7.

47 Crossley (1994) does not discuss the education of Manchu women at all.

48 Elliott (2001a, 253–55). Many girls married at a rather early age, before they turned twenty.

49 Du Jiaji (2003).

50 I have not found evidence that any of the Manchu women poets in this selection had to present themselves in person at the palace for selection for service as *xiunü*. Ding Yizhuang (2014, 3–4); Elliott (2001a, 253–55). Wang Shuo (2004) argues that this system was only fully formalized by the middle of the eighteenth century.

51 In the early decades of the nineteenth century, the wife of the Manchu grandee Ying-he (1771–1840), a woman of the Sakeda clan, wrote a treatise for the education of her grandchildren titled *Guanshengge jiayan*, with chapters on topics such as filial piety, respect, motherly care, humanity, diligence, and frugality (Yinghe 1991, 246).

52 The earliest references to *gegu* date from the Tang dynasty, when we also find the first references to the medicinal value of human flesh (Chaves 1986; Groot 1969, 4:357–406; Knapp 2015; Lu 2008, 152–56; Qiu Zhonglin 1996; T'ien 1988, 149–61; Yü 2001, 338–47).

53 Her act of *gegu* and her eventual suicide were greatly praised in a long poem by Lady Tongjia. Tongjiashi, *Wenshilou hexuan*, 4b–5b; Tongjiashi, *Xuchuang yake*, 2:5a–b.

54 Crossley (1990, 159).

55 There are more Manchu women poets who never married. One was Xuecheng (1725–1752), a younger sister of the provincial governor Ya-er-ha-shan (d. 1759). "She suffered from a debilitating disease and vowed to stay with her parents till her death. She loved to read

books and discuss examples of chastity and loyalty from past and present. About to die, she requested to be cremated, but Lord Ya refused to do so. He composed a grave inscription for her and had her buried. She authored *Plain Words* (Suyan) in one scroll" (Zhenjun 1973, 4:39b). Her collection has been preserved. Another Manchu woman poet who never married was Yuling, who passed away at the age of seventeen in 1872, after which her brother A-ke Zhan-zhen had her seventeen surviving poems formally published in the small collection *Yunlan zhuangge yigao*, with a long formal preface by Yousheng Yuqing, dedicatory poems by six different persons, and his own loving postface in which he narrates her obsession with versifying and blames a vulgar quack for her untimely death.

56 Ying-he (1771–1840) placed the poems he had written to his wife during her life and the poems lamenting her together in a special section at the end of his poetry collection. He attached extensive commentaries to his poems lamenting her, turning this section into a loving memoir (Yinghe 1991, 241–47).

57 For reasons unknown, Gu Taiqing was forced by her mother-in-law to leave the princely mansion upon the death of her husband and live elsewhere with her children. It has often been stated that her mother-in-law threw her out because she was romantically involved with the famous southern Han-Chinese poet and statecraft-thinker Gong Zizhen (1792–1841). For a highly romanticized account of that alleged affair, see McAleavy (1963, 13–28). Huang Shizhong (2006) argues that Gu Taiqing was a young widow when she married Yi-hui, and that she was expelled from the family home by Yi-hui's mother upon the latter's death because she was considered bad luck. Her mother-in-law, I think, also may have thrown her out because Yi-hui treated her like his wife upon the death of his consort, rather than properly marrying a second consort, who by her own status and the support of her family would have been much better placed to take care of the household.

58 Many of these widows will have relied on family capital and support from relatives, but in contrast to Chinese widows, Manchu widows were also entitled to government support, in one way or another, through the banner administration (Ding Yizhuang 2014, 4–6).

59 These two lines are highly praised by Dong Wencheng (1987, 134–35) as an indictment of feudal patriarchy.

60 For a general description of the reading materials of Ming-Qing women, see Han Shuju (2009). In the extensive notes to the poems lamenting his wife, Ying-he mentions her regret that she had not been able to study when she was young because her family was poor and so took up reading with a vengeance in her thirties. As to her readings, he mentions the Four Books, the *Rites* (Lijing), and the *Selections of Refined Literature* (Wenxuan), alongside a number of medical texts. He also mentions some primers and introductory readings in history that she had printed (Yinghe 1991, 246). According to ECCP (933), Ying-he's wife "achieved some skill as a writer" but she seems to have been primarily active as a painter (she also practiced finger-painting).

61 In the collection of Lingwen Zhuyou, *Xuxuang yinguan shigao* (9b–10b), we find a set of three poems on a painting of Shi Xiangyun, one of the female characters in the novel. Even earlier, Guizhen Daoren wrote a poem on a painted fan that showed Shi Xiangyun and the nun Miaoyu (*Bingxuetang shi*, 44b; Widmer 2006, 141). The story of the novel was also popularized through plays and ballads. The earliest female reader of the novel may have been Lady Tongjia: four of her poems borrow phrases or lines from poems in Cao's work (Zhan Song 2015). On Lady Tongjia and her son Chun-ying as early readers of *Honglou*

meng, see Hu Xiaowei (1996); Lu Gong and Hu Xiaowei (1987); Zhou Ruchang (1987).

62 Widmer (2006).

63 Gu Taiqing's poems on her excursions in and around Beijing are discussed by Yanning Wang (2014a, 115–45).

64 Xun Liu (2004). Lady Husihali repeatedly (*Xiuyu xiaocao* 6:3a; 6:4b) refers to the study of the *Tianxian zhengli*, a work by the Ming-dynasty meditation master Wu Shouyang (1574–1644), the "putative founder of the Wu-Liu school" of inner alchemy (Kohn 2000, 613, 632–33, 635–36; Pregadio 2008, 1046–47; 1049–50).

65 For a recent survey of the scholarship on Manchu ethnicity, see Shao (2011, 6–10). None of these studies pay attention of the ethnicity of Manchu women as distinct from Manchu men.

66 Elliott (2001a, 246–55); Ding Yizhuang (1999); Zhou Hong (2005).

67 The rare Manchu girls who presented themselves in Han Chinese dress for the triannual *xiunü* selection were rebuked severely. Shuo Wang (2004).

68 The relatively high status of these women poets among the Manchu sets them apart from the types of lower-class Manchu women that are satirized in some "youth books" (also known as bannermen's tales, *zidishu*), such as "The 'Eating Crabs' Youth Book" translated by Elliott (2001b). Also see Stent (1878, 142–48).

69 Elliott (1999) notes a spectacular rise in officially registered "chaste widows" among Manchu women from the early years of the Qianlong period on, and contrasts this "sinicization" of Manchu women with the consistent attempts of the Qianlong emperor to strengthen the ethnic distinctiveness of Manchu men. He concludes, "This suggests that the Qianlong boom in widow chastity was more than just an effort to acquire Confucian legitimacy, and more, even, than just a leap in the pace of acculturation. Promoting widow chastity affirmed the control of Manchu males over the nuptiality and fertility of Manchu women, giving them further control over the reproduction of Banner people and Qing power" (71). Also see Theiss (2004, 25–54) for a discussion of the ongoing formulation of Qing government policy on female chastity. The information on Manchu family life and Manchu women in youth books has been exhaustively collected by Guo Xiaoting (2013, 120–78). Unfortunately, in her section on Manchu women (154–78) she relies heavily on youth book adaptations of episodes from traditional plays and novels, which are set in a Chinese society and depict Han Chinese women, for her analysis of the values and attitudes of Manchu women (166–78).

70 ECCP, 578–79.

71 Zhenjun (1973, 4:37b). The temporary character of a marriage may be stressed in poetry by comparing bride and groom to birds that roost in one grove for a while but soon fly off in different directions.

72 Cf. the discussion of this poem in Elliott (2014, 351–54). Wen-kang (ca. 1810–ca. 1870) in the final chapter of his novel *A Tale of Love and Heroism* (Ernü yingxiong zhuan) offers a hilarious description of the consternation in the banner family of his protagonists when the youngest son is posted to Urumchi (an appointment that with the help of friends in high places is changed to an appointment to Shandong).

73 For a recent survey of English-language scholarship on traditional Chinese women's literature, see Idema (2012). For a recent survey of Chinese scholarship on women writers of the Qing dynasty see Yao Min (2013).

74 Widmer (2009).

75 A few of the Manchu women poets on occasion express a conventional admiration for Han dynasty prose and High Tang verse.

76 Duomin Huiru, *Yiqiangge yishi*, 19b.

77 In the relevant volumes of the four-volume *Manzu wenxue shi* (Zhao Zhihui 2012; Ma Qingfu 2012; and Deng Wei 2012), the coverage of Manchu women authors is incomplete and often based, it would appear, on the selections in anthologies such as Xu Shichang (1995), while some women writers who are discussed are placed in the wrong period. Zhang Juling (2014) contains several articles on Gu Taiqing, but none on other Manchu women writers.

1. THE WOMEN OF THE NALAN FAMILY

1 ECCP, 577–78.

2 Yang Yongjun and Huang Yinong (2013, 341–42).

3 Huang Yinong (2014, 219).

4 Xing-de's wife Lady Lu (1657–1677) was also highly literate. In 1684, when he accompanied the Kangxi emperor on his first Southern Tour, Xing-de acquired the Jiangnan courtesan Shen Wan as his concubine. Shen Wan is known as the author of a collection of lyrics entitled *Xuanmenglou ci* (Lyrics of the selected dreams loft). Five of her lyrics were included in the late seventeenth-century anthology of female-authored lyrics *Zhongxiang ci* (Shu ji: 10b–11a).

5 On Kui-xu as a poet see Zhao Zhihui (2012, 218–30).

6 Kuixu (1993, "Fanli").

7 On Ajige, see ECCP, 4–5.

8 Zhao Xun (2000, 37).

9 Ibid., 38.

10 Ibid., 35.

11 Ibid., 49. The "Inner Rules" (Neize) is a chapter of the *Liji*, one of the Five Classics. As the title suggests, this chapter provides ritual prescriptions for women. The term is also used as a general designation for moral tracts for women.

12 Ibid., 50.

13 ECCP, 924–25.

14 ECCP, 926–27.

15 The troubled relation of the Kangxi emperor and his heir-apparent are described in great detail in Wu (1979). On Kui-xu's role in the events of 1708, see Durand (1991, 206–7).

16 ECCP, 915–20.

17 In 1737 the Qianlong emperor, at the request of a grandson of Xing-de, gave permission to remove the inscription.

18 Yang Yongjun and Huang Yinong (2013, 356–57).

19 Huang Yinong argues that the Sibo household with six girls and one boy may have been one of the sources of inspiration for Cao Xueqin in writing the *Honglou meng*. See Huang Yinong (2012); Huang Yinong (2014, 241–58); and Yang Yongjun and Huang Yinong (2013). Other theories that argue for a connection between the Ming-zhu household and the novel tend to focus on Xing-de.

20 Hong Ying (1995); Zhang Jiasheng (1989); Zhu Zhuxian (1997).

21 Shen Shanbao (2010, 417) quotes two of these poems as representative of Miss Nalan's work. The persons discussed in these poems are all well known from the stories of the wars following the collapse of the Qin dynasty and resulting in the establishment of the Han dynasty (206 BCE–220 CE).

22 Sibo gave birth to four daughters and one boy, but the latter passed away before his father. See Yang Yongjun and Huang Yinong (2013, 352–53).

23 Yang Yongjun and Huang Yinong (2013, 353–55).

24 He reached this rank in 1724 but was removed from his position in 1725.

25 James Legge (1971a, 44; the transcription has been adapted).

26 Idema and Grant (2004, 17–42).

27 Fashishan (2005, 29).

28 Tiebao (1992, 1687).

29 For a survey of this genre as practiced by women poets, see Wang (2014, 31–65). She analyzes the *nü youxian* poems (poems on roaming among the immortals as a woman) of four Qing-dynasty women poets (including Gu Taiqing), and makes the following bold claim: "The emergence of *nü youxian* also signifies a new contemporary gender consciousness. From the perspective of content, authorship, and readership, *nü youxian* poems are written by women, about women, and probably mainly for women. In these poems, the authors reinscribe male notions of the meaning and nature of the transcendent world to challenge the so-called fixed gender spaces of the inner and the outer" (37). It should be pointed out, however, that the female protagonists in these poems almost exclusively meet with female immortals during their travels through celestial realms.

30 The famous poet Tao Qian (Yuanming; 365–417) narrates in the preface to one of his poems the story of a fisherman who, upon passing through a peach blossom grove, accidentally enters a rural community of order and harmony. The inhabitants tell him that their ancestors had fled the wars following the collapse of the Qin dynasty and that since then their community had not had any contacts with the outside world. Hightower (1970, 254–58); Owen (1996, 309–10). Peach Blossom Spring has become the proverbial designation for a rural utopia.

31 A handwritten note accompanying this poem reads: "A girl should not say such words, and she also should not write poems on such topics." The poem is written from the perspective of the virtuous Concubine Ban who had been banished to the Palace of Eternal Trust after Emperor Cheng (r. 32–7 BCE) had become enamored of the dancer Flying Swallow Zhao (Zhao Feiyan), which whom he cavorted in the Zhaoyang Hall. The Phoenix Carriage is the conveyance of the emperor who no longer visits Concubine Ban. The virtue and fate of Concubine Ban was a popular topic in traditional Chinese poetry, also in poetry by women. See Idema and Grant (2004, 77–82; 148–49). The anonymous commentator may have felt that a topic that hints at sexual frustration and female jealousy was improper for an unmarried girl.

32 The full moon that is reflected in all streams but remains the same is a common image for the Buddha-nature that is present in every human being.

33 Manjusri is the Bodhisattva of wisdom.

34 The Yellow Springs are a common designation for the realm of the dead.

35 A medallion?

36 Zhenwu is the warlike god of the north who was widely venerated in the Ming and Qing

dynasties, also by the ruling houses. The main temple complex dedicated to the deity is located on Mount Wudang in Hubei province.

37 *Shiyu hejie* also contains on pages 14a–15a an essay titled "On Instructing Sons" (Xunzi shuo) addressed to Ning-xiu.

38 A daughter should obey her father, a wife her husband, and a widow her grown-up son. This is referred to as "threefold obedience." "Fourfold virtue" refers to proper behavior, proper speech, proper bearing, and proper diligence.

39 Literally, hauling water and pounding rice.

40 *The Book of Odes* and *The Book of Documents* are two of the Five Classics.

41 Short lines are lines of four syllables as commonly found in *The Book of Odes*, one of the Five Classics.

42 Widows who devote themselves to the education of their children often compare themselves to the mother of the fourth-century BCE philosopher Meng Ke (Mencius). Twice she moved house to provide her son with the right surroundings: when she lived near a market her son started to play butcher, so she moved, but she moved again when at this new location he started to play at being an undertaker. When her son one day came back from school and said: "The same!" in answer to her question what he had learned that day, she cut the cloth she was weaving to impress on him that a piece of cloth was only completed by repeating the same action of throwing the shuttle any number of times, and that he too would have to stay at his studies in order to complete his formation.

43 The poet Song Yu lived in the third century BCE; the dates of the poet Shen Yue are 441–513.

44 During the wars of the fourth and third centuries BCE that would end with the conquest of the Chinese world by the western state of Qin, the statesman Su Qin at one moment concurrently served as the prime minister of the six states opposing Qin. The poet Sima Xiangru (172–118 BCE) was once handsomely paid by Empress Chen for writing a poem in her voice in which she expressed her lasting love for her husband Emperor Wu (r. 140–87 BCE) who had discarded her in favor of another woman.

45 Yingzhou is one of the floating islands of the immortals in the Eastern Ocean.

46 Shuangcheng and Feiqiong are both well-known female immortals. In many romantic stories girls select their husband by throwing an embroidered ball into a crowd of suitors—the one who catches the ball will be the groom.

2. A PRISONER'S MOTHER AND WIFE

1 When Neng-tai took the initiative in 1787 to have these collections printed, he entrusted the project to the editorial care of Gan Yunyuan (1718–1794), a well-known literatus of the time (Tongshan, *Bocui shanfang shi*, 12a).

2 Enhua (2006, 98); Zhao Zhihui (2012, 151, 157).

3 On Su-nu, see ECCP, 692–94.

4 Both Yin-si and Yin-tang died later that year under suspicious circumstances while in prison. Both were formally expelled from the imperial clan, to be posthumously restored to their positions only in 1778.

5 Li Wenhai (2000, 79; twentieth day of the Fifth Month of 1724 [July 10]); 200 (twenty-eighth day of the Fifth Month of 1726 [June 27]).

6 Quoted in Tiebao (1992, 1682).

7 For a discussion of Nurturing Simplicity's poetry see Zhu Jiji (2011, 102–7).

8 Songshan, *Yuliantang shi* 7:3a.

9 Ibid., 2:18b

10 Ibid., 1:19b.

11 Ibid., 2:26a.

12 Ibid., 6:25a

13 The poetry of the Master of Orchid Study is very briefly discussed in Ma Qingfu (2012, 187–88), where she is treated, however, as a poet of the Jiaqing-Daoguang period. Also see Zhu Jiji (2011, 87–91).

14 Confucius.

15 ECCP, 694.

16 Yun Zhu (1831a, 9:4a–4b).

17 Yun Zhu (1831a, 9:4a–4b).

18 Choosing her neighbors and destroying her weaving were the actions by which the widowed mother of Meng Ke (Mencius) achieved her son's education.

19 Because migrating geese fly in formation, the single goose became a common symbol for loneliness.

20 "Heaven's Pipes" refers to the sounds of nature.

21 The pine is a symbol of loyalty and fidelity because it stays green even in winter. The plum likewise is a symbol of chastity and purity because it will flower even in winter.

22 That is, on meeting her husband.

23 Yang Jisheng (1516–1555) was a metropolitan official who denounced the corruption of the powerful prime minister Yan Song (1480–1565). After Yang had been questioned under torture, he was severely beaten and thrown in jail. Eventually he was condemned to death. More than a decade later, the verdict was reversed and Yang received the title of Loyal and Concerned Duke. The story was adapted for the stage as *Mingfeng ji* (The crying phoenix), one of the most popular plays of the Ming dynasty. See DMB, 2:1503–5, and 1586–91.

24 Guan Longfeng was a loyal official who was killed because he protested against the crimes of Jie, the evil last ruler of the Xia dynasty. Bi Gan was a close relative of Zhou, the evil last king of the Shang dynasty. When he protested against Zhou's actions, the latter had his breast opened because he wanted to see whether the heart of a sage indeed had seven holes as was said.

25 Wang Mang (45 BCE–23 CE) was a powerful minister during the final years of the Western Han dynasty who eventually usurped the throne to found the short-lived Xin dynasty (9CE–23CE). Cao Cao (155–220) was a fiendishly cunning warlord who imposed his will on the court during the final decades of the Eastern Han dynasty (25–220).

26 Misery and longing waste one's figure away.

27 The Seventh Night is the night of the seventh day of the Seventh Month. This is the only time when the Weaving Maiden and Oxherd are allowed to meet. Weaving Maiden and Oxherd are two stars on opposite sides of the River of Heaven (the Milky Way). Because they neglected their duties following their wedding, they were separated by the Jade Emperor, who allowed them only one meeting each year. On the Seventh Night the magpies form a bridge across the River of Heaven for the couple.

28 Threefold Peace refers in Daoist Inner Alchemy to the stage of meditation that the heart

achieves harmony and the soul is happy.

29 Zhuo Wenjun was a young widow who had returned to her natal home in Linqiong, where she allowed herself to be seduced by the dashing young poet Sima Xiangru when he played a love song on the zither. The couple eloped and operated a wine shop in the market place of Chengdu, until her wealthy father relented and gave her her dowry. After Sima Xiangru had made a career at court, he fell in love with a younger woman, inducing Zhuo Wenjun to compose the White Hair Lament (*Baitou yin*), lamenting her fate (Idema and Grant 2004, 108–12).

3. CHASTITY AND SUICIDE: XIGUANG

1 Tiebao (1992, 1692).

2 ECCP, 219–21.

3 According to Du Xun (2012, 2:470) Xiguang was Yi-song-a's second wife when she married him in 1771; she became a widow only two years later. If this information is reliable, it means that Ai-bi-da cannot have been instrumental in convincing her not to immediately follow her husband in death as stated in the account of the event in the *Qingshi gao* that is translated here.

4 Quoted in Tiebao (1992, 1692–93). On the career of Shu-he-de, see ECCP, 659–61.

5 Yun Zhu (1831b, 4:51b–52a). *Langui baolu* is a voluminous compilation of biographies of virtuous women. See Mann (1997, 208–14).

6 Zhenjun (1973, 4:36a).

7 QSG, 14159. I have been unable to locate the poem by the Qianlong emperor (if, indeed, he ever wrote it).

8 For a general study of women's suicide poetry of the Qing, see Fong (2001).

9 The Xies were one of the most powerful families of the Eastern Jin dynasty of the fourth century. Xiguang compares herself here to the famous woman poet Xie Daoyun. Once, when her uncle the prime minister Xie An (320–385) tested his nephews on their poetical skills, he concluded that the line proposed by his niece was far superior. Idema and Grant (2004, 136–46).

10 "Red tears" are tears mixed with rouge and/or blood. The Yellow Sources or Yellow Springs refer to the realm of the dead.

11 The King of Emptiness refers to the Buddha.

12 *Xichao yayong ji yuji* places old-style poems ahead of modern-style poems, but I have moved this poem to the end of my selection because it was her final work.

13 For the poems exchanged between the loving couple Qin Jia and Xu Shu (second century?), see Idema and Grant (2004, 132–36). Later tradition turned Xu Shu into a chaste widow who disfigured her face when her brothers tried to force her to remarry.

14 A classic description of a perfect couple, filled with mutual respect.

15 The "urchins deep inside" are the urchins between the heart and the diaphragm that appeared in a dream and sealed the death of Duke Jing of Jin.

16 Bodao is one of the names of Deng You (d. 326). During the chaotic years of the end of the Western Jin dynasty he abandoned his only son in order to save the orphaned son of his younger brother. Despite this virtuous act he remained without sons for the rest of his life.

17 Cai Yong's (132–192) only daughter was Cai Yan. As a young widow she was abducted by a

Xiongnu prince, to whom she bore two sons. When she was later ransomed by the powerful warlord Cao Cao, she had to abandon her boys. She is credited with three long poems in which she describes her sufferings (Idema and Grant 2004, 112–27).

18 Bran and chaff are the food one is reduced to eating when suffering great poverty.

4. MOURNING ROYALTY:
LADY ZHOUJIA, LADY TONGJIA, AND LADY FUCHA

1 On Tong Guogang and his male descendants, see ECCP, 794–95. Tong Guogang, a favorite uncle of the Kangxi emperor, originally belonged to one of the Chinese banners but was reassigned to a Manchu banner when he claimed to be of Manchu descent. From that moment the family's surname was changed to Tongjia. Some scholars believe that Cao Xueqin's novel *Honglou meng* was inspired by the story of the Tongjias, whose glory during the Kangxi reign was followed by precarious survival during the Yongzheng era.

2 The crow is an emblem of filial piety, as it reputedly feeds its elderly parents to repay them for all their care.

3 The Four Books are the *Analects*, the *Mencius*, the *Great Learning*, and the *Central Harmony*, with the commentary of the Neo-Confucian thinker Zhu Xi (1130–1200), who had selected these four texts as the basic writings of Confucianism. Zhu Xi was also the author of *Xiaoxue* (Earliest studies).

4 A poem lamenting her death dating from 1759 is included in Lady Tongjia's *Lüchuang yingao*, 2:3a–b.

5 Duling here refers to the Tang poet Du Fu (712–770), who in his poems often laments the dispersal of his family.

6 The actual number is thirty-four. The collection consists of eight seven-syllable regulated poems entitled "Weeping for My Father" (Kufu shi), four five-syllable regulated poems entitled "Dreaming of My Father on a Winter Night" (Dongye mengfu), and two seven-syllable quatrains entitled "Thinking of Father on a Spring Day" (Chunri sifu). These are followed by two sets of poems entitled "Weeping for My Mother" (Kumu shi), one consisting of ten seven-syllable regulated poems, and one consisting of the same number of five-syllable regulated poems. The collection of the Harvard-Yenching Library also includes a manuscript of this collection, which contains two additional poems entitled "Thinking of Father on a Spring Day" (one a quatrain, one a seven-syllable regulated poem).

7 A selection of Ru-song's poems was printed in 1789 as *Yiqing shushi shichao*. This collection contains no poems addressed to his wife.

8 Rawski (1998, 78). The Qianlong emperor was disappointed by the sons of the fourth-generation heir because they could not speak Manchu and their archery skills were poor. He then selected Ru-song as "the best" from a much larger pool of Dorbo descendants. Ru-song's equestrian skills probably contributed to his selection.

9 QSG, 9032.

10 This revision of earlier historiography is discussed in detail by Pamela K. Crossley (1999, 281–336). The revision tended to stress the purity of the Manchu race, and to downplay the role of Chinese officials in the establishment of the Qing and the conquest of China.

11 Ru-song also posthumously received this rank.

12 For the revision of the judgment on Dorgon, see Rawski (1998, 79–81, 105, 219); Zhou Yuanlian and Zhao Shiyu (1993, 464–75).

13 But Chun-ying was chided shortly before his death by the Jiaqing emperor for overstepping the bounds of his authority. QSLZ, 41–42.

14 QSLZ, 39–40; QSG, 9033. Chun-ying's second son, Xi-en (1784–1852), held a string of high positions (interrupted by several degradations) during the first half of the nineteenth century. The last Prince Rui survived the collapse of the Qing dynasty; upon his death his sons squandered the family fortune on Western gadgets. The princely mansion was sold in 1923, and in 1933 it was turned into a private middle school. The grounds are now occupied by the Beijing No. 24 Middle School (Wang Lanshun 2014). Life inside the princely mansion in its last few years is described by Jin Jishui and Zhou Shachen (1988).

15 A brief account of the life and poetry of Lady Tongjia is provided by Mo Limin (2010); a more detailed study is provided by Dong Wencheng (1987). Neither of these articles mentions *Lüchuang yingao.*

16 Tongjiashi, *Lüchuang yingao,* 1:29b.

17 A copy of this collection is preserved in the Peking University Library where it is classified as a manuscript.

18 This is the nun Mingben. This highly literate woman hailed originally from Suzhou; after much traveling she settled in Beijing. She authored several works and also practiced poetry and painting. She has a short biography in Zhenhua, *Xu biqiuni zhuan,* juan 5.

19 One work by Lady Tongjia that I have not seen is her *Wubei tai fujin zhuan fu Wubei tai fujin shi,* which to judge from its title might be a biographical sketch of Lady Zhoujia followed by (a selection of) her poems. The only known copy of this work is kept in the Library of Peking University and is currently inaccessible because it is being restored.

20 Rusong, *Yiqing shushi shichao,* 24a. The curtains of the first line are the bed curtains.

21 Tongjiashi, *Lüchuang yingao* 1:43a–44b.

22 Her son Chun-ying's collection also contains poems mourning the death of a fifth and a sixth brother.

23 On Bo Shaojun's poems see Idema (2011); Idema (2013); McLaren (2010); Robertson (1992, 88–95).

24 Lady Tongjia's earliest poem following the rhymes of the Female Scribe of Practiced Seclusion in *Lüchuang yingao* 2:15b dates from 1765. "Thirteen" should therefore read "thirty." Thirteen is the age at which Lady Tongjia started studying poetry with the Elder of Cypress Fragrance. Lady Zhoujia's *Yunchuang yingao* also contains several poems following the rhymes of poems by the Female Scribe of Practiced Seclusion.

25 This is an allusion to a poem from the *Odes,* which is said to contain words of advice by a wise wife to her husband.

26 Prince Shen is Yun-xi (or Yin-xi; 1711–1758), the twenty-first son of the Kangxi emperor, who was an active literary patron.

27 Tongjiashi, *Xuchuang yake,* contains several poems written in answer to poems by Plum Kiosk.

28 Tongjiashi, *Xuchuang yake* 2:14a-b contains poems addressed to Luo Shilan (Luo Qilan?), but the collection contains none that are addressed to Hu Shilan.

29 ECCP, 921.

30 On Ying-he, see ECCP, 931–33.

31 Chun-ying's poems were after his death collected as *Xubaiting shichao* and printed in 1806.

32 Yinghe, "*Xubaiting ji* xu," 2b–3a, in Chunying (1806).

33 The poem most likely dates from 1780. Chun-ying's *Xubaiting shichao* opens with a (much shorter) poem entitled *Zishu*, which is explicitly dated to that year.

34 QSLZ, 51.

35 Several near final poems in the second scroll of *Xuchuang yake*, such as "Monkey Show," have their counterparts in Chun-ying's *Xubaiting shichao*. These poems of Chun-ying date, at their latest, from 1800. If he wrote them at the request of his mother (as suggested by Ying-he), these poems by Lady Tongjia also would date at the latest from 1800.

36 This collection was apparently not available to Dong Wencheng (1987) and Mo Limin (2014). Both scholars also ignore her *Baoshantang jiaxun*.

37 In the *sao* mode, lines of unequal length are broken in the middle by the meaningless particle *xi*. This type of line is often used in poems that give expression to extreme emotions.

38 Lady Fucha's father was the famous general Fu-heng (d. 1770). ECCP, 252–53.

39 Lu Gong and Hu Xiaowei (1989, 490–91; 503–4).

40 *Danxiang shichao*, 4a.

41 Clear and Bright is a spring festival when relatives visit the graves of deceased family members to offer sacrifices and repair the graves.

42 The ambition to stay loyal to her deceased husband and not remarry.

43 The Lantern Festival was celebrated on the night of the fifteenth day of the First Month of the year, the first night of the year with a full moon.

44 When coming across one of his students sleeping during the day, Confucius remarked: "Rotten wood cannot be carved" (*Lunyu* V, 10).

45 The Kun is a giant fish that is mentioned in the first chapter of the *Zhuangzi*, where it represents the untrammeled existence made possible by superior insight.

46 I understand "frost of the Ninth Month" as a reference to the whiteness of crabmeat.

47 The expression *hengxing*, which is here translated as "sideways movement," usually means "to run wild, to run amok, to be on a rampage."

48 The author most likely wrote this poem in 1753, on the eve of her marriage.

49 *Guining* (returning to one's parental home) refers to a short visit by a married woman to the house of her own parents.

50 Ru-song.

51 The word translated as "silk" is *si*, which has the same pronunciation as *si* (thought, longing).

52 A parting song.

53 The "red brush" refers to the works composed by women; the "green records" refer to historical chronicles; in ancient times records were kept on strips made of wood or bamboo.

54 The manuscript version of this poem carries the following authorial note: "The *Taishang ganying pian* states: if one wishes to become a terrestrial immortal, one has to do three hundred good deeds." The *Taishang ganying pian* is a moral tract that had circulated widely since the Song dynasty.

55 Ding Lan, who is said to have lived during the Han dynasty, is famed as one of the

"Twenty-Four Exemplars of Filial Piety." Following the death of his parents, he had lifelike wooden statues carved.

56 The author's younger brother apparently died before the death of his mother, but he had been married, and his wife had given birth to a son.

57 Bamboo was, and is, used for making paper.

58 The fourth-century Xie Daoyun was China's most famous female poet, but her fame rested on a single line in which she compared snow to willow floss (Idema and Grant 2004, 137).

59 Legend has it that the soul of Du Yu, an ancient emperor of Shu (modern Chengdu), upon his death was turned into the cuckoo (*dujuan*) that sadly cries, shedding tears of blood. The azalea too is called *dujuan* because its flowers have been dyed red by the tears of the bird.

60 Jambudvipa is the Buddhist designation of the world in which humans live and suffer. But as this is also the continent on which the historical Buddha Shakyamuni preached his dharma, it also provides the opportunity to escape from suffering if we accept his message that all suffering originates from attachment, which is vain because all existence in final analysis is empty.

61 Double Springs is one of the many designations for the world of the dead.

62 The "jade vase" is the moon.

63 In traditional China the night was divided into five watches of equal length.

64 *Tu* (*Sonchus oleraceus*) is a vegetable with a very bitter taste.

65 The seventh night of the Seventh Month is the only moment in the year when Weaving Maiden and Oxherd, two stars and lovers separated by the Heavenly River (the Milky Way; also known as the Silver River), are allowed to meet. If it rains on this night, the rain is said to be the couple's tears on parting. Cf. Robertson (1992, 95–96).

66 The "one-inch square" refers to the heart.

67 A boy is said to be a "lad" (*tong*) on turning fifteen years of age (by Chinese reckoning).

68 One sprig of flowering winter plum in a vase.

69 The author's parents died at a relatively early age, and the author did not follow her husband in death by committing suicide.

70 1753.

71 The first-century recluse Liang Hong refused to see his new wife Meng Guang when she appeared before him in all her finery, so she dispensed with her jewelry, and when offering him his food, "lifted the tray as high as her eyebrows."

72 1754.

73 This phrase derives from the "Small Preface" to one of the texts in the *Book of Odes*, which is said to contain the words of admonishment of a wise consort, urging her husband to attend to his duties at court, where the early morning audience took place at dawn.

74 1762.

75 When Zi Zhang, one of the disciples of Confucius, had inquired about correct behavior, he wrote the words of the master down on his sash (*Lunyu* XV, 6).

76 He did not pursue sensual pleasures.

77 1770.

78 This line suggests that our poet had had made up her mind to follow her husband in death.

79 This phrase denotes that the disease was incurable.

80 The "abandoned forest" here refers to the family graveyard outside the city.

81 Sincere feelings of friendship, which also persist in adversity, are called "thick."

82 The words for "thread" (*si*) and "thought/longing/yearning" (*si*) are homophones.

83 1773.

84 These two phrases both are clichés for a poor widow raising and teaching her son.

85 1775.

86 In traditional China women plucked their eyebrows and painted on eyebrows curved like willow leaves.

87 Clear and Bright is a spring festival during which one visits the graves of the ancestors.

88 The "treasure in the palm" refers to a beloved young child.

89 "Cap and gown" refer to the dress of officials; it is meant to remind those who wear it of their moral duties toward the community.

90 A portrait of Chun-ying, dated to 1796, is reproduced in Stuart and Rawski (2001, 147).

91 Shouts and blows with his staff are means the Chan master used to awaken his disciples to sudden insight to help them see through their illusions.

92 *Norms for Women* (Nüfan) is a treatise on the moral education of women by a certain Lady Liu of the Ming dynasty.

93 *Instructions for Women* (Nüxun) is the title of both a short essay ascribed to the second-century scholar Cai Yong (132–192), and a treatise in twelve chapters of 1508 by the wife of the Zhengde emperor (r. 1506–1521).

94 The *Classic of Filial Piety for Women* (Nü Xiaojing) was written by Lady Zheng (first half of the eighth century). The work is modeled on the *Classic of Filial Piety* and consists of eighteen chapters, in which Ban Zhao answers questions from her disciples. For a translation see Ebrey (2001) and Robin Wang (2003, 372–90). Also see Murray (1988; 1990).

95 The Four Books here appear to refer to the Four Books for Women, the titles of which are listed at the end of the next paragraph. Full translations of the Four Books for Women are found in Martin-Liao (1984, 93–177). The first three texts are also translated in Robin Wang (2003, 177–88, 327–40, 372–90). Modern Chinese editions may be found in Zhang Fuqing (1996).

96 The *Analects for Women* (Nü Lunyu) is traditionally ascribed to Song Ruoxin (early ninth century). The text consists of twelve chapters and comes with a preface ascribed to Ban Zhao. Idema and Grant (2004, 54–57). For a full translation see Robin Wang (2003, 327–40).

97 Idema and Grant (2004, 17–42).

98 *Instructions for the Inner Quarters* (Neixun) of 1407 was written by Empress Wen, the wife of the Yongle emperor (r. 1403–1424).

99 Tairen was the wife of King Wen (eleventh century BCE); she is often mentioned as a model of all female virtues.

100 "Hexagonal drum songs" (*bajiaogu*) is the general designation for a number of short narrative ballads that were highly popular among the Manchus of Beijing from the Qianlong period onward. See Ma Qingfu (2012, 393–97).

101 The famous female poet Xie Daoyun lived in the middle of the fourth century and was renowned for her quick wit. See Idema and Grant (2004, 136–44).

5. SACRIFICE AND FRIENDSHIP: BINGYUE

1 Yun Zhu (1831a, 6:1a).

2 ECCP, 120–23, 856–58.

3 When the Jiaqing emperor in 1799 dismissed Yi-xing as governor of Jiangsu and banished him to Xinjiang (most likely because of Yi-xing's close connection to the toppled He-shen), he characterized him as "an arrogant alcoholic who extorted special gifts from his subordinates" (Guy 2010, 139). Yi-xing was a specialist in the Manchu language and in the final years of the Qianlong era compiled the *Qingwen buhui* (1786; revised by his son-in-law Fakjinge in 1802), a dictionary of nearly eight thousand phrases (Crossley and Rawski 1993); he used his enforced leisure in Xinjiang to compile a handbook for colloquial Manchu titled *Yongyan zhizhi* (Song Bing 2013). Having redeemed himself in this manner, he was recalled to the capital in 1803 and could resume his career.

4 ECCP, 587–90.

5 Shen Yanfang, "Muzhiming," in *Yueshan shiji*. See also Yixing, "Xian dafu shiji gongji," in *Yueshan shiji*.

6 Du Xun (2012, 466 [no. 5840]).

7 Gui-pu not only printed the writings of his father but also those by some other relatives. He described this project in the "Xian dafu shiji gongji" printed at the end of Heng-ren's *Yueshan shiji*.

8 Women do not follow any of the "schools" that dominated Qing dynasty poetry by men.

9 Legge (1971a, 8–10).

10 *The Book of Odes* contains two poems with the title "Cypress Boat" (Bozhou), but none of them is found in the section Xiaoya (Lesser Elegantiae). Both are found in the Guofeng (Airs of the States). The first is found in Beifeng (Legge 1971a, 38–40), the second in Yongfeng (Legge 1971a, 91–93).

11 That is, her husband.

12 Despite the date of the two prefaces, the collection may only have been printed after Yi-xing's return from Xinjiang in 1803. Bingyue mentions that Lady Tongjia read her printed collection only in 1806.

13 The Tang-dynasty poet Li Bai (701–762) was famed for his unbridled expression.

14 The Yellow Springs refer to the realm of the dead. The author sees from time to time her husband in a dream.

15 The formation of migrating geese in flight is often compared to a line of brothers.

16 Cedrela and daylily are common symbols for father and mother.

17 Song Yu (third century BCE) is traditionally considered to be the author of "Zhaohun" (Summoning the soul), one of the poems in the *Chuci*.

18 For an alternative translation of this poem and an analysis, see Xiaorong Li (2012, 79–81).

19 The First Emperor of the Qin dynasty (221–210 BCE) had all books burned that did not conform to his legalist policies (including the Confucian Classics).

20 The concept of hell and its punishments was introduced into China by Buddhism, so was still unknown in China during the Qin (221–208 BCE) and Han (206 BCE–220 CE) dynasties.

21 The Buddha.

22 Guizhen Daoren mentioned this set of poems in the opening lines of her poem lamenting the death of Bingyue twenty years later (*Bingyuetang shi*, 65a).

23 The full moon symbolizes togetherness and reunion. The word for "fence" (*li*) has the same pronunciation as the word for "parting" or "separation" (*li*).

24 That is to say, by being reborn in a next life as an animal that will serve you.

25 The italicized words in this poem are the ones supplied by Shanxi to complete the damaged text in the original manuscript, as we learn from the note she appended: "As for the *Drafts of Chantings from Cold Study* by the female scribe Bingyue of the imperial clan—her poetic talent is rich and her expression is original. She has been famous in the inner quarters for quite some time, and she is capable of adding luster to us women of the imperial house. Now I found this *Continuation* in a basket filled with old books. Alas, the last page was damaged, which could not but fill one with regret. So now I have added a few words in order to complete the poem—a dog's tail added to the mink, a joke in the eyes of cognoscenti! —Written by the Female Scribe of the Imperial Clan Shanxi."

6. A TOMBOY IN A SILLY DRESS: MENGYUE

1 This pseudonym is based on the following item in the *Analects*: "The Master said of Zichan that he had the way of the gentleman on four counts: he was respectful in the manner in which he conducted himself; he was reverent in the service of his lord; in caring for the common people he was generous; in employing their services he was just" (*Lunyu* V, 16; translation adapted from Confucius [1979, 78]).

2 Miaolianbao (1836, 5:15a).

3 Guy (2010, 150–52).

4 Mengyue, *Zhuwu shichao*, 39a.

5 For Yin-ti, see ECCP, 929–30.

6 For the Qianlong emperor's appreciation of Hong-shang, see Meng Fanyong (2015).

7 Fashishan.

8 Fashishan (2002, 745–46); Fashishan (2015, 1186–87).

9 The Bodhisattva Guanyin. One of her attributes is a willow wand placed in a vase of pure water.

10 Bingling Gong, the third son of the Great Thearch of the Eastern Marchmount (Mount Taishan) is also venerated as the god of fire.

11 The pole star is an often used symbol for the emperor. When girls reached marriageable age, they plucked out their eyebrows and painted on eyebrows curved like the antennae of a moth.

12 When Meng Guang first presented herself to her husband, the first-century recluse Liang Hong, she dressed herself in all her finery, but her husband refused to see her until she had dressed quite simply.

13 In the manuscript this poem is placed between bold brackets, probably indicating that this poem should be excised when cutting the printing blocks for publication.

14 According to ancient legend, the goddess Nüwa repaired the dome of heaven when it crashed after a rebelling god had broken one of the eight columns that separate heaven and earth. The legend of Nüwa making her stones is referred to in the opening pages of the famous eighteenth-century novel *Honglou meng*.

15 Chu refers to the area of modern Hubei and Hunan. The Yellow Crane Tower is found in Wuhan, on a little hill to the south of the confluence of the Han and the Yangzi (the "River" in the description). Legend told that the place had once been visited by an immortal who had flown off in the shape of a crane. Parrot Island used to be a little island in the Yangzi that is nowadays joined to the riverbank. One of the most famous regulated poems of the Tang dynasty was written by Cui Hao (ca. 695–ca. 760) upon his visit to this spot.

16 Xining is the modern capital of Qinghai. In the second half of the eighteenth century the region had only recently been incorporated into the Qing Empire.

17 Yan Hui, Confucius' favorite disciple, lived in extreme poverty.

18 The seeds of elm trees are called coins; the sprouts are bamboo sprouts. High officials were allowed to display a prescribed number of spears outside the gate of their mansion as a symbol of status.

19 Lord Getian is one of the emperors of a mythic past, when simplicity reigned and everyone was happy.

20 "Oyster-tower" is the Chinese expression for a mirage at sea.

21 Master Zhuang of Meng is the ancient philosopher Zhuang Zhou (fourth/third century BCE) who taught absolute relativity.

22 The Western Paradise of the Buddha Amitabha.

23 Wang Zhaojun was a palace lady in the reign of Emperor Yuan (r. 48–33 BCE). She failed to attract the emperor's attention, and when the Xiongnu offered to make peace if their ruler would be given a Chinese princess in marriage, she volunteered to go. When the Xiongnu ruler died, she married his son, as was the local custom. Her children would play a major role in the relations between the Xiongnu and the Han. It was believed that her grave on the steppe remained green throughout the year. According to later legend Wang Zhaojun failed to attract the attention of Emperor Yuandi because he selected his bedmates on the basis of portraits; trusting in her own beauty, Wang Zhaojun had refused to bribe the painter, who had painted her as an ugly woman. When the emperor saw her in the flesh after she had been selected for marriage to the barbarian prince, he was stricken by her beauty but had to let her go in order to avoid war. The story of Wang Zhaojun became a popular topic in Chinese poetry and was often adapted for the stage (Idema and Grant 2004, 91–95). For more detailed discussions see Eoyang (1982); Hung (2003); and Kwong (1986). For a discussion of the use of the Wang Zhaojun legend in twentieth-century culture and politics see Bulag (2002, 63–102). Bulag wrongly states that "very few poems about Wang Zhaojun were written by women" (101).

24 A "simple zither" is a zither without strings.

25 On achieving a certain rank in the bureaucracy, one could apply for a corresponding honorary title for one's parents.

26 The one drop of pure water dispensed by Guanyin's willow wand brings blessings and insight.

27 This last line refers to a poem on the enlightenment of a nun that was first recorded in the thirteenth century and reads: "All day long I searched for spring but nowhere did I find it— / On sandals of straw I trekked through the clouds atop the hill. / When I returned, I smiled and plucked a sprig of flowering plum, / One sniff and I found that all of spring was there in this twig" (Idema and Grant 2004, 158).

28 The shrine erected in honor of her grandfather.

29 When traveling south on the Grand Canal one would cross the Yangzi (the river) from Guazhou and travel from Zhenjiang further southward on the Grand Canal. Golden Mountain, home to a famous monastery, was a little island in the Yangzi near Zhenjiang (the island is now connected to the shore).

30 The Blessed Isles are the floating islands of the immortals in the Eastern Ocean.

7. UNBRIDLED ENERGY: YINGCHUAN

1 Yun Zhu (1831a, 15:1a). Ba-ke-tang-a (Baktanga) was born in 1718 and had a modest career.

2 ECCP, 717–18. On Tie-bao as a poet see Li Jinxi (1998); Ma Qingfu (2012, 147–55); Zhang Juling (1990, 135–68).

3 *Shiqi tie* and *Sushi zixu tie* are well-known calligraphy models for cursive or "grass" script. *Shiqi tie* provides examples of the cursive script of Wang Xizhi (321–379); the *Sushi zixu tie* is the most famous example of the "wild grass" script of the Tang monk Huaisu (b. 737). Calligraphy models usually are rubbings of carvings based on the calligraphy of masters. For a general introduction to Chinese calligraphy as an art and a discipline see Billeter (1990).

4 Tiebao (1999, 3a–4b).

5 Ibid., 24a.

6 These two lines describe the young Yingchuan's diligence as a proper housewife by waking her husband in time for the court audiences at dawn and by devoting all her time to needlework.

7 An ironic reference to the seal of a high official.

8 Tiebao (2002, 2:12b–13a).

9 On Yingchuan's character and poetry, see Zhang Juling (1990, 136–37).

10 Shen Shanbao (2010, 478–79) not only quotes a few poems by Yingchuan, but also mentions that her daughters Shaoru and Xiuhuang (perhaps the daughters born by Ms. Ma?) were well versed in poetry too, and proceeds to quote two poems by Shaoru.

11 Langfeng is Yu-bao (1759–1798), a younger brother of Tie-bao, who also served in the Hanlin Academy and ended his career as the vice president of the Board of Civil Office (ECCP, 718). The autumn hunt refers to the Qianlong emperor's annual hunting trip at Mulan, beyond the Great Wall. See Elliott (2004).

12 Clear and Bright is a spring festival celebrated at the beginning of the Third Month. On this day families visit the graves of their ancestors.

13 As the wife of one of the highest officials, Yingchuan was allowed to attend the first formal audience of the Jiaqing emperor following the abdication of the Qianlong emperor. The author refrains from describing the new emperor directly.

14 Lady Lengzhai is Bingyue. Tie-bao had written a preface for her first collection of poetry.

15 Li Taibai is the famous Tang-dynasty poet Li Bai (701–762), well-known for his unbridled expression.

16 The Mountain-Sea Pass (Shanhaiguan) guards the spot where the Great Wall meets the sea.

8. RELEASING BUTTERFLIES: WANYAN JINCHI

1 On Lady Cai and Lady Gao, see the introduction, note 8.
2 Yuan Mei (1716–1798). ECCP, 955–57. The "River" refers to the Yangzi.
3 Tie-bao (1752–1824). ECCP, 717–18.
4 The poetry of Wanyan Jinchi is briefly discussed in Ma Qingfu (2012, 185–87). It would appear that this discussion is based on the selection of her poems included in Xu Shichang (1995).
5 A reference to a well-known poem of the Tang dynasty in which a young bride who is expected to cook a meal for her new family for the first time asks her husband's younger sister how his parents like their congee.
6 Luanyang is another name for Chengde.

9. SEEKING REFUGE IN TRUTH: GUIZHEN DAOREN

1 On this person see Ding Yizhuang (2006, 7). The modern scholar Deng Zhicheng (Deng Zhicheng 2012, 298) recorded in 1945 that he had read an edition of the works of Guizhen Daoren that included a preface by Ying-he.
2 Guizhen Daoren's father was Chen Tingfang, a well-known Confucian scholar.
3 This reflects the widespread belief that talent would shorten a woman's life.
4 This would appear to be a rather late age for marriage at the time. If Guizhen Daoren lived at home up to that time studying with her father it may explain the presence in the first part of her collections of a considerable number of poems addressed to her father or harmonizing with his works. One may wonder to what extent Guizhen Daoren's late marriage was linked to the strong resentment of the gender limitations that were imposed on her, as expressed in one of her earliest poems, "Writing Down my Deepest Feelings."
5 This Fuzhou is located in Shaanxi Province.
6 This person is also mentioned by Yingchuan in her collection (*Ruting shigao*, 2:26a), but I have been unable to identify her. The poems directed to Jingyi Zhuren in Guizhen Daoren's collection provide no precise information. The deferential language in many of them suggests, however, a considerable status difference between the two women. One is tempted to identify Jingyi Zhuren with Lady Tongjia but she is not known to have used this pseudonym, calling herself Tianran Zhuren. From a poem lamenting Jingyi Zhuren (*Bingxuetang shi*, 53a) we learn that Guizhen Daoren met Jingyi Zhuren for the first time in 1804.
7 Bingyue.
8 Bingyue mentions in one of her poems that Guizhen Daoren was the teacher of one of her granddaughters.
9 While a large number of rhyme categories are quite "broad," i.e., include a great number of words that share that particular rhyme, other rhyme categories may be quite "narrow," i.e., include only a very limited number of words that share that particular rhyme. When poetry was practiced as a social game, poets might challenge each other by setting not only a particular theme but also by assigning a specific narrow rhyme.
10 The Jade Clepsydra refers to the palace water clock.
11 Golden Cudgel is here used as translation of *jinwu*. The original meaning of this term is not clear, but it is often understood to refer to a special weapon or a gold-tipped baton. The term was also used at times in the designation of one of the units of the Imperial Guard.

12 The Silver Toad refers to the moon that is said to be inhabited by a toad.

13 The Triple Terrace (Santai) refers to an asterism made of three pairs of stars that correspond to the Three Dukes (Sangong), a common designation for the highest dignitaries of the realm.

14 When the poet Sima Xiangru left Chengdu for the capital he left an inscription on a bridge outside Chengdu, vowing he would not return unless riding a five-horse carriage.

15 Ban Zhao's brother Ban Chao (32–102) was so disgusted with his clerical duties as a young man that "he threw away his brush" to pursue a career in the military. As a general he established Chinese control in the oasis cities of Inner Asia.

16 "Watching heaven from the bottom of a well" is a common phrase to refer to limited experience and narrow-mindedness. The explorer Zhang Qian, sailing down the Yellow River on a raft, eventually found himself sailing the River of Heaven (the Milky Way).

17 The Three Isles are the floating islands of the immortals in the Eastern Ocean. According to other traditions, the Eastern Ocean is home to the Ten Lands of the immortals.

18 The "road to Shu" refers to the road from Chang'an (modern Xi'an) through the steep Qinling Mountains to Chengdu. One of the best known poems of the Tang dynasty poet Li Bai is his "How Hard the Road to Shu" (Shudao nan). See for instance Liu and Lo (1975, 104–6) for an English translation.

19 One of the common ways in late imperial China to seek contact with the dead was through the procedure of planchette writing. The medium held a T-shaped stick and drew lines in a plate filled with ashes or sand; these lines were then transcribed by an assistant as Chinese characters. The revelations often were in verse.

20 A "feathered gentleman" refers to a Daoist priest. Some famous immortals of ancient times wore cloaks made of feathers.

21 The Yellow Springs refer to the world of the dead.

22 The *jiazi* year here must refer to 1804.

23 Qu Yuan (ca. 300 BCE) is credited with the authorship of a number of poems in the *Chuci* in which the author laments the moral corruption of the times when evil men and flattering courtiers are appointed to high office but loyal officials are dismissed and banished to the wilds. Qu Yuan became a symbol for unrecognized talent, not only in the poetry by men but also in the poetry by women. See Yanning Wang (2014b). In one piece in the *Chuci* a fisherman advises Qu Yuan to adapt himself to the ways of the world.

24 Yao and Shun are perfect rulers from a mythical past. The Master refers to Confucius.

10. TRAVELING THROUGHOUT THE EMPIRE: BAIBAO YOULAN

1 ECCP, 428–30.

2 ECCP, 430.

3 Crossley (1990, 128–33).

4 Cf. *Lunyu* XVII, 7.

5 Idema and Grant (2004, 77–82).

6 For Su Hui (third century?) and her palindrome, see Idema and Grant (2004, 127–31).

7 Sima Xiangru was the major poet of the second century BCE.

8 Xie Daoyun was highly praised by her uncle Xie An (320–385) for her line comparing snowflakes to willow floss. Idema and Grant (2004, 136–44).

9 "Other mountains" here refers to teachers and critics. The allusion is based on the following lines in *The Book of Odes*: "With stones of other mountains / One can polish his own jade."

10 The First Emperor of Qin (r. 221–210 BCE) is said to have perused "five cartloads of documents" (*wuche zhi shu*) each day (at these times such documents were usually written on strips of bamboo or wood, which goes a long way to explain the volume).

11 Pine and bamboo are common symbols of loyalty and fidelity in adversity because they stay green even in winter.

12 Cedrela and daylily symbolize one's father and mother.

13 "Hovering Clouds" (Tingyun) is the title of a poem by Tao Qian (365–417) that according to its preface expresses his longing for his friends. For a translation and discussion, see Hightower (1970, 11–15).

14 Cf. the following passage from the preface to *The Book of Odes*: "When emotions are stirred within, they are manifested in words. When these words are not sufficient, they are accompanied by sighs. When these sighs are not sufficient, we extend the words and sing them."

15 One of the common designations for lyrics is *shiyu* (extensions of poetry). Baibao Youlan here uses this characterization of lyrics in order to stress that her sentiments in writing in this genre are the same as those she expresses in her poems.

16 Yu Xin (513–581).

17 Bao Zhao (d. 466).

18 Cao Zhi (192–232).

19 Liu Zhen (170?–217).

20 Bao Linghui (fifth century) was a younger sister of Bao Zhao. One of her works (now lost) was "One Hundred Vows."

21 This fifth character in this lines reads *shun* (to suck) in the version reproduced in Baibao Youlan's collection, but *ru* (to eat) in the version in Bin-liang's collected writing. The last two characters of the line are *boya* (corktree sprouts), which I take as an image for the slivers of flesh because of the well-known medical qualities of the Amur cork tree. My translation of this line is tentative.

22 Bin-liang, *Baochongzhai shiji*, 35:91b. The poem dates from the year 1846, and must have been written shortly before Bin-liang's departure for Lhasa. The "pheasant-rig" is mentioned in *The Book as Odes* as a carriage decorated with pheasant feathers in which a lady rides to court. On Bin-liang as a poet, see Ma Qingfu (2012, 156–61).

23 ECCP, 620–21.

24 Most likely because her anthology project was exclusively focused on *shi* as indicated by its title.

25 It is difficult to square this statement with the content of the collection, which strongly suggests that Baibao Youlan accompanied Gui-liang to every posting up to at least 1845.

26 As the Taiping Tianguo rebellion had originated in southernmost China, the rebels were often characterized as "Cantonese rebels," even though by this time the overwhelming majority of the rebel troops must have been raised locally in the Jiangnan area.

27 A part of the city of Hangzhou was briefly occupied by the rebels in 1860.

28 For brief discussions of her poetry, see Deng Wei (2012, 85–89), and Fu Tao (2015). On her educational poems, see Fu Tao (2014). Fu Tao apparently has no access to the 1856 edition of Baibao Youlan's works.

29 Tea brewed using melted snow is considered to be the height of sophistication.

30 Yijun refers to modern Yichang, a major port on the Yangzi in western Hubei.

31 Badong refers to eastern Sichuan, where the Yangzi passes through the Three Gorges.

32 The "River" refers to the Yangzi.

33 The ancient state of Chu covered the area of Hubei and Hunan.

34 Xiang Chang (Ziping) lived in the early decades of the first century CE. When summoned to court, he refused to serve under the usurper Wang Mang and returned home. After he had arranged the marriage of his sons and daughters, he abandoned his family and with friends roamed the famous mountains. "You" in the final line refers to the author's deceased husband.

35 The ancient state of Shu had its capital at Chengdu, so Shu is often used in poetry as a designation for Sichuan.

36 The Pearl River is the designation of the West River once it has passed Guangzhou.

37 "The pair of urchins" refer to a critical illness.

38 The Zhang River is one of the source rivers of the Gan River in Jiangxi.

39 "Legs of sunlight" are shafts of sunlight shining through the clouds.

40 South of Hangzhou the Qiantang River is called the Fuchun River.

41 The Kitchen God (also known as the God of the Stove) sported the grand title of Arbiter of Fate. Each year on the twenty-third day of the Twelfth Month he departed to heaven to report on the deeds of the family that housed him. To ensure that he would only report good things, his lips were smeared with sugar before his departure.

42 The *Changes* are *The Book of Changes*, one of the Five Classics.

43 *Songs of the South* is the translation of *Chuci* popularized by David Hawkes. Many of the poems in the *Chuci* are ascribed to Qu Yuan.

44 "An otter's sacrifice" refers to a useless activity.

45 Penglai is one of the floating islands of the immortals in the Eastern Ocean.

46 Langyuan is one of the many names of the realm of the immortals.

47 "Fighting flowers" (*doucao*) refers to a game in which the participants try to collect as many as possible different flowers.

48 In the night before his death, the Tang poet Li He (790–816) dreamed he was summoned to heaven in order to write an inscription for a newly completed Jade Tower.

49 "Little Monk" is apparently the childhood name of Lin-zhi.

50 Chang'an (modern Xi'an) was the capital of both the Western Han and the Tang dynasties. Here it refers to Beijing, the capital of the Manchu Qing dynasty.

51 Mount Heng in Hunan Province is the sacred mountain of the south.

52 Middle Prime refers to the fifteenth of the Seventh Month, the date of the Ghost Festival.

53 "The Long Sagebrush" is one of the titles in *The Book of Odes*. In this song an orphan gives expression to his frustration at having been unable to repay his parents for all their toil and suffering on his behalf.

54 These poems most likely were written when Lin-zhi started his formal schooling under a tutor.

55 A floating stick is completely at the mercy of winds and waves.

56 Vimalakirti was a layman whose understanding of the dharma surpassed even that of the Buddha's most eminent disciples.

57 Lianyou (Lotus Friend) refers to Naxun Lanbao.

58 When sailing up a river with blooming peach trees on both its banks, a fisherman from

Wuling inadvertently discovered the utopian world of Peach Spring Fount. See Hightower (1970, 254–58).

59 Lao Laizi is one of the twenty-four exemplars of filial piety: when his parents were old and senile, he dressed up as a little boy in colorful clothes in order to make them believe they were still young.

60 The local magistrate is often called a "father-and-mother official."

61 In the early empire, salaries were paid in grain, and two thousand bushels was the salary of a prefect.

62 Tianzhu (India) is one of Hangzhou's major Buddhist monasteries. It is located to the west of Hangzhou's scenic West Lake. There are actually three monasteries carrying that name: Lower Tianzhu, Middle Tianzhu, and Upper Tianzhu, collectively known as the Three Zhu. Tianzhu is a major center for the veneration of Guanyin, the Bodhisattva of Compassion.

63 Hangzhou's West Lake is one of China's most famous scenic spots.

64 The Six Bridges and Orphan Island are some of the famous sights of Hangzhou's West Lake.

11. A PROUD DESCENDANT OF CHINGGIS KHAN: NAXUN LANBAO

1 The Mongol woman poet Xichun coauthored a collection with her husband, the provincial administration commissioner Foxi Qiaxian. Zhenjun (1973 4:38b). Foxi served as provincial administration commissioner for Sichuan in 1726 and 1727. Du Xun (2012, 2:471) quotes one poem by Xichun titled "Spring Morning" (Chunxiao): "The morning air ripples the curtain waves, / And a light breeze then feebly passes. / Her makeup done, there's nothing she can do / But softly teach the parrot some new words." An even earlier Mongol woman poet may have been the wife of Jinangnuke. This woman of the Borjigit clan authored a now lost collection titled *Beigui ji* (Returning north), which included a poem titled "Leaving through the Old Northern Gate" (Chu gu beikou), which describes the sights and her feelings as she crosses Juyongguan on a trip from Beijing to her homeland: "North of the gate the way is rough and rocky, / It hardly allows passage for my cart. / The single pass provides a narrow roadway; / The thousand hills embrace the central land. / The evening falls and strengthens homeward longing, / The clouds that open offer a wide vista. / Alas that I, as tender as a willow, / Will on this journey suffer wind and dust" (Du Xun 2012, 2:466). This may well be the only poem by a Mongol woman poet of the Qing dynasty that is directly inspired by the landscape beyond the Great Wall.

2 Sun Yuzhen (1991).

3 Aruna (2006, 2009a, 2009b); Bai Daixiao (1992); Mi Yanqing (2014); Wang Longgeng (1982); Wei Zhonglin (1989); Yun Feng (1987); Zhao Xiangbi (1982).

4 Li Qingzhao (1084–1156?) is best known for her *ci* lyrics. See Egan (2013). Bao Xiaohua (2011) offers an extended comparison of Li Qingzhao and Naxun Lanbao and lamely concludes: "Both of them were born in a family of public officials. Both were well-educated. Some of their poems also express strong feelings about their country and people. They bravely rebelled against the feudal ethics and patriarch [sic] morals, pursuing their ideals. The difference between the two is that the works of Naxun Lanbao show the characteristics of her ethnic background, while the works of Li Qingzhao more often express rage and sorrow" (211).

5 ECCP, 648–50.

6 Ding Yizhuang (2006); Da Jiaji (2006). Naxun Lanbao's date of birth is often mistakenly given as 1801.

7 ECCP, 648–50; Deng Wei (2012, 365–79). Sheng-yu is best known for his work on Manchu and Mongol history.

8 This text is also included in the first scroll of Shengyu (1910). Naxun Lanbao's collection also includes a long preface by the scholar and official Li Ciming (1830–1894). On Li, see ECCP, 493.

9 For the social poetry of Naxun Lanbao, see Fu Yixuan (2009).

10 "At the instigation of some powerful person this year an academician dug out the poem on seeing off her brother in my mother's collection, said that she had forgotten her roots and asked for an edict to destroy the printing blocks, hoping to topple me. But thanks to Heaven's Grace his request was not granted." Interlinear notes to a lyric to the tune Jinlüqu titled "My Classmate Wang Taofu Asked Me to Inscribe His Mother's *Jiaoweige yiji*" (Wang Taofu tongnian shu ti taifuren Jiaoweige yiji) in the fourth scroll of his *Yuhuage yiji* (Shengyu 1908). *Jiaoweige yiji* was a small collection of thirty-three poems by Lu Deyi (1820–1865) that had been compiled by her second son, Wang Yanwei (Taofu; 1843–1904) and printed in 1875.

11 ECCP, 209–11. Jiang Zhongshen's poems were collected as *Huancuitang shigao.*

12 "Pushing and pounding" refers to a careful consideration and reworking of each word of a line of verse.

13 *The Book of Odes* is traditionally divided into four sections. The first of these is Airs of the States, which is itself subdivided into fifteen sections, of which the "Songs of Zhou" (Zhou nan) is the first. Most of the songs in this section were, according to the traditional interpretation, composed in honor of the wife of King Wen, praising her for her many virtues. The Four Beginnings are the opening poem of each of the four main sections of *The Book of Odes.*

14 *The Book of Odes* includes a number of texts that, according to the traditional exegetes, had been composed by women.

15 "Floriate" (*hua*) designates the area and culture of China proper.

16 The Wastelands refer to the areas beyond the land of the barbarians, outside the transformative influence of the virtue of the Son of Heaven.

17 Lady Zhang Mengti refers to Zhang Qieying (1792–after 1863). She hailed from Changzhou, and lived with her husband in Beijing from 1829 to 1844, and again from 1847 to 1853. She was widely regarded as one of the finest women poets of her age. In Beijing, her best female friend appears to have been Shen Shanbao.

18 Youlan is Baibao Youlan, who left Beijing for Jinhua in 1856, when her son had been appointed as prefect of that city.

19 Yellow Turbans is a conventional designation of rebels, after a rebellion of the late second century. Here it refers to the Taiping Tianguo movement.

20 Luanyang here refers to the Manchu summer capital Chengde. In the last year of the Second Opium War (1856–60), the Xianfeng emperor and his court fled there when a combined English and French expeditionary force approached Beijing.

21 The famous Song-dynasty poet Su Shi (1036–1101) was banished to Hainan from 1097 to 1100. He died on his way back to the capital.

22 Yang Guifei, the favorite concubine of the Xuanzong emperor (r. 712–756) of the Tang

dynasty (617–906), loved to eat lychees. As soon as these tropical fruits were ripe, they would be delivered by mounted courier to the court in Chang'an (modern Xi'an). In later ages this has often been cited as a prime example of the extravagance that doomed Xuanzong's reign.

23 Ink Princess refers to Foyunbao.

24 Lucky Luster (Jiguang) is the name of a mythic breed of horses from Inner Asia.

25 The Isle of Penglai is one of the three floating islands of the immortals in the Eastern Ocean. This would suggest that the "true practice" of Guizhen was primarily Daoist in inspiration.

26 Duke Huan of Qi once met an elderly man in Maiqiu. This man turned out to be eighty-three. When he was asked to bless the duke, he said: "I pray Your Majesty may live to an old age, despising treasure but treasuring your men. Next I pray that Your Majesty may not be ashamed to learn and may not hate to seek counsel from his subordinates—if you have wise men at your side, they will be the persons to admonish you. Lastly I pray that Your Majesty will commit no crime toward the common people."

12. FROM HENGYANG TO BEIJING: LINGWEN ZHUYOU

1 ECCP, 617–20. The Taiping Tianguo rebellion is reflected in Lingwen Zhuyou's collection by poems on the fall of Yangzhou and of Nanjing. She had passed through these cities earlier when traveling from Hengyang to Beijing, as we learn from other poems in her collection.

2 The title page calligraphy was done by Shang Qiheng (b.1866). A sister of Shang Qiheng was married to a brother of Empress Cixi.

3 Nie Yinniang and Hongxian are female knight-errants immortalized in short stories of the Tang dynasty. For translations, see Kao (1985, 357–61, 363–70).

4 In recognition of her chaste widowhood.

5 Ouyang Xiu (1007–72).

6 Many works in *The Book of Odes* were ascribed to women by the traditional commentators.

7 Zhuo Wenjun was a young widow when she was seduced by the dashing young poet Sima Xiangru. Cai Yan was a young widow when she was abducted by a Xiongnu chieftain, to whom she bore two children; after she had been ransomed, she married for a third time. Zhu Shuzhen lived during the twelfth century. According to the preface to her collection, she was unhappily married, and some modern critics even believe that her poems prove that she had a lover while married. See Idema and Grant (2004, 244–56).

8 The period of Spring and Autumn refers to the period covered by the *Annals of Spring and Autumn*, a chronicle for the ancient state of Lu for the years 721–463 BCE. The *Annals of Spring and Autumn* were believed to have been edited by Confucius and were counted as one of the Five Classics. Gong Jiang of Wei is, according to the Mao commentary of *The Book of Odes*, the author of "Cypress Boat."

9 Boji was the wife of Duke Gong of Song (r. 588–576 BCE). When her dwelling one night caught fire, she refused to flee because a married woman should not go out at night without a chaperone, and as a result she lost her life in the conflagration (Kinney 2014, 68–70).

10 In 681 BCE, Shuji, a younger daughter of the Duke of Lu who had been married as a lesser consort to the lord of Ji, did not return to her natal home in Lu after it had destroyed Ji, but joined her husband's younger brother in the state of Qi out of loyalty to her late husband (Legge 1971b, 88–89).

11 Tao Ying was a woman in the ancient state of Lu. Widowed at an early age, she supported herself and her son by spinning and weaving. When someone proposed marriage to her, she refused, expressing her abiding loyalty to her late husband in a song praising the loyalty of the yellow goose to its deceased partner (Kinney 2004, 82–83).

12 Peng Yulin had proceeded to Guangdong with 4,000 Hunan veterans in the context of the Sino-French War (1884–85).

13 "Baturu" (Brave) was a high merit distinction conferred solely for active service in the field.

14 For a brief discussion of Lingwen Zhuyou's poetry see Gao Xingfan (2007). A short note on her poetry is included in Deng Wei (2012, 397).

15 In this couplet Ban probably refers to the virtuous Concubine Ban, whose best known work was a *shi* poem; the "lush lyrics of the Song" may perhaps refer to the *ci* lyrics of the Song dynasty woman poet Li Qingzhao.

16 When in the mythic past a rebel broke one of the eight pillars separating heaven and earth, the goddess Nüwa repaired the dome of heaven.

17 The changing attitudes of people depending on one's status and wealth.

18 Upper-class women used to pluck their eyebrows and paint on artificial ones that were nicely curved. The high official Zhang Chang (first century BCE) was such a devoted husband that he painted his wife's eyebrows for her.

19 The "bronze jar" is the jar of the clepsydra into which the water drops down throughout the night. As the widow stays awake throughout the night, her heart is broken by this incessant sound.

20 Meng Liang was the devoted wife of the first-century recluse Liang Hong.

21 In traditional China the year consisted of twelve months of twenty-nine or thirty days. In order to make sure that the lunar year would not depart too much from the solar year, Chinese astronomers inserted additional (intercalary) months into the calendar when necessary, so one year could, for instance, have a regular Seventh Month followed by an intercalary Seventh Month.

22 During the Taiping Tianguo rebellion the city of Yangzhou was captured three times by the rebels, and three times retaken by the government troops. The first time the rebels captured the city was in 1853, the third time was in 1858. In view of the last line, the poem most likely refers to the fall of the city in 1858. As the home of the Anhui salt merchants, the city had enjoyed decades of prosperity in the eighteenth century. The destruction caused by the fighting troops on both sides was enormous. See Tobie Meyer-Fong (2009, 40–43).

23 Ji'er refers to her son Ji-shun.

24 This is a line from "Quanxue pian" (Exhortation to study), a poem written by Emperor Zhenzong (r. 997–1022) of the Song dynasty.

25 Salt was a government monopoly and responsible for a large part of the state income. Essential as it was for housekeeping, it was an expensive commodity for citizens.

26 The five watches of the night were marked by a roll on the drums from the drum tower that was found in every city.

13. THE MODEST PURSUIT OF A MINOR WAY: DUOMIN HUIRU

1 In general anthologies of Chinese poetry, the main bulk consisted of poetry by men. Their poetry could be followed by special chapters devoted to the poetry of women, Buddhist monks, Daoist priests, foreigners, and ghosts.

2 Weston (2004, 38).

3 For an extensive discussion of Duomin Huiru's poetry, see Yu Yuehua (1994; reprinted in Deng Wei 2012, 157–63).

4 The grounds of Spoon Garden are today part of the main campus of Peking University and the location of the foreign students' dorm.

5 The "River's Southland" (Jiangnan) is a common designation for the area south of the Yangzi and east of Nanjing.

14. A POET FROM THE HOMELAND: LADY HUSIHALI

1 For a generous introduction to Lady Husihali's life and work, see Zhan Song (2012).

2 Zhou Ruchang (1976, 2:1108–9), quoting Lady Husihali's poems on the *Honglou meng* she wrote at the age of thirteen, suggests that her early poems may have been corrected by her teachers and her parents. Zhan Song (2012, 43–44) suggests that she also may have edited her own poems at some later date when compiling her collection and providing notes.

3 *Liaoyang xianzhi erbian* (1928, image 474).

4 Ibid. Local gazetteers from some of Hui-ge's later postings praise him for the restoration of buildings and for the support of modern education.

5 Hui-ge had these poems reprinted in 1901 as *Quanjie changdu zhizhici, Quanmin gaiguo congshanci Fu Guixun shierze* (Bamboo songs warning against prostitution and gambling, Lyrics urging the people to change their faults and follow the good, with Twelve instructions for the inner chambers; Zhan Song 2012). The social dislocations caused by the Taiping Tianguo rebellion and other anti-Qing movements resulted in a renewed emphasis on spreading the message of traditional morality throughout society, for instance by means of lectures on the Sacred Edict. In order to reach the illiterate lower classes this moral message was also spread by songs and ditties. Hui-ge's activities in this respect were certainly not unique. Cf. Meyer-Fong (2013, 30–34).

6 *Yichun xianzhi* (1940, image 1323–24).

7 On the ritual duties of officials during droughts, see Snyder Reinke (2009).

8 Xie Lingyuan and Bao Linghui are famous women poets of the fourth and fifth century respectively. See Idema and Grant (2004, 136–44; 48–52).

9 On Ban Zhao and her *Instructions for my Daughters*, see Idema and Grant (2004, 17–42).

10 Probably sessions to explain the contents of the Sacred Edict to the population at large.

11 According to one early source, "Shun created the five-stringed zither and sang the song of the southern wind." The content of that song is quoted in another early song as "When the southern wind is sweet, / It can release the trouble of us people; / When the southern wind is timely, / It can enlarge the prosperity of us people."

12 Zhan Song (2012, 40) argues that Lady Husihali must have been still alive in 1901 because Hui-ge did not use any of the customary designations for a deceased wife when he wrote his preface for the reprinting of his and her moral songs.

13 *Zi* refers to midnight (11 p.m.–1 a.m.), *wu* to noon (11 a.m.–1 p.m.).

14 Penglai is one of the floating islands of the immortals in the Eastern Ocean.

15 These two lines describe Lin Daiyu, one of the female protagonists of the novel. Because of karmic causes she can never declare her love for the novel's male protagonist, and she dies the night he marries another girl. The "paradise of parting's pain" (*lihentian*) is the highest of the thirty-three heavens in Buddhist cosmology.

16 *Qian* stands for yang, *kun* for yin.

17 According to some ancient Chinese sources, the earth is supported by a giant turtle.

18 Shenyang ("the northern bank of the Shen"), also known as Shenjing or Mukden, was the secondary capital of the Qing dynasty.

19 By the nineteenth century, "bamboo branch lyrics" (*zhuzhi ci*) had come to designate humorous or satirical quatrains in a simple language. For recent studies on opium use in nineteenth-century China, see Dikötter et al. (2004); McMahon (2002); and Zheng (2005). Lady Husihali focuses on opium addiction among women. For a studio photograph of a Manchu woman with an opium pipe, see Zheng (2005, 118).

20 In Chinese the opium pipe is called *qiang* (lance, gun). For a discussion of the implications of this name see McMahon (2002, 112).

21 "Beasts that spit out smoke" are incense burners in the shape of real or mythical animals.

22 The Liuzhou Peninsula and the Korean Peninsula?

23 The legend of Mulan tells the story of a girl who dresses as a boy to take her elderly father's place in the army. She returns home after twelve years without her fellow soldiers ever guessing that she might be a girl. Kwa and Idema (2010).

24 The rickshaw was a Japanese invention to replace the carrying chair and the wheelbarrow. When first introduced in the late nineteenth century it was a spectacular improvement over these earlier forms of transport.

25 The traditional Lantern Festival was celebrated during the full moon of the First Month. Illuminations brightened the night and men and women thronged the streets.

26 In a well-known story from the Tang dynasty, a student on his way to the capital to take the examinations makes a stop at an inn in Handan. Waiting for the yellow millet gruel of his meal to be cooked, he has a dream in which he has a spectacular career. When he wakes up, he realizes that our worldly existence is only a dream.

27 Before the destruction wrought by the mid-century Taiping Tianguo rebellion.

28 The Taiping Tianguo rebels who had made Nanjing their capital.

29 The Bodhisattva refers to the Bodhisattva Guanyin.

30 The "Two Souths" (Ernan) refer to the two first sections of the Airs, the first part of *The Book of Odes*. The first song of *The Book of Odes* is a wedding song, implying, according to the traditional commentators, that marriage is the basis of society.

31 Zhuo Wenjun was a young widow when she allowed herself to be seduced by the dashing young poet Sima Xiangru (179–118 BCE).

32 This Lady Fan may have been a local celebrity from Yuanzhou.

33 Bao Xuan, who lived during the Han dynasty, so impressed his teacher Huan that the latter gave him his daughter as wife. Bao Xuan returned her rich dowry, and his wife joined him in farm work without any complaint.

GLOSSARY OF CHINESE CHARACTERS

A-er-jing-a 阿爾京阿
A-gong 嗄公
A-han-tai 阿漢泰
Ai-bi-da 愛必達
A-ke Zhan-zhen 阿克占震

Baibao Youlan 百保友蘭
Baitou yin 白頭吟
Baiyunguan 白雲觀
bajiaogu 八角鼓
Ban Chao 班超
Ban Zhao 班昭
Bao Linghui 鮑令暉
Bao Xuan 鮑宣
Bao Zhao 鮑照
Bao Zhihui 鮑之惠
Bao-en 寶恩
Bao-kang 寶康
Baoshantang jiaxun 寶善堂家訓
Baoyan 葆妍
Baqi shiyuan xiaozhuan 八旗詩媛小傳
Baqi tongzhi 八旗通志
Baqi yiwen bianmu 八旗藝文編目
Beifeng 北風
Beigui ji 北歸集
benzhai cangban 本宅藏版
Bi Gan 比干
Bingling Gong 炳靈公
Bingyue 冰月
Bin-liang 斌良
Bin-yue 斌越
Bixia yuanjun 碧霞元君
Bo Shaojun 薄少君
Bodao 伯道
Boji 伯姬
Boxiang laoren 柏香老人
Boya 伯牙
boya 檗牙
bozhou 柏舟
burugui 不如歸

Cai Dianqi 蔡殿齊
Cai Wan 蔡琬
Cai Yan 蔡琰
Cai Yong 蔡邕
Cai Yurong 蔡毓榮
Cao Cao 曹操
Cao Xueqin 曹雪芹
Cao Zhenxiu 曹貞秀
Cao Zhi 曹植
Chang'e 嫦娥
Chaofanshi huafan 超範室畫範
Chen 陳
Chen Tingfang 陳廷芳
Cheng-an 成安
Cheng-shuo 承碩
Chong-bao 崇保
Chu gu beikou 出古北口
Chuci 楚辭
Chunqinwang fu 醇親王府
Chunri sifu 春日思父
Chunxiao 春曉
Chun-ying 淳穎
ci 詞
"Ci Shilan nüshi jianzeng yuanyun" 次石蘭女史見贈元韻
Concubine Ban 班婕妤
Consort Shu 淑妃
Cui Hao 崔顥

Dailü caotang yishi 帶綠草堂遺詩
Danxiang yingao 淡香吟稿
Danxiang Zhuren 淡香主人
Deng You 鄧攸
De-yong 德勇
Ding Lan 丁蘭
Ding-chang 定長
Dong'e shi yijia shigao 東鄂氏一家詩稿
Dongqingguan shi 冬青館詩
Dongwu 東悟
Dongye mengfu 冬夜夢父
doucao 鬥草

Du Fu 杜甫
Du Xun 杜珣
Du Yu 杜宇
Duan-en 端恩
dujuan 杜鵑
Duke Huan 桓公
Duke Xing 興
Duling 杜陵
Duo-fu 多福
Duomin Huiru 多敏惠如

E 猗
E-lun-dai 鄂崙岱
Emperor Cheng 成帝
Emperor Wu 武帝
Emperor Yuan 元帝
Empress Chen 陳皇后
Empress Wen 文皇后
En-hua 恩華
En-liang 恩良
En-long 恩隆
Ernan 二南
Ernü yingxiong zhuan 兒女英雄傳

fanli 凡例
Fashishan 法式善
Feimo 費莫
Feiqiong 飛瓊
Feng 馮
Feng Fan 馮播
Fengyi 鳳儀
Foxi Qiaxian 佛喜恰仙
Foyunbao 佛芸保
fu 賦
Fuxi 伏義
Fuxue 婦學
"Fuzeng Luo Shilan Nüshi" 賦贈駱石蘭女史

Gan Yunyuan 甘運源
Gao Jingfang 高景芳
Gao Qi 高琦
Gao Qizhuo 高其倬
gegu 割股
Geng Jingzhong 耿精忠
Geng Juzhong 耿聚忠
Gong Danting 宮淡亭
Gong Jiang 共姜
Gong Zizhen 龔自珍
Grand Secretary Fu 福
Gu Taiqing 顧太清
"Gu Taiqing Yihui shehui jiaowang zhuyao renwu biao" 顧太清奕繪社會交往主要人物表
Guan Longfeng 關龍逢
Guanshengge jiayan 觀生閣家言
Guihai yin 閨海吟
Guihu yishi 閨壺遺詩
Gui-liang 桂良
guining 歸寧
Gui-pu 桂圃
Guizhen Daoren 歸真道人
Guochao guige shi chao 國朝閨閣詩鈔
Guochao guixiu zhengshi ji 國朝閨秀正始集
Guochao guixiu zhengshi xuji 國朝閨秀正始續集
Guochao guixiushi liuxuji 國朝閨秀詩柳絮集
Guofeng 國風
Guoluoluo 郭洛羅

hao 號
He Fu 何福
"He Luo jiefu Peixiang yuanyun" 和駱節婦佩香元韻
Hecun shichao 合存詩鈔
Heng-en 恆恩
Heng-ren 恆仁
hengxing 横行
He-she-li Ba-ni-hun 赫舍里巴尼渾
He-shen 和珅
He-shun 和順
He-you 鶴友
Honglou meng 紅樓夢
Hongloumeng ying 紅樓夢影
Hong-shang 弘晌
Hongxian 紅線
Hongxue yinyuan tuji 鴻雪因緣圖記
Hongxuexuan shiwenji 紅雪軒詩文集
Hu 胡

Hu Wenkai 胡文楷
hua 華
Huaisu 懷素
Hualiang 畫梁
Huan 桓 (surname)
Huancuitang shigao 環翠堂詩稿
Huang Zhimo 黃秩模
Hui-ge 惠格

Ji 纪
Ji Yun 紀昀
Ji Zha 季扎
Jian-fu 健夫
Jiang Zhongshen 蔣重申
Jiangxi huanyou jishi 江西宦遊紀事
Jiangyou suihuan jishi 江右隨宦紀事
Jie 桀
Ji'er 吉兒
Ji-guang 吉光
Jinangnuke 吉囊努克
Jing-an 靜菴
Jing-lin 景麟
Jing-ting 凈庭
Jingyi 靜怡
Jingyi Furen 靜怡夫人
Jingyi Zhuren 靜怡主人
Jing-zheng 敬徵
Jinlüqu 金縷曲
jinwu 金吾
Jin-zhai 藎齋
Ji-shun Rong-fan 吉順榮帆
juan 卷
jueju 絕句

Kong Shangren 孔尚仁
Kua-dai 夸代
"Kufu shi" 哭父詩
Kui-fang 揆芳
Kui-qing 奎慶
Kui-xu 揆敘
"Kumu shi" 哭母詩
Kun 坤
kuzi 哭子

Lady Chang 常氏
Lady Fan 范氏
Lady Fucha 富察氏
Lady Han 韓氏
Lady Husihali 扈斯哈里氏
Lady Geng 耿氏
Lady Liu 劉氏
Lady Lu 盧氏
Lady Tongjia 佟佳氏
Lady Zhaojia 兆佳氏
Lady Zheng 鄭氏
Lady Zhoujia 周佳氏
Lang-feng 閬夆
Langui baolu 蘭閨寶錄
Langyuan 閬苑
Lanxuan Nüshi 蘭軒女史
Lanxuan Zhuren 蘭軒主人
Lanxue ji 蘭雪集
Lao Laizi 老萊子
Lao Yuan'en 勞沅恩
Lenghongxuan ci 冷紅軒詞
Lenghongxuan shiji 冷紅軒詩集
Lenghongxuan xuji 冷紅軒續集
Lengyue shantang shiji 冷月山堂詩集
Lengzhaiyin chugao 冷齋吟初稿
Lengzhai Zhuren 冷齋主人
li 籬 (fence)
li 離 (separation, parting)
Li Bai 李白
Li Ciming 李慈銘
Li He 李賀
Li Hongzhang 李鴻章
Li Jinchun 李錦春
Li Qingzhao 李清照
Li Taibai Lou 李太白樓
Liang Hong 梁鴻
Lianyou 蓮友
Lianzhai sanshou 蓮齋三壽
Lichao guiya 歷朝閨雅
Lidai funü zhuzuo kao 歷代婦女著作考
Liexin ji 裂心集
lihentian 離恨天
Liji 禮記
Lijing 禮經
Lin 林

Lin Daiyu 林黛玉
Lingnan Nüshi Meixuan 嶺男女史梅軒
Lingwen Zhuyou 齡文竹友
Lin-qing 麟慶
Lin-zhi 麟趾
Liu Keyi 劉可毅
Liu Yuxi 劉禹錫
Liu Zhen 劉楨
"Long Yaomei ge" 龍么妹歌
Lord Getian 葛天氏
Lu Deyi 盧德儀
luan 鸞
Luo Qilan 駱綺蘭
Luo Shilan 駱石蘭
Lüchuang yingao 綠窗吟稿
lüshi 律詩
Lüzhu 綠珠

Ma ruren 馬孺人
Maiqiu 麦邱
Manzhou guige shichao 滿洲閨閣詩鈔
Manzu wenxue shi 滿族文學史
Master Zhuang 莊子
Meihuayin 梅花引
men 門
Meng 蒙
Meng Guang 孟光
Meng Ke 孟珂
Menghuage shigao 夢華閣詩稿
Mengyue 夢月
Mian-cheng 綿成
Miaolianbao 妙蓮保
Miaoyu 妙玉
ming 名
Mingben 明本
Ming-chang qi-chu 明長啟初
Mingfeng ji 鳴鳳記
Ming-rui 明瑞
Ming-sheng 明繩
Ming-wan 明紈
Mingyuan shihua 名媛詩話
Ming-zhu 明珠
Miss Nalan 納蘭氏
"Muzhiming" 墓誌銘

Nalan Xing-de 納蘭性德
Na-mu-tu 那穆圖
Nanmiao 南廟
Naxun Lanbao 那遜蘭保
Neixun 內訓
Neize 內則
Neng-tai 能泰
Nian Gengyao 年羹堯
Nie Yinniang 聶隱孃
Ning-xiu 寧秀
Nü Lunyu 女論語
Nü Xiaojing 女孝經
nü youxian 女遊仙
Nüfan 女範
Nüjie 女誡
Nüwa 女媧
Nüxun 女訓

Ochang 鄂昌
Ortai 鄂爾泰
Ouyang Xiu 歐陽修

pailü 排律
Peilanxuan xiuyu cao 佩蘭軒繡餘草
Peng Yulin 彭玉麟
Peng Yunzhang 彭蘊章
Penglai 蓬萊
Prince Gong 恭親王
Prince Kang 康王
Prince of the Blood Zhuang 莊親王
Prince Shen of the Second Rank 慎郡王
Prince Su 肅王
Pu-zhao 普照

Qian 乾
Qin Jia 秦嘉
Qingdai guige shiren zhenglüe 清代閨閣詩人徵略
Qing-gui 慶桂
Qingren shuohui erbian 清人說匯二編
Qingwen buhui 清文補彙
Qing-yue 慶岳
Qi-shi 齊什 (七十)
Qiudeng kenü tu 秋燈課女圖
Qiusheng fu 秋聲賦

Qiuyan 秋煙
qu 曲
Qu Yuan 屈原
Quanjie changdu zhizhici, Quanmin gaiguo congshanci Fu Guixun shierze 勸戒娼賭竹枝詞勸民改過從善詞附閨訓十二則
Quanxue pian 勸學篇
Quli 曲禮

ren 人
Rongyin 榮蔭
ru 茹
Ruijuzhuang 瑞菊莊
Rui-liu 瑞六
Rui-yuan 瑞元
Ru-song 如松
Ruting shicao 如亭詩草
Ruting shigao 如亭詩稿

sangong 三公
santai 三台
San-yin 三蔭
sao 騷
Servant Woman Li 李氏
Shang Qiheng 尚其亨
Shangguan Wan'er 上官婉兒
Shanhaiguan 山海關
Shanxi 善憙
Shaoru 少如
Shen 沈
Shen Shanbao 沈善寶
Shen Wan 沈 宛
Shen Yanfang 沈延芳
Shen Yue 沈約
Sheng-yu 盛昱
shi 詩
Shi Chong 石崇
Shi Kefa 史可法
Shi Shuyi 施淑儀
Shi Xiangyun 史湘雲
Shilan 石蘭 (alternative name of Luo Qilan)
Shilan 師蘭 (Wanyan Jinchi's sister)
Shiqi tie 十七帖
Shi-tang 式堂
shiyu 詩餘
Shiyu hejie 詩餘合解
Shuangcheng 雙成
"Shudao nan" 蜀道難
Shuji 叔姬
shun 吮
Shurong 淑榮
si 思 (thought, longing)
si 絲 (thread)
Sibo 思柏
Sima Xiangru 司馬相如
Siyan Zhuren 四焉主人
Song Ruoxin 宋若莘
Song Ruozhao 宋若昭
Song Yu 宋玉
Song-chun 松椿
Song-shan 嵩山
Song-zhong-feng 嵩中峰
Su Hui 蘇蕙
Su Qin 蘇秦
Su Shi 蘇軾
Sufang 素芳
Suhui 素卉
Suiwei leicao 繐帷泪草
Sushi zixu tie 素師自序帖
Suwan Duo-ling 蘇完多齡
Suxinren 素心人
Suyan 素言

tai 台
Tai-fei-yin 檯費蔭
Taiping Tianguo 太平天國
Tairen 太任
Taishang ganying pian 太上感應篇
Tao Liang 陶樑
Tao Qian 陶潛 (Yuanming 淵明)
Tao Ying 陶嬰
Taohua shan 桃花扇
Taoyuan ji 桃園記
Tianran Zhuren 天然主人
"Tianwen" 天問
Tianxian zhengli 天仙正理
Tianzhi ouwen 天咫偶聞
Tianzhu 天竺

tici 題辭
Tie Ye-ting 鐵冶亭
Tie-bao 鐵保
Tingqiuxuan guizhong tongren ji 廳秋軒閨中同人集
Tingqiuxuan zengyan 聽秋軒贈言
"Tingyun" 停雲
tong 童
Tong Guogang 佟國綱
Tong-shan 峒山
Tong-yuan 桐園
tu 荼

waifan nüshi 外籓女史
Wang Mang 王莽
Wang Qisun 王豈孫
Wang Shao 王韶
"Wang Taofu tongnian shu ti taifuren Jiaoweige yiji" 王弢甫同年屬題太夫人焦尾閣遺集
Wang Xizhi 王羲之
Wang Yanwei 王彥威
Wang Zhaojun 王昭君
Wanyan Chong-hou 完顏崇厚
Wanyan Jinchi 完顏金墀
Wanyan Yun Zhu 完顏惲珠
Wen Huacheng 文化成
Wen-duan 文端
Weng Fanggang 翁方綱
Wenhuang Xianghua 文篁香花
Wen-kang 文康
Wen-liang 文梁
Wenshilou hexuan 問詩樓詩選
Wen-xi 文禧
wu 午
Wu Sangui 吳三桂
Wu Shouyang 伍守陽
Wu Xiuying 吳秀英
Wubei tai fujin zhuan fu Wubei tai fujin shi 五輩太福晉傳附五輩太福晉詩
wuche zhi shu 五車之書
Wula 烏拉
Wumen shihua 梧門詩話
Wusi cuncao 烏私存草
Wuyunzhu 烏雲珠

xi 兮
Xi Shi 西施
"Xian dafu shiji gongji" 先大夫詩集恭記
"Xianbi Han Taishuren xingzhuang" 先妣韓太淑人形狀
Xiang Chang 向長
Xiangcen 湘岑
Xiaoxue 小學
Xiaoya 小雅
Xichao yasong ji 熙朝雅頌集
Xichao yasong ji yuji 熙朝雅頌集餘集
Xichun 熙春
Xie An 謝安
Xie Daoyun 謝道韞
Xie Lijuan 謝麗娟
Xi-en 禧恩
Xieyunlou xiaogao 寫韻樓小稿
Xiguang 希光
Xin-shao-yuan 辛紹元
xing 姓
xingling 性靈
Xiuhuang 修篁
xiunü 秀女
xiuyu 繡餘
Xiuyu shigao 繡餘詩稿
Xiuyu xiaocao 繡餘小草
Xiyou Nüshi 習幽女史
Xiyuan shichao 西園詩鈔
Xizhen 錫縝
Xu 徐
Xu Shu 徐淑
Xuanmenglou ci 選夢樓詞
Xuanzong 玄宗
Xubaiting ji xu 虛白亭集序
Xubaiting shichao 虛白亭詩鈔
Xuchuang yake 虛窗雅課
Xuecheng 學誠
Xuelou jiangshou 雪樓講授
Xueqin 雪琴
Xu-gu 虛谷
xuji 續集
"Xunzi shuo" 訓子說

Ya-er-ha-shan 雅爾哈善
Yan Hui 顏回
Yan Song 嚴嵩
Yang 楊
Yang Guifei 楊貴妃
Yang Jisheng 楊繼盛
Yangyizhai Nüshi 養易齋女史
Yangyizhai Zhuren 養易齋主人
Yan-shan 燕山
yanzi 雁字
Yan-zuo 延祚
Yehe Zao-wang-bao 葉河竈王保
Ye-ting 冶亭
yi 一
Yi-hui 奕繪
Yingchuan 瑩川
Ying-he 英和
Ying-jun 瀛俊
Ying-zhi 英志
Yin-reng 胤礽
Yin-si 胤禩
Yin-tang 胤禟
Yin-ti 胤禔
Yin-xi 胤禧
Yin-zhen 胤禛
Yiqing shushi shichao 怡情書室詩鈔
Yi-sang-a 伊桑阿
Yi-song-a 伊嵩阿
Yi-sun 宜孫
Yi-xin 奕訢
Yi-xing 宜興
Yongfeng 鄘風
Yong-fu 永福
Yong-gui 永貴
Yong-shou 永壽
Yong-xi 永錫
Yongyan zhizhi 庸言知旨
Yong-zhao 永釗
You-sheng Yu-qing 友生餘慶
youxianci 遊仙詞
Yu Xin 庾信
Yuan Jianzhai 袁簡齋
Yuan Mei 袁枚
Yu-bao 玉保
yuchi 玉尺
Yu-de 玉德
Yueshan shihua 月山詩話
Yueshan shiji 月山詩集
Yuhua 毓華
Yuhuage yiji 鬱華閣遺集
Yulian tang shiji 余廉堂詩集
Yuling 毓靈
Yun Zhu 惲珠
Yunchuang xiansheng 芸窗先生
Yunchuang yingao 芸窗吟稿
Yunlan zhuangge yigao 蘊蘭妝閣遺稿
Yun-xi 允禧
Yunxiang 韻湘
Yunxiangguan yishi 芸香館遺詩
Yunzhenxuan xiaocao 蘊真軒小草
Yuxiu 毓秀
Yuxuan 玉軒

Zhang Chang 張敞
Zhang Hongsheng 張宏生
Zhang Mengti 張夢緹
Zhang Qian 張騫
Zhang Qieying 張縚英
Zhang Xuecheng 章學誠
Zhang Yuniang 張玉娘
Zhang Zongyuan 張宗元
Zhao Feiyan 趙飛燕
"Zhaohun" 招魂
Zhaorong 昭容
Zhen-jun 震鈞
Zhenwu 真武
zhihun 指婚
Zhong Ziqi 鍾子期
Zhong-shan-ting 忠善亭
Zhongxiang ci 眾香詞
Zhou 紂
Zhou nan 周南
Zhu Shuzhen 朱淑真
Zhu Xi 朱憙
Zhuang Zhou 莊周
Zhuangjie 壯介
Zhu-liang 朱亮
Zhuo Wenjun 卓文君
Zhuo-li 卓立
Zhuwu shichao 竹屋詩鈔

Zhuyou 竹友
zhuzhi ci 竹枝詞
zi 子 (cyclical character)
zi 字 (style name)
Zi Chan 子產
Zi Zhang 子張
zidishu 子弟書
Ziping 子平
Ziren 子仁
"Zishu" 自述
"Zishu ge" 自述歌
Ziyou 子猷

BIBLIOGRAPHY

MAJOR COLLECTIONS OF MANCHU AND MONGOL WOMEN POETS

Baibao Youlan 百保友蘭. *Lenghongxuan shiji* 冷紅軒詩集; *Lenghongxuan xuji* 冷紅軒續集; *Lenghongxuan ci* 冷紅軒詞. Woodblock edition (1857?). Prefaced by Prince Gong 恭親王 (1833–1898), 1855; Peng Yunzhang 彭蘊章 (1791–1862), 1855; Tao Liang 陶樑, 1855; *Tici* by Lianzhai sanshou 蓮齋三壽; Foyunbao 佛芸保; Li Jinchun 李錦春; Bin-liang 斌良 (1784–1847). Preface by the author, 1837. Postfaces by Lao Yuan'en 勞沅恩 (1802–1858), 1856; Lin-zhi 麟趾, 1857.

———. *Lenghongzhai shiji*. 2 *juan*. Woodblock edition, 1875. Reprinted in *Meiguo Hafo daxue Hafo Yanjing tushuguancang Ming Qing funü zhushu huikan*, edited by Fang and Yi, vol. 2:371–94. Preface by Naxun Lanbao, 1873. Calligraphy of title page (1875) by Xizhen 錫縝.

———. *Lenghongzhai shiji*. 2 *juan*. Woodblock edition, 1882. Title page calligraphy (1875) by Xizhen. Preface by Naxun Lanbao, 1873. Postface by Chong-bao 崇保, 1882.

Bingyue 冰月. *Lengzhaiyin chubian* 冷齋吟初編. 2 *juan*. Woodblock edition of the early nineteenth century. Preface by Tie-bao 鐵保, 1798; preface by author, 1798.

———. *Lengzhaiyin xubian* 冷齋吟續編. 2 *juan*. Woodblock edition of the early nineteenth century.

Duomin Huiru 多敏惠如. *Yiqiange yishi* 逸蒨閣遺詩. Woodlock edition of the late nineteenth century. Preface by Liu Keyi 劉可毅 (d. 1900), 1893. Postface by Bao-kang 寶康, n.d.

Fucha Shi 富察氏. *Danxiang shichao* 淡香吟稿. Woodblock edition.

Guizhen Daoren 歸真道人. *Bingxuetang shi* 冰雪堂詩. Woodblock edition of the middle of the nineteenth century. Preface by Yuhua 毓華, 1840, followed by two regulated poems by Ming-chang Qi-chu 明長啟初. Postface by Chengshuo 承碩, 1834.

Husihali Shi 扈斯哈里氏. *Jiangxi huanyou jishi* 江西宦遊紀事. Lithographic edition.

———. *Xiuyu xiaocao fu Jiangyou suihuan jishi* 繡餘小草附江右隨宦記事. Lithographic edition of the Shanghai shuju 上海書局 of 1903. Prefaces by Chen Hongzhang 陳鴻章 (1896); Wen Huacheng 文化成; Chen Jingxian 陳景賢; and Shen Lin 沈麟. Title page inscription by Bao Xueqing 鮑雪卿.

Lanxuan Zhuren 蘭軒主人. *Lanxuan shi* 蘭軒詩. 1 *juan*. Woodblock edition of the second half of the eighteenth century. Prefaces by An-yi-nong 安肄農, 1758; Yehe Zao-wang-bao 葉河竈王保, 1769; Duo-fu 多福, 1765. Postfaces by Songshan, 1755; He Fu 何福, 1754.

Lingwen Zhuyou 齡文竹友. *Xuxiang yinguan xiaocao* 絮香吟館小草. Woodblock edition of the second half of the nineteenth century. Preface by Peng Yulin 彭玉麟, n.d. Title page calligraphy by Shang Qiheng 尚其亨, dated 1886.

Mengyue 夢月. *Zhuwu shichao* 竹屋詩鈔. Manuscript of the early nineteenth century. Preface by author, 1808. Editorial principles.

Nalanshi 納蘭氏. *Xiuyu shigao* 繡餘詩藁. Woodblock edition of the early eighteenth century. Preface (damaged) by Yongshou 永壽, n.d.

Naxun Lanbao 那遜蘭保. *Naxun Lanbao shiji* 那逊兰保诗集. In *Naxun Lanbao shiji sanzhong* 那逊兰保诗集三种, edited by Sun Yuzhen 孙玉溱, 9–75. Hohhot: Neimengu daxue chubanshe, 1991.

———. *Yunxiangguan yishi* 芸香館遺詩. Woodblock edition of 1874. Reprinted in *Meiguo Hafo daxue Hafo Yanjing tushuguancang Ming Qing funü zhushu huikan*, edited by Fang and Yi, vol. 2:353–70. Preface by Li Ciming 李慈銘 (1830–1894), 1874. Postface by Sheng-yu 盛昱, 1874. Title page calligraphy (1874) by Xizhen.

———. *Yunxiangguan yishi*. Lithographic edition, 1928.

Sibo 思柏 and Gong Danting 宫淡亭. *Hecun shichao* 合存詩抄. 4 *juan*. Woodblock edition of the mid-eighteenth century. Reprinted in *Qingdai shiwenji huibian*, vol. 223:551–610. Prefaces by Gong Danting, 1738; Shibo, 1738.

———. *Shiyu hejie* 詩餘合解. Woodblock edition of the mid-eighteenth century. National Library, Beijing. Reprinted in *Qingdai shiwenji huibian*, vol. 223:611–19. Preface by Gong Danting, 1742.

Tongjia Shi 佟佳氏. *Baoshantang jiaxun* 寶善堂家訓. Woodblock edition of the early nineteenth century. Preface by author, 1800.

———. *Ku fumu shi* 哭父母詩. Manuscript (Harvard-Yenching Library).

———. *Liexin ji* 裂心集. Woodblock edition, earliest years of the nineteenth century (1802?).

———. *Lüchang yingao* 綠窗吟稿. Manuscript. Reprinted in *Nankai tushuguan xijian Qingren bieji congkan*; reprinted in *Qingdai guixiuji congkan*.

———. *Suiwei lei cao* 繐帷泪草. Woodblock edition, second part of the eighteenth century.

———. *Wenshilou hexuan* 問詩樓合選. Woodblock edition, second part of the eighteenth century. Preface by author, 1792. Postface by Cao Zhenxiu 曹貞秀, 1792.

———. *Wusi cun cao* 烏私存草. Woodblock edition, second part of the eighteenth century. Preface by author, 1776.

———. *Xuchuang yake* 虛窗雅課. *Chuji* 初集; *erji* 二集. Woodblock edition of the early nineteenth century (1810). Reprinted in *Meiguo Hafo daxue Hafo Yanjing tushuguancang Ming Qing funü zhushu huikan*, edited by Fang and Yi, vol. 1:75–101. Reprinted in *Qingdai shiwenji huibian*, vol. 391. Preface by Qing-gui 慶桂, n.d. Postface by Ying-he 英和, 1805.

Wanyan Jinchi 完顏金墀. *Lüyunxuan shiji* 綠芸軒詩集. Woodblock edition of the second part of the nineteenth century. Preface by Naxun Lanbao 那遜蘭保, 1873.

Yangyizhai Zhuren 養易齋主人. *Yangyizhai shi* 養易齋詩. 1 *juan*. Woodblock edition of the late eighteenth century. Postface by Song-shan 嵩山, 1789.

Yingchuan 瑩川. *Ruting shigao* 如亭詩稿. 2 *juan*. Woodblock edition of the first half of the nineteenth century. Prefaces by Li Zonghan 李宗瀚, 1828; Pan Shi'en 潘世恩, 1827; Yang Yizeng 楊懌曾, 1827; Feng Yuanxi 馮元錫, 1827; Xie Zhao 謝照, n.d. Postface by Rui-yuan 瑞元, 1828.

Zhoujia Shi 周佳氏. *Yunchuang yingao* 芸窗吟稿, woodblock edition. Preface by Kui-qing 奎慶, n.d.; postface by Ru-song 如松, n.d.

GENERAL BIBLIOGRAPHY

Aruna 阿如那. 2006. "Mengguzu 'Yi'an jushi' Naxun Lanbao: Jiating, minzu, xingbie dui qi shige chuangzuo de yingxiang" 蒙古族易安居士那遜蘭保家庭民族性別對其詩歌的影響. *Hulunbei'er xueyuan xuebao* 14 (3): 41–43.

———. 2009a. "Shiji *Yunxiangguan yishi* ticai fenxi" 詩集芸香館遺詩題材分析, *Changsha daxue xuebao* 23 (1): 73–74.

———. 2009b. "Shiji *Yunxiangguan yishi* suo fanyingchulai de minzu jingshen" 詩集芸香館遺詩所反映出來的民族精神. *Neimenggu minzu daxue xuebao* 15 (1): 4–5.

Bai Daixiao 白代晓. 1992. "Naxun Lanbao ji qi *Yunxiangguan yishi*" 那逊兰保及其芸香馆遗诗. *Neimenggu shehui kexue*, no. 6: 95–98.

Bao Xiaohua 包晓华. 2011. "Mengguzu nüshiren Naxun Lanbao yu Li Qingzhao zhi bijiao" 蒙古族女诗人那逊兰保与李清照之比较. *Dalian minzu xueyuan xuebao* 13 (2): 110–12; 122.

Billeter, Jean François. 1990. *The Chinese Art of Writing*. New York: Rizzoli International Publications.

Binliang 斌良. *Baochongzhai shiji* 抱冲齋詩集. Woodblock edition.

Bodde, Derk, and M. L. C. Bogan. 1994. *Annual Customs and Festivals in Peking with Manchu Customs and Superstitions*. Reprint, Taipei: SMC Publications.

Brunnert, H. S. and V. V. Hagelstrom. n.d. *Present Day Political Organization of China*. Reprint, n.p.

Bulag, Uradyn E. 2002. *The Mongols at China's Edge: History and the Politics of National Unity*. Lanham, MD: Rowman and Littlefield Publishers.

Cao Zhenxiu 曹貞秀. *Xieyunxuan xiaogao* 寫韻軒小稿. Woodblock edition. Reprinted in *Meiguo Hafo daxue Hafo Yanjing tushuguancang Ming Qing funü zhushu huikan*, edited by Fang Xiujie and Yi Weide, 4:275–309. Guilin: Guangxi shifan daxue chubanshe.

Cha Zhengxian 查正贤, ed. 2010. *Jiangnan nüxing biejie erbian* 江南女性别集二编. 2 vols. Hefei: Huangshan shushi.

Chang, Kang-I Sun. 1997. "Ming and Qing Anthologies of Women's Poetry and Their Selection Strategies." In *Writing Women of Imperial China*, edited by Ellen Widmer and Kang-I Sun Chang, 147–70. Stanford, CA: Stanford University Press.

Chang, Kang-i Sun, and Haun Saussy, eds. 1999. *Women Writers of Traditional China*. Stanford, CA: Stanford University Press.

Chaves, Jonathan. 1986. "Moral Action in the Poetry of Wu Jia-ji (1618–1684)." *Harvard Journal of Asiatic Studies* 46 (2): 387–469.

Chen Shuiyun 陳水雲. 2005. "Gu Chun yanjiu de shiji huigu" 顧春研究的世紀回顧. *Manzu yanjiu*, no. 2: 104–11.

Chunying 淳穎. 1806. *Xubaiting shichao* 虛白亭詩鈔. In *Qingdai shiwenji huibian*, vol. 466:409–61.

Confucius. 1979. *The Analects (Lun yü)*. Translated by D. C. Lau. Harmondsworth, UK: Penguin.

Crossley, Pamela Kyle. 1990. *Orphan Warriors: Three Manchu Generations and the End of the Qing World*. Princeton, NJ: Princeton University Press.

———. 1994. "Manchu Education." In *Education and Society in Late Imperial China, 1600–1900*, edited by B. A. Elman and Alexander Woodside, 340–78. Berkeley: University of California Press.

———. 1997. *The Manchus*. Cambridge, MA: Blackwell.

———. 1999. *A Translucent Mirror: History and Identity in Qing Imperial Ideology*. Berkeley: University of California Press.

Crossley, Pamela Kyle, and Evelyn S. Rawski. 1993. "A Profile of the Manchu Language in Ch'ing History." *Harvard Journal of Asiatic Studies* 53 (1): 63–102.

Cui Xiujing 崔琇景. 2010. "Qian-Jia zhi ji nüxing zuojia de wenxue jiaoyou guanxi ji qi yiyi—yi Luo Qilan wei li" 乾嘉之际女性作家的文学交游关系及其意义以骆綺兰为例. *Suzhou daxue xuebao*, no. 3: 55–59.

Deng Hongmei 邓红梅. 2000. *Nüxing ci shi* 女性词史. Jinan: Shandong jiaoyu chubanshe.

Deng Wei 邓伟, ed. 2012. *Manzu wenxueshi* 满族文学史. Vol. 4. Shenyang: Liaoning daxue chubanshe.

Deng Zhicheng 邓之诚. 2012. *Deng Zhicheng wenshi zhaji* 邓之诚文史札记. Edited by Deng Rui 邓瑞. Nanjing: Fenghuang chubanshe.

Dikötter, Frank, Lars Laaman, and Zhou Xun. 2004. *Narcotic Culture: A History of Drugs in China*. Chicago: Chicago University Press.

Ding Yizhuang 定宜庄. 1999. *Manzu di funü shenghuo yu hunyin zhidu yanjiu* 满族的妇女生活与婚姻制度研究. Beijing: Beijing daxue chubanshe.

———. 2001. "Zhenji, gexing yu caigan: Lun Qingchao ruguan hou Manzu funü di bianhua he tedian" 贞节, 个性与才干: 论清朝入关后满族妇女的变化和特点. *Zhejiang xuekan*, no. 6: 120–24.

———. 2006. "'Wu meng dao saibei, you yi gong wenzhang' Qingdai Menggu nüshiren Naxun Lanbao de shenshi yu xiezuo" 無夢到塞北有義工文章 清代蒙古女詩人那遜蘭保的身世與寫作. Paper presented at the conference Chinese Women through a Modern Lens, Cambridge, MA, June 2006.

———. 2014. "Guanyu Qingdai Manzu funüshi yanjiu de ruogan sikao" 关于清代满族妇女史的若干思考. *Jilin shifan daxue xuebao*, no. 6: 1–7, 14.

Dong Wencheng 董文成. 1986. "Jiechu de Manzu nüshiren Tongjiashi" 杰出的满族女诗人佟佳氏. In *Manzu luncong* 满族论丛, 122–37. Shenyang: Liaoning daxue chubanshe.

Du Jiaji 杜家驥. 2001. "Qingchao di Man-Meng lianyin" 清朝的满蒙联姻. *Lishi jiaoxue*, no. 6: 15–18.

———. 2003. *Qingchao Man-Meng lianyin yanjiu* 清朝满蒙联姻研究. Beijing: Renmin chubanshe.

———. 2006. "Qingdai Mengguzu nüshiren Naxun Lanbao jiqi xiangguan wenti kaozheng" 清代蒙古族女詩人那遜蘭保及其相關問題考證. *Minzu yanjiu*, no. 3:86–93.

Du Xun 杜珣. 2000. *Zhongguo lidai funü wenxue zuopin jingxuan* 中国历代妇女文学作品精选. Beijing: Zhongguo heping chubanshe.

———. 2012. *Guihai yin* 閨海吟. 2 vols. Beijing: Hualing chubanshe.

Durand, Pierre-Henri. 1991. *Lettrés et pouvoirs: Un process littéraire dans la Chine impériale*. Paris: Éditions de l'École des Hautes Études en Sciences Sociales.

Ebrey, Patricia Buckley, trans. 2001. "*The Book of Filial Piety for Women* Attributed to a Woman Née Zheng (ca. 730)." In *Under Confucian Eyes, Writings on Gender in Chinese History*, edited by Susann Mann and Yu-yin Cheng, 47–70. Stanford, CA: Stanford University Press.

Egan, Ronald. 2013. *The Burden of Female Talent: The Poet Li Qingzhao and Her History in China*. Cambridge, MA: Harvard University Asia Center.

Elliott, Mark C. 1999. "Manchu Widows and Ethnicity in Qing China." *Comparative Studies in Society and History* 41 (1): 33–71.

———. 2001a. *The Manchu Way: The Eight Banners and Ethnic Identity in Late Imperial China*. Stanford, CA: Stanford University Press.

———. 2001b. "The 'Eating Crabs' Youth Book." In *Under Confucian Eyes: Writings on Gender in Chinese History*, edited by in Susann Mann and Yu-yin Cheng, 263–82. Berkeley: University of California Press.

———. 2004. "The Qing Hunt at Mulan." In *New Qing Imperial History: The Making of Inner Asian Empire at Qing Chengde*, edited by James A Milward et al., 66–83. London: RoutledgeCurzon.

———. 2014. "Frontier History: Periphery as Center in Qing History." *Frontiers of History in China* 9 (3): 336–60.

Enhua 恩华, comp. 2006. *Baqi yiwen bianmu* 八旗艺文編目. Edited by Guan Jixin 関纪新. Shenyang: Liaoning minzu chubanshe.

Eoyang, Eugene. 1982. "The Wang Chao-chün Legend: Configurations of the Classic." *Chinese Literature: Essays, Articles, Reviews* 4:3–22.

Fang Xiujie 方秀潔 (Grace S. Fong) and Yi Weide 伊維德 (Wilt L. Idema), eds. 2009. *Meiguo Hafo daxue Hafo Yanjing tushuguancang Ming Qing funü zhushu huikan* 美國哈佛大學哈佛燕京圖書館藏明清婦女著述彙刊. 5 vols. Guilin: Guangxi shifan daxue chubanshe.

Fashishan 法式善. 2002. *Cunsutang wen xuji* 存素堂文續集. In *Xuxiu Siku quanshu*, 1476.

———. 2005. *Wumen shihua hejiao* 梧門詩話合校. Edited by Zhang Yinpeng 張寅彭and Qiang Diyi 強迪藝. Nanjing: Fenghuang chubanshe.

———. 2015. *Fashishan shiwen ji* 法式善詩文集. Edited by Liu Qingshan 劉青山. 2 vols. Beijing: Renmin chubanshe.

Fisher, Thomas S. 1978. "New Light on the Accession of the Yung-cheng Emperor." *Papers on Far Eastern History* 17:103–36.

Fong, Grace S. 2001. "Signifying Bodies: The Cultural Significance of Suicidal Writings by Women in Ming-Qing China." *Nan Nü* 3:105–42.

———. 2008a. *Herself an Author: Gender, Agency, and Writing in Late Imperial China*. Honolulu: University of Hawai'i Press.

———. 2008b. "Private Emotion, Public Commemoration: Qian Shoupu's 'Poems of Mourning.'" *CLEAR* 30:19–30.

———. 2012. "Autobiographical Subjects: Ming-Qing Women's Poetry Collections as Sources for Women' Life Histories." In *Overt and Covert Treasures: Essays on the Sources for Chinese Women's History*, edited by Clara Wing-Chung Ho, 369–410. Hong Kong: Chinese University Press.

Fu Tao 伏涛. 2014. "Baibao Youlan 'Jiaozi shi' tanwei" 百保友兰教子诗探微. *Chuxiong shifan xueyuan xuebao* 29 (8): 47–51.

———. 2015. "Shidai yinying xiade nüshi xintai—Yi Dao-Xian nianjian Changbai nüshi shiren Baibao Youlan weili" 时代阴影下的女史心态—以道咸年间长白女史诗人百宝友兰为例. *Huabei daxue xuebao* 16 (4): 73–77.

Fu Yixuan 傅苡嫙. 2009. "Mengguzu nüshiren Naxun Lanbao (1824–1873) jiaoyoushi xilun" 蒙古族女詩人那訓蘭保 (1824–1873) 交遊詩析論. *Dongfang renwen xuezhi* 8 (4): 191–210.

Gao Chunhua 高春花. 2014. "Man-Han jiazu ronghe yu chucai yangde zhi dao—Lan Qingdai nüshiren Yun Zhu de caiming huode yu chucao celüe" 满汉家族融合与处才养德之道—论清代女诗人恽珠的才名获得与处才策略. *Heilongjiang minzu congkan* 142:130–34.

Gao Xingfan 高兴璠. 2007. "Qingdai manzu nüzhen shiren Lingwen" 清代满族女真诗人龄文. *Manzu wenxue*, no. 2: 58–59.

Grant, Beata. 2009. "The Poetess and the Precept Master: A Selection of Daoist Poems by Gu Taiqing." In *Texts, Performance, and Gender in Chinese Literature and Music: Essays in Honor of Wilt Idema*, edited by Machiel van Crevel, Tian Yuan Tan, and Michel Hockx, 325–40. Leiden: Brill.

Groot, J. J. M. de. 1969. *The Religious System of China*. 6 vols. Reprint, Taipei: Ch'eng-wen.

Guo Xiaoting 郭晓婷. 2013. *Zidishu yu Qingdai qiren shehui yanjiu* 子弟书与清代旗人社会研究. Beijing: Zhongguo shehui kexue chubanshe.

Guy, R. Kent. 2010. *Qing Governors and Their Provinces: The Evolution of Territorial Administration in China, 1644–1796*. Seattle: University of Washington Press.

Hamilton, Robyn. 1997. "The Pursuit of Fame: Luo Qilan (1755–1813?) and the Debates about Women and Talent in Eighteenth-Century Jiangnan." *Late Imperial China* 18 (1): 39–71.

———. 2010. "The Unseen Hand: Contextualizing Luo Qilan and her Anthologies." In *The Inner Quarters and Beyond: Women Writers from Ming through Qing*, edited by Grace S. Fong and Ellen Widmer, 107–40. Leiden: Brill.

Han Shuju 韩淑举. 2009. "Ming-Qing nüxing yuedu huodong tanxi" 明清女性阅读活动探析, *Tushuguan gongzuo yu yanjiu* 155:63–68.

Hightower, James Robert. 1970. *The Poetry of T'ao Ch'ien*. Oxford: Clarendon Press.

Ho, Clara Wing-chung. 1994. "Conventionality versus Dissent: Designations of the Titles of Women's Collected Works in Qing China." *Ming Qing yanjiu* 3:47–90.

———, ed. 1998. *Biographical Dictionary of Chinese Women: The Qing Period, 1644–1911*. Armonk, NY: M.E. Sharpe.

———. 1999. "Encouragement from the Opposite Gender: Male Scholars and Women's Publications in Ch'ing China." In *Chinese Women in the Imperial Past: New Perspectives*, edited by Harriet Zurndorfer, 308–53. Leiden: Brill.

———, ed. 2012. *Overt and Covert Treasures: Essays on the Sources for Chinese Women's History*. Hong Kong: Chinese University Press.

Hong Ying 紅鶯. 1995. "Manzu nüshiren Nalan shi" 滿族女詩人納蘭氏. *Manzu yanjiu*, no. 2: 24.

Hu Wenkai 胡文楷. 1985. *Lidai funü zhuzuo kao* 歷代婦女著作考. Rev. ed. Shanghai: Shanghai guji chubanshe.

———. 2008. *Lidai funü zhuzuo kao* 歷代婦女著作考, revised by Zhang Hongsheng 張宏生. Shanghai: Shanghai guji chubanshe.

Hu Xiaowei 胡小伟. 1996. "Ruiqinwang Chunying tihongshi yu *Hongloumeng* chaoben de zaoqi liuchuan" 睿亲王淳颖题红诗与红楼梦钞本的早期流传. *Hongloumeng xuekan*, no. 4: 307–25.

Huang Shizhong 黄仕忠. 2006. "Gu Taiqing de xiqu chuangzuo yu qi zaonian jingli" 顧太清的戲曲創作與其早年經歷. *Wenxue yichan*, no. 6: 88–160.

Huang Yanli 黄嫣梨. 2002. *Qingdai si da nüciren* 清代四大女词人. Shanghai: Hanyu dacidian chubanshe.

Huang Yinong 黄一农. 2012. "Cong Nalanshi si jiemei de hunyin xitan *Honglou meng* de benshi" 从纳兰氏姊妹的婚姻析探红楼夢的本事. *Qingshi yanjiu*, no. 4: 1–14.

———. 2014. *Erchongzou: Hongxue yu Qingshi de duihua* 二重奏:紅學與清史的對話. Xinzhu: Guoli Qinghua daxue chubanshe.

Huang Zhimo 黄秩模, comp. 2011. *Guochao guixiushi Liuxuji jiaobu* 國朝閨秀詩柳絮集校補. Edited by Fu Qiong 付瓊. 4 vols. Beijing: Renmin chubanshe.

Hung, Eva, ed. 2003. *The Faces of a Chinese Beauty: Wang Zhaojun*. Special issue, *Renditions*, nos. 59–60.

Idema, Wilt L. 1999. "Male Fantasies and Female Realities: Chu Shu-chen and Chang Yü-niang and their Biographers." In *Chinese Women in the Imperial Past: New Perspectives*, edited by Harriet Zurndorfer, 19–52. Leiden: Brill.

———. 2010. "Poetry, Gender and Ethnicity: Manchu and Mongol Women Poets in Beijing (1775–1875)." In *Hsiang Lectures on Chinese Poetry*, edited by Grace Fong, 5:1–28. Montreal: Centre for East Asian Research, McGill University.

———. 2011. "The Biographical and the Autobiographical in Bo Shaojun's *One Hundred Poems Lamenting My Husband*." In *Beyond Exemplary Tales: Women's Biography in Chinese History*, edited by Joan Judge and Ying Hu, 230–45. Berkeley: University of California Press.

———. 2012. "Writing Women of Dynastic China: A Bibliographical Survey of English-Language Scholarship." *Guoji Hanxue yanjiu tongxun/Newsletter for International Chinese Studies* 6:20–63.

———. 2013. "Bo Shaojun and her *One Hundred Poems Lamenting My Husband*." *Nan Nü* 15 (2): 317–32.

Idema, Wilt L., and Beata Grant. 2004. *The Red Brush: Writing Women of Imperial China*. Cambridge, MA: Harvard University Asia Center.

Jin Jishui 金寄水 and Zhou Shachen 周沙尘. 1988. *Wangfu shenghuo shilu* 王府生活实录. Beijing: Zhongguo qingnian chubanshe.

Kao, Karl S. Y. 1985. *Classical Chinese Tales of the Supernatural and the Fantastic: Selections from the Third to the Tenth Century*. Bloomington: Indiana University Press.

Ke Yuchun 柯愈春. 2001. *Qingren shiwenji zongmu tiyao* 清人詩文集綜目提要. Beijing: Beijing guji chubanshe.

Kinney, Anne Behnke. 2014. *Exemplary Women of Early China: The* Lienü zhuan *of Liu Xiang*. New York: Columbia University Press.

Knapp, Keith. 2015. "Chinese Filial Cannibalism: A Silk Road Import?" In *China and Beyond in the Medieval Period*, edited by Dorothy Wong and Gustav Heldt, 135–49. Amherst, NY: Cambria Press.

Ko, Dorothy. 1994. *Teachers of the Inner Chambers: Women and Culture in Seventeenth-Century China*. Stanford, CA: Stanford University Press.

Kohn, Livia, ed. 2000. *Daoism Handbook*. Leiden: Brill.

Kuixu 揆敍. 1993. *Lichao guiya* 歷朝閨雅. Woodblock edition. Reprinted in *Siku weishoushu jikan* 10:30. Beijing: Beijing chubanshe.

Kwa, Shiamin, and Wilt L. Idema. 2010. *Mulan: Five Versions of a Classic Chinese Legend with Related Texts*. Indianapolis: Hackett.

Kwong Hing-foon. 1986. *Wang Zhaojun: Une héroïne chinoise de l'histoire à la légende*. Paris: Collège de France Institut des Hautes Études Chinoises.

Laamann, Lars, ed. 2013. *Critical Readings on the Manchus in Modern China (1616–2012)*. 4 vols. Leiden: Brill.

Legge, James. 1971a. *The Chinese Classics with a Translation, Critical and Exegetical Notes, Prolegomena, and Copious Indexes, In Five Volumes*. Vol. 4, *The She King, Second Edition*. Reprint, Taipei: Wenshizhe chubanshe.

———. 1971b. *The Chinese Classics with a Translation, Critical and Exegetical Notes, Prolegomena, and Copious Indexes, In Five Volumes*. Vol. 5, *The Ch'un Ts'ew with the Tso Chuen, Second Edition*. Reprint, Taipei: Wenshizhe chubanshe.

Li, Waiyee. 2014. *Women and National Trauma in Late Imperial Chinese Literature*. Cambridge, MA: Harvard University Asia Center.

Li, Xiaorong. 2009. "Gender and Textual Politics during the Qing Dynasty: The Case of the *Zhengshi ji*." *Harvard Journal of Asiatic Studies* 69 (1): 75–107.

———. 2012. *Women's Poetry of Late Imperial China: Transforming the Inner Chambers*. Seattle: University of Washington Press.

Li Jinxi 李金希. 1998. "Qingdai Manzu shiren Tiebao" 清代滿族詩人鐵保. *Minzu wenxue yanjiu* 1998 (3): 41–48.

Li Ping 李萍. 1999. "Naxun Lanbao zhuiqiu nüxing jiefang, ziyou he fandui fengjian lijiao de sisiang" 那遜蘭保追求女性解放自由和反對封建礼教的思想. *Qianyan*, no. 2: 52–54.

Li Wenhai 李文海, ed. 2000. *Qingshi biannian* 清史編年. Vol. 4, *Yongzheng chao* 雍正朝. Beijing: Zhongguo renmin daxue chubanshe.

Liang Yizhen 梁乙真. 1958. *Qingdai funü wenxueshi* 清代婦女文學史. Taipei: Taiwan zhonghua shuju.

Liaoyang xianzhi erbian 遼陽縣志二編. 1928. In Erudition database.

Liu, Wu-chi, and Irving Yucheng Lo, eds. 1975. *Sunflower Splendor: Three Thousand Years of Chinese Poetry*. Garden City, NY: Anchor Books.

Liu, Xun. 2004. "Visualizing Perfection: Daoist Paintings of Our Lady, Court Patronage, and Elite Female Piety in the Late Qing." *Harvard Journal of Asiatic Studies* 64 (1): 57–115.

Liu Mengxi 劉夢溪. 2015. "Hongxue yanjiu de jicheng zhi zuo: Du Huang Yinong jiaoshou *Erchongzou: hongxue yu Qingshi de duihua*" 紅學研究的集成之作: 讀黃一農教授二重奏: 紅學與清史的對話. *Qinghua xuebao* 45 (1): 143–49.

Liu Xiaomeng 刘小萌. 2008. *Qingdai Beijing qiren shehui* 清代北京旗人社会. Beijing: Zhongguo shehui kexueyuan chubanshe.

Lu, Tina. 2008. *Accidental Incest, Filial Cannibalism, and other Peculiar Encounters in Late Imperial Chinese Literature*. Cambridge, MA: Harvard University Asia Center.

Lu Gong 路工 and Hu Xiaowei 胡小伟. 1987. "Xin faxian de Rui qinwang Chunying 'Du *Shitou ji* oucheng'" 新发现的睿亲王淳颖读石头记偶成. *Guangming ribao*, July 15.

———. 1989. "Yishou xinfaxian de tihongshi: Rui Gong qinwang Chunying 'Du *Shitou ji* oucheng' shi kaoxi" 一首新发現旳题紅诗: 睿恭亲王淳颍读石头记偶成诗考析. *Honglou meng yanjiu jikan* 14:489–514.

Lu Xingji 卢兴基. 2005. *Gu Taiqing ci xinshi jiping* 顾太清词新释辑评. Beijing Zhongguo shudian.

Ma Qingfu 马清福, ed. 2012. *Manzu wenxueshi* 满族文学史. Vol. 3. Shenyang: Liaoning daxue chubanshe.

Ma Rihan 马日罕. 2014. "Gudai Mengguzu Hanwen chuangzuo yanjiu xianzhuang zongshu yu chonggu" 古代蒙古族汉文创作研究現状綜述与重估. *Chifeng xueyuan xuebao* 35 (9): 25–27.

Mann, Susan. 1992. "'Fuxue' (Women's Learning) by Zhang Xuecheng (1738–1801): China's First History of Women's Culture." *Late Imperial China* 13:40–62.

———. 1995. "Talented Women in Local Gazetteers of the Lingnan Region during the Eighteenth and Nineteenth Centuries." *Jindai Zhongguo funüshi yanjiu* 3:123–41.

———. 1997. *Precious Records: Women in China's Long Eighteenth Century*. Stanford, CA: Stanford University Press.

———. 2005. "The Virtue of Travel for Women in Late Imperial China." In *Gender in Motion. Divisions of Labor and Cultural Change in Late Imperial and Modern China*, edited by Bryna Goodman and Wendy Larson, 55–74. Lanham, MD: Rowman and Littlefield, 2005.

———. 2007. *The Talented Women of the Zhang Family*. Berkeley: University of California Press.

Martin-Liao, Tienchi. 1984. *Frauenerziehung im Alten China: Eine Analyse der Frauenbücher.* Bochum: Brockmeyer.

McAleavy, Henry. 1963. *A Dream of Tartary: The Origins and Misfortunes of Henry P'u Yi.* London: George Allen and Unwin.

McCraw, David. 1996. "Out from Qing Boudoirs: Songs by a Merchant-Class Lesbian and a Hypergamous Manchu." In *Constructions and Confrontations: Changing Representations of Women and Feminism, East and West, Selected Essays,* edited by Christina Bacchilega and Cornelia N. Moore, 121–39. Honolulu: University of Hawai'i Press.

McLaren, Anne E. 2010. "Lamenting the Dead: Women's Performance of Grief in Late Imperial China." In *The Inner Quarters and Beyond: Women Writers from Ming through Qing,* edited by Grace S. Fong, and Ellen Widmer, 49–77. Leiden: Brill.

McMahon, Keith. 2002. *The Fall of the God of Money: Opium Smoking in Nineteenth-Century China.* Boston: Rowman and Littlefield.

Meng, Liuxi (Louis). 2007. *Poetry as Power: Yuan Mei's Female Disciple Qu Bingyun (1767–1810).* Lanham, MD: Lexington Books.

Meng Fanyong 孟繁勇. 2015. "Cong Hongshang jiangzhi an kan Qianlong di dui Shengjing jiangjun de yange jianguan" 从弘晌降职案看乾隆帝对盛京将军的严格监管. *Lantai shijie,* no. 18: 5–6.

Meyer-Fong, Tobie. 2009. "Gathering in a Ruined City: Metaphor, Practice and Recovery in Post-Taiping Yangzhou." In *Lifestyle and Entertainment in Yangzhou,* edited by Lucie Olivová and Vibeke Børdahl, 37–61. Copenhagen: NIAS Press.

———. 2013. *What Remains: Coming to Terms with Civil War in 19th Century China.* Stanford, CA: Stanford University Press.

Mi Yanqing 米彦青. 2014. "Meng Han shige jiaoliu shiyu zhongde Naxun Lanbao chuangzuo" 蒙汉诗歌交流視域中的那逊兰保创作. *Suzhou daxue xuebao,* no. 4: 140–45.

Miaolianbao 妙蓮保, comp. 1836. *Guochao guixiu Zhengshi xuji* 國潮閨秀正始續集. Woodblock edition, Hongxiangguan 紅香館.

Mo Limin 莫立民. 2010. "Tongjia shi yu *Xuchuang yake*" 佟佳氏与虚窗雅课. *Manzu yanjiu,* no. 4: 77–81.

Murray, Julia. 1988. "The *Ladies' Classic of Filial Piety* and Sung Textual Illustration: Problems of Reconstruction and Artistic Context." *Ars Orientalis* 18:95–129.

———. 1990. "Didactic Art for Women: The *Ladies' Classic of Filial Piety.*" In *Flowering in the Shadows: Women in the History of Chinese and Japanese Painting,* edited by Marscha Weidener, 27–53. Honolulu: University of Hawai'i Press.

Owen, Stephen. 1996. *An Anthology of Chinese Literature: Beginnings to 1911.* New York: W. W. Norton.

Pregadio, Frabrizio, ed. 2008. *The Encyclopedia of Taoism.* London: Routledge.

Qiu Zhonglin 邱仲麟. 1996. "Buxiao zhixiao: Tang yilai gegu liaoqin xianxiang de shehuishi chutan" 不孝之孝唐以來割股療親現象的社會史初探. *Xin shixue* 6 (1): 49–92.

Rawski, Evelyn S. 1998. *The Last Emperors: A Social History of Qing Imperial Institutions.* Berkeley: University of California Press.

Rhoads, Edward J. M. 2000. *Manchu and Han: Ethnic Relations and Political Power in Late Qing and Early Republican China, 1861–1928.* Seattle: University of Washington Press.

Robertson, Maureen. 1992. "Voicing the Feminine: Constructions of the Gendered Subject in Lyric Poetry by Women of Medieval and Late Imperial China." *Late Imperial China* 13:63–110.

———. 1997. "Changing the Subject: Gender and Self-Inscription in Authors' Prefaces and *Shi* Poetry." In *Writing Women in Late Imperial China*, edited by Ellen Widmer and Kang-i Sun Chang, 171–217. Stanford, CA: Stanford University Press.

———. 2010. "Literary Authorship by Late-Imperial Governing-Class Chinese Women and the Emergence of a 'Minor Literature.'" In *The Inner Quarters and Beyond: Women Writers from Ming through Qing*, edited by Grace S. Fong and Ellen Widmer, 375–86. Leiden: Brill.

Rowe, William T. 2009. *China's Last Empire: The Great Qing*. Cambridge, MA: Harvard University Press.

Rusong 如松. 1789. *Yiqing shushi shichao* 怡情書室詩鈔. Woodblock edition. Reprinted in *Qingdai shiwenji huibian*, vol. 391:611–32.

Schmidt, J. D. 2008. "Yuan Mei (1716–98) on Women." *Late Imperial China* 29 (2): 129–85.

Shan Shili 單士釐, ed. 1912. *Guixiu Zhengshi zaixuji* 閨秀正始再續集. Gui'an: Qianshi.

Shao Dan. 2011. *Remote Homeland, Recovered Borderland: Manchus, Manchoukuo, and Manchuria, 1907–1985*. Honolulu: University of Hawai'i Press.

Shen Shanbao 沈善寶. 2010. *Mingyuan shihua*. In *Qingdai guixiu shihua congkan* 清代閨秀詩話叢刊, compiled by Wang Yingzhi 王英志, 1:337–613. Nanjing: Fenghuang chubanshe.

Shengyu 盛昱. 1908. *Yuhuage yiji* 鬱華閣遺集. In Erudition database.

———. 1910. *Yiyuan wenlüe* 意園文略. In Erudition database.

Shi Shuyi 施淑儀, comp. 1971. *Qingdai guige shiren zhenglüe* 清代閨閣徵略. Taipei: Dingwen shuju.

Snyder-Reinke, Jeffrey. 2009. *Dry Spells: State Rainmaking and Local Governance in Late Imperial China*. Cambridge, MA: Harvard University Asia Center.

Song Bing 宋冰. 2013. "Man-Han hebi *Yongyan zhizhi* zuozhe Yixing xiaokao" 满汉合璧庸言知旨作者宜兴小考. *Manyu yanjiu* 57:44–47.

Songshan 嵩山. *Yuliantang shi* 余廉堂詩. Woodblock edition of the second half of the eighteenth century in *Dong'e shi yijia shigao* 東鄂氏一家詩稿.

Stent, George Carter. 1878. *Entombed Alive and Other Songs, Ballads, etc. from the Chinese*. London: William H. Allen and Co.

Stuart, Jan, and Evelyn S. Rawski. 2001. *Worshiping the Ancestors: Chinese Commemorative Portraits*. Stanford, CA: Stanford University Press.

Sun Yuzhen 孫玉溱, ed. 1991. *Naxun Lanbao shiji sanzhong* 那遜蘭保詩集三種. Hohhot: Neimenggu daxue chubanshe.

Tan Zhengbi 谭正璧. 1984. *Zhongguo nüxing wenxue shihua* 中国女性文学史话. Beijing: Baihua wenyi chubanshe.

Theiss, Janet M. 2004. *Disgraceful Matters: The Politics of Chastity in Eighteenth-Century China*. Berkeley: University of California Press.

Tiebao 鐵保, comp. 1992. *Xichao yasong ji* 熙朝雅頌集. Edited by Zhao Zhihui 趙志輝. Shenyang: Liaoning daxue chubanshe.

———, comp. 1999. *Mei'an zibian nianpu* 梅庵自編年譜. In *Beijing tushuguan zhenben niankan congkan*, 119. Beijing: Beijing tushuguan chubanshe.

———. 2002. *Meian shichao* 梅庵詩鈔. In *Xuxiu siku quanshu*, 1476.

T'ien Ju-k'ang. 1988. *Male Anxiety and Female Chastity: A Comparative Study of Chinese Ethical Values in Ming-Ch'ing Times*. Leiden: Brill.

Tongshan 峒山. *Bocui shanfang shi* 栢翠山房詩. Woodblock edition of the second half of the eighteenth century in *Dong'e shi yijia shigao* 東鄂氏一家詩稿.

Waley-Cohen, Joanna. 1991. *Exile in Mid-Qing China: Banishment to Xinjiang, 1758–1820*. New Haven: Yale University Press.

Wang, Robin R. 2003. *Images of Women in Chinese Thought and Culture: Writings from the Pre-Qin Period through the Song Dynasty*. Indianapolis: Hackett.

Wang, Shuo. 2004. "The Selection of Women for the Qing Imperial Harem." *Chinese Historical Review* 11 (2): 212–22.

Wang, Yanning. 2010. "Qing Women's Poetry on Roaming as a Female Transcendent." *Nan Nü* 12 (1): 65–102.

———. 2012. "Behind 'Burning': Women Writers' Self-Censorship and Self-Promotion." *Frontiers of Literary Study in China* 6 (4): 490–510.

———. 2014a. *Reverie and Reality: Poetry on Travel by Late Imperial Chinese Women*. Lanham, MD: Lexington Books.

———. 2014b. "Fashioning Voices of Their Own: Three Ming-Qing Writers' Use of Qu Yuan's Persona and Poetry." *Nan Nü* 16 (1): 59–90.

Wang Lanshun 王兰顺. 2014. "Liangzuo Ruiwangfu, yibu *Honglou meng*" 两座睿王府一部紅楼梦. *Beijing dang'an*, no. 4: 55–59.

Wang Longgeng 王龙耿. 1982. "Mengguzu nüshiren Naxun Lanbao Lianyou" 蒙古族女诗人那逊兰保蓮友. *Neimenggu funü*, no. 1: 22–23.

Wang Weiping 王伟萍. 2014. "Cong Luo Qilan 'Qiudeng kenü tu' kan Qingshi de mujiao" 从骆绮兰秋灯课女図看清世的母教. *Qianyan*, nos. 363–64: 227–30.

Wang Yingzhi 王英志, comp. 2010. *Qingdai guixiu shihua congkan* 清代閨秀詩話叢刊. 3 vols. Nanjing: Fenghuang chubanshe.

Wei Zhonglin 魏中林. 1989. "Xin qing zi de shi shu wei/qing shen zhi hao ji shi kan: Qingdai Mengguzu nüshiren Naxun Lanbao shige chuangzuo jianlun" 心清自得诗书味 情深只好寄诗看：清代蒙古族女诗人那逊兰保诗戨创作简论. *Minzu wenxue yanjiu*, no. 6: 55–60.

Wenhuang Xianghua 文篁湘華. 1883. *Peilanxuan xiuyu cao* 佩蘭軒繡餘艸. Woodblock edition.

Wenkang 文康. 1980. *Xianü qiyuan (yuanming Ernü yingxiong zhuan)* 侠女奇缘原名儿女英雄传. Nanning: Guangxi renmin chubanshe.

Weston, Timothy B. 2004. *The Power of Position: Beijing University, Intellectuals, and Chinese Political Culture, 1898–1929*. Berkeley: University of California Press.

Widmer, Ellen. 2006. *The Beauty and the Book: Women and Fiction in Nineteenth-Century China*. Cambridge, MA: Harvard University Asia Center.

———. 2009. "Guangdong's Talented Women of the Eighteenth Century." In *Text, Performance, and Gender in Chinese Literature and Music: Essays in Honor of Wilt Idema*, edited by Maghiel van Crevel, Tian Yuan Tan, and Michel Hockx, 293–309. Leiden: Brill.

———. 2011. "Women as Biographers in Mid-Qing Jiangnan." In *Beyond Exemplar Tales: Women's Biography in Chinese History*, edited by Joan Judge and Ying Hu, 246–61. Berkeley: University of California Press.

Wu, Silas H. 1979. *Passage to Power: K'ang-his and His Heir Apparent, 1661–1722*. Cambridge, MA: Harvard University Press.

Xiangcen 湘岑. *Menghuage shigao* 夢花閣詩稿. n. p., n.d.

Xishan badachu daoyou 西山八大処导遊. 2004. Beijing: Badachu gongyuan.

Xu Shichang 徐世昌, comp. 1995. *Qingshi hui* 清詩匯. Beijing: Beijing chubanshe. Original title *Wanqingyi shihui* 晚晴簃詩匯, 1929.

Xu Shumin 徐樹敏 and Qian Yue 錢岳, comps. 1689. *Zhongxiang ci* 眾香詞. Woodblock edition.

Xu Sufeng. 2006. "The Rhetoric of Legitimation: Prefaces to Women's Poetry Collections from the Song to the Ming." *Nan Nü* 8 (2): 255–89.

Yang Yongjun 楊勇軍 and Huang Yinong 黃一農. 2013. "*Honglou meng* yu Nanlan zhu jiemei zhi shengping shiji" 紅樓夢與納蘭諸姊妹之生平事迹. *Zhonghua wenshi luncong* 111:341–62, 403–5.

Yao Min 姚敏. 2013. "Jin ershiyu nian Qingdai zhishi nüxing wenti yanjiu zongshu" 近二十年清代知识女性问题研究综述. *Xuelilun* 14: 228–30.

Yichun xianzhi 宜春縣志. 1940. In Erudition database.

Yinghe 英和. 1991. *Enfutang biji shichao nianpu* 恩福堂筆紀詩鈔年譜. Beijing: Beijing guji chubanshe.

Yü Chün-fang. 2001. *Kuan-yin: The Chinese Transformation f Avalokiteśvara*. New York: Columbia University Press.

Yu Yuehua 于月华. 1994. "Nüshiren Duomin yu *Yiqiange yishi*" 女诗人多敏与逸倩阁遗诗. *Manzu yanjiu*, no. 2: 51–55.

Yuling 毓靈. 1872. *Yunlan zhuangge yigao* 蘊蘭妝閣遺稿. Woodblock edition.

Yun Feng 云峰. 1987. "Qingdai Mengguzu nüshiren Naxun Lanbao shige shuping" 清代蒙古族女诗人那逊兰保诗戬述评. *Zhongnan minzu xueyuan xuebao* 25:41–44.

Yun Zhu 惲珠, comp. 1831a. *Guochao guixiu Zhengshi ji* 國潮閨秀正始集. Woodblock edition, Hongxiangguan 紅香館.

———, comp. 1831b. *Langui baolu* 蘭閨寶錄. Woodblock edition, Hongxiangguan.

———. [1994?] *Hongxiangguan shicao yijuan hiyu yijuan* 紅香館詩草一卷詩餘一卷. In *Congshu jicheng xubian*, vol. 134. Shanghai: Shanghai shudian.

———. 2010. *Hongxiangguan shicao yijuan fu Hongxiangguan shiyu*紅香館詩草一卷附紅香館詩餘. In *Qingdai shiwenji huibian*, vol. 499. Shanghai: Shanghai guji chubanshe.

Yuncha Waishi 云槎外史. 1988. *Honglou meng ying* 紅樓夢影. Beijing: Beijing daxue chubanshe.

Zhan Song 詹颂. 2009. "Dao-Xian shiqi jingshi Man Han nüxing de wenxue jiaoliu yu chuangzuo—Yi Shen Shanbao *mingyuan shihua* wei zhuyao kaocha xiansuo" 道咸时期京师满汉女性的文学交流与创作—以沈善宝名媛诗话为主要考察线索. *Minzu wenxue yanjiu*, no. 4: 123–28.

———. 2012. "Husihalishi de shige chuangzuo yu Wan-Qing shehui" 扈斯哈里氏的诗戬创作与晚清社会. *Minzu wenxue yanjiu*, no. 2: 39–44.

———. 2015. "Tongjiashi fanghongshi kaolun" 佟佳氏仿红诗考论. *Hongloumeng xuekan*, no. 6: 165–82.

Zhang Fuqing 张福清, comp. 1996. *Nüjie: Nüxing de jiasuo* 女诫女性的枷鎖. Beijing: Zhongyang minzu daxue chubanshe.

Zhang Guangcai 张广才. 2013. "Jin bainian Gu Taiqing yanjiu zongshu" 近百年顾太清研究綜述. *Hubei shehui kexue*, no. 11: 136–39.

Zhang Jiasheng 张佳生. 1989. "Qingdai manzu funü shiren gaishu" 清代满族妇女诗人概述. *Manzu yanjiu*, no. 1: 80–86.

Zhang Juling 张菊玲. 1990. *Qingdai Manzu zuojia wenxue gailun* 清代满族作家概论. Beijing: Zhongyang minzu xueyuan chubanshe.

———. 2014. *Jihui yanjuan ku Cao hou: Manzu wenxue lunji* 几回掩卷哭曹侯:满族文学论文集. Shanyang: Liaoning minzu chubanshe.

Zhang Juling, Guan Jixin 関紀新, and Li Hongyu 李紅雨, eds. 1987. *Qingdai Manzu zuojia shici xuan* 清代满族作家诗词选. Changchun: Shidai wenyi chuanshe.

Zhang Lingyu 張聆雨. 2012. "Qingdai nüxing zhushu chuban tujing kao" 清代女性著述出版途徑考. *Gudian wenxian yanjiu* 15:146–67.

Zhang Zhang 張璋, ed. 1998. *Gu Taiqing Yihui shi ci heji* 顧太清奕繪詩詞合集. Shanghai: Shanghai guji chubanshe.

Zhao Xiangbi 赵相璧. 1982. "Qingdai Mengguzu nüshiren Naxun Lanbao" 清代蒙古族女诗人那逊兰保. *Neimenggu shehui kexue,* no. 4: 96–99.

Zhao Xun 赵迅. 2000. *Nalan Chengde jiazu muzhi tongkao* 纳兰成德家族墓志通考. Beijing: Wenjin chubanshe.

Zhao Zhihui 赵志辉, ed. 2012. *Manzu wenxueshi* 满族文学史, vol. 2. Shenyang: Liaoning daxue chubanshe.

Zheng Yangwen. 2005. *The Social Life of Opium in China*. Cambridge: Cambridge University Press.

Zhenjun 震鈞. 1973. *Tianzhi ouwen* 天咫偶聞. Woodblock edition. Reprinted in *Jindai Zhongguo shiliao congkan,* vol. 219. Taipei: Wenhai chubanshe.

———. 1991. *Baqi shiyuan xiaozhuan* 八旗詩媛小傳. Reprinted in *Jindai Zhongguo shiliao sanban,* vol. 625. Taibei: Wenhai chubanshe.

Zhong Huiling 鍾慧玲. 2000. *Qingdai nüshiren yanjiu* 清代女詩人研究. Taipei: Liren.

Zhou Hong 周虹. 2005. *Manzu funü shenghuo yu minsu wenhua yanjiu* 满族妇女生活与民俗文化研究. Beijing: Zhongguo shehui kexue chubanshe.

Zhou Ruchang 周如昌. 1976. *Honglou meng xinzheng* 紅楼梦新证. 2 vols. Beijing: Renmin chubanshe.

———. 1987. "Qing xin Rui qinwang ti *Hong* shi jie" 清新睿王题紅诗解. *Hebei shifan daxue xuebao,* no. 2: 16–20.

Zhou Yuanlian 周远廉 and Zhao Shiyu 赵世瑜. 1993. *Huangfu shezhengwang Duo'ergun* 皇父摄政王多尔衮. Changchun: Jilin wenxue chubanshe.

Zhu Jiji 朱吉吉. 2011. "Qingdai Manzu nüshiren yanjiu" 清代滿族女詩人研究. Master's thesis, Zhejiang University.

Zhu Zhuxian 祝注先. 1997. "Qingdai Manzu, Mengguzu de funü shige" 清代滿族蒙古族的詩歌. *Zhongnan minzu xueyuan xuebao,* no. 4: 82–86.

INDEX